T0129150

Dragon Chaser

A MEMOIR

Mark Lloyd

iUniverse, Inc.
Bloomington

DRAGON CHASER
A MEMOIR

iUniverse books may be ordered through booksellers or by contacting:

iUniverse
1663 Liberty Drive
Bloomington, IN 47403
www.iuniverse.com
1-800-Authors (1-800-288-4677)

Because of the dynamic nature of the Internet, any web addresses or links contained in this book may have changed since publication and may no longer be valid. The views expressed in this work are solely those of the author and do not necessarily reflect the views of the publisher, and the publisher hereby disclaims any responsibility for them.

Any people depicted in stock imagery provided by Thinkstock are models, and such images are being used for illustrative purposes only.

Certain stock imagery © Thinkstock.

ISBN: 978-1-4759-9454-4 (sc)
ISBN: 978-1-4759-9455-1 (hc)
ISBN: 978-1-4759-9456-8 (e)

Library of Congress Control Number: 2013910783

Printed in the United States of America.

iUniverse rev. date: 6/14/2013

CONTENTS

Part 3 Holding Our Own

Part 4 The Amazon Basin

Part 5 Inside the Beltway

PREFACE

This book is dedicated to my children, for I never shared much about my work with any of you. I was always busy—gone, really. I vanished early in your lives, sentencing us to our irregular reunions. During those times we spent together, I didn't dwell on my work. You didn't inquire much, anyway.

Erik, later on when you and Kevin stayed with me that summer in Thailand, you got a peek at my lifestyle, but not much of my mission in that exotic land halfway around the world. Actually, I never thought you were attracted to my choice of profession, so imagine my surprise and delight when you chose to travel much the same road I had. Your sister may not welcome this, but a couple of my grandsons seem interested, though they are young and early interests are subject to change.

I didn't start out meaning to end up where I have, but how many of us ever did? We may start out on our journeys with a map to guide the way, but maps cannot limit life's events from changing our courses. Perhaps I should go back to where it all started and thank the army for setting me on the path I chose. Yes, the army gave me a glimpse of that trail, one that I followed without stopping to ponder or question.

Regardless, I want to tell all of you some of my tale as I know it, which gives me fulfillment at this juncture. Perhaps by sharing my story with you and others, each of you can better tell yours to those who follow, because every one of us has a story to tell.

I now carry the badge and credentials of a retired Drug Enforcement Administration (DEA) agent. Those credentials serve to represent the path taken through thirty-six years of public service to reach this point. This story relates some of the recollections of my time spent in the army, the

Los Angeles Police Department, and the DEA—the successes and failures, the satisfactions and regrets.

My account is most likely ranked as old history now. As many of the issues that were current for me have since changed so much, some may wonder if it is worth returning to them at this hour. But I think it is those changes, really, that make this account worthwhile. Changes help us to realize that history is not something that "was"; it's something that "is." Doesn't each succeeding generation, as it encounters and tolerates its own experiences in life, sometimes wonder about what drove the previous generations to act as they did in similar circumstances? How they handled it? To that end, hopefully I can illustrate some of the differences between then and now. I won't say "this is the way it should be," but rather "this is the way I experienced it."

Attitudes about the subjects of war and crime have changed considerably—what is thought now to be widespread truth was not believed forty years ago or was not true at that time. Phrases like "the domino theory" and "the war on drugs" have lost their meaning. Revisionist history, trendy ideas, social change, and the immense impacts of television and the Internet have distorted a good deal over the past half century. So I shall attempt to set a few subjects straight (straight as I saw them, an eyewitness) in small and unimportant matters as well as in wider aspects.

That is my reason for writing—not a history, for that has been done better than I could do, or even a concise, detailed narrative, for I haven't got that kind of memory—simply what I know and remember. And I can remember much, because a man's past never leaves him. He may try to block it out, forget it, but it always seems to come back and grab him.

Looking back over sixty-odd years, memory of life extends like a long, winding stretch of road with bumps in it here and there. The bumps are those moments, whether they are key life events or not, that live in the mind forever. The smooth stretches between are obscure, dimly recalled times when I remember what generally happened but cannot be sure of the dates or all of the tiny details. I'm sure it is the same with most everybody. A peculiar attribute of human memory is that it does not clasp only the great and momentous; sometimes utter trivia and unimportant notes become as etched in the mind as matters of life and death. Those trifling moments and occasions, however, are the fine weave in the rough fabric of our lives. By touching and handling that fabric, we recall events, both major and minor, that in their whole define who we are and why we are that way.

Of course, I usually have not used real names in order to protect personal privacy, and at times I have combined characters and events for the same purpose or for the sake of clarity. The conversations quoted may not be word for word; who could ever remember every spoken word? But they are entirely faithful in meaning, subject, and style. It all is as I remember it.

Much of this book centers on enduring a year fighting in a war and a lifetime chasing the dragon of illicit drug trafficking. Anyone chancing to read this who is employed in either of those two honorable activities recognizes that while the faces of war and of crime have altered through new technologies, the basics—meeting the enemy on the battlefield and catching the criminal—have never changed since Agamemnon stood before Troy or Cain murdered Abel.

PROLOGUE

The prime minister of Thailand, Thaksin Shinawatra, nodded and told me, "You need two million dollars and you shall have it. I have a special fund, and I can give you the money without having to wait for cabinet approval."

On that day in May 2004, Prime Minister Thaksin had just officially dedicated and opened the new training facility for the International Law Enforcement Academy (ILEA) in Bangkok. After his speech before the crowd of Thai officials, US embassy officials, and police executives from the thirteen East Asian countries that received training at ILEA, US Ambassador Hutchens and I gave Thaksin a tour of the new, ultramodern academy. At an architect's model showing ILEA's buildings, I had pointed out the as yet unfunded student dormitory and, on impulse, asked Thaksin for two million dollars.

While conducting our courses at temporary training facilities, I had worked for two and a half years to get the new academy funded and built, and that day was special to me. I had accomplished what I set out to do when I accepted the assignment as the academy director.

Earlier, in July 2001, I was serving as the commander of the San Diego Narcotic Task Force. Eighty narcotics investigators from nineteen San Diego County law enforcement agencies comprised the task force. With work I found always interesting and challenging, I enjoyed the unique drug enforcement and political issues that arose in making that mixed-bag organization succeed.

I was due for mandatory retirement in four more years, and I had begun thinking ahead to that life, waiting for the day when I no longer carried a badge and gun. For twenty-nine years I had been part of organizations removed from regular society, for in law enforcement it was "us" and "them." Leaving that would be challenging—but welcome.

An announcement had come out from DEA headquarters advertising a position in Bangkok as the director of the recently opened International Law Enforcement Academy. The job would entail being seconded to the State Department, which sponsored ILEA. After reading the announcement, I had passed on it, preferring not to live abroad anymore—I had already served eleven years in other countries, and I was weary of foreign-world living. Soon after, I received a call from the chief of DEA training at our academy in Quantico asking me to reconsider since my Asian experience and Thai language ability would ensure DEA did not lose the position to other federal agencies vying for the assignment. We talked, he was persuasive, and in the end I agreed to take the job.

ILEA proved to be the ideal transitory stage between living in the protective cocoon of the badge and the outside world. With a mind-set not unlike that of a longstanding convict facing the worry of sudden parole, I used ILEA as my halfway house and eased out of law enforcement.

I took satisfaction in directing a progressive training academy that annually taught more than a thousand foreign police. Overseeing the construction of a beautiful academy building may have been the highlight of my professional career—as something tangible, it certainly was my legacy. But the defining period of my life was not commanding a narcotics task force or directing a law enforcement academy in Thailand. That period began years earlier when I was a young soldier in a country at war.

PART ONE

Soldiering

1

The Green Machine

Standing in that crowd, I felt alone, completely isolated. On a dreary January day in 1968, I found myself at the army induction center in Seattle, Washington. I had arrived with several hundred other young men, and we were going into the army.

They stood waiting and talking, huddled together in small groups for protection from what lay ahead. The conversations spun around guesswork—where would the army send us? I heard comments such as, "I'm a trained mechanic, so I'm set," or "I have almost two years of college and I can type—I'll see you in the office." One guy said, "I had a year of premed college; I'm sure to be a medic."

As for myself, I had neither skills nor aspirations, so I kept my mouth shut and just listened to the nervous chatter around me. The suspense and speculation grew until someone came in and shouted at us to shut up and listen.

A master sergeant, he was lean and wiry, standing before us flagpole straight with head held high. His impressive stance commanded our attention. He looked us in the eye and declared, "I heard your bleatings, and I know you all want to know what the army has in store for you. Some of you think you're qualified for this job or want to train for that job. Let me tell you now so you can stop sniveling and begin getting your minds right. We have a war going on, and this month the army needs infantrymen.

Every last one of you is going to the infantry, and four months from today you all will be on your way to Vietnam. Start getting ready."

Complete silence trailed that sobering introduction. Wasting not ten seconds on our stillness, the sergeant followed up by reading out thirty or so names, ordering those people off to the side as they answered up. He directed them to exit out a side door. As they started toward the door, he informed them they would serve their two years of military service in the Marine Corps. Watching them shuffle out, slumping like condemned men, was depressing, since nobody had realized the marines were also drafting. Oddly enough, it had a calming effect on the rest of us, as if we had just dodged a bullet.

Only one and a half years earlier, I had graduated from high school. After working during the summer, I had gone to college, attending Brigham Young University. At the end of my first year, I was married and had a new son. That summer of 1967 I worked in Los Angeles at a large mortuary company. Mortuary work was as morbid as it sounds, being around death. Having to observe families' sadness, the occasional bickering over who in the family received what assets and who had to pay for funeral costs was a depressing business. Working the many funerals for boys coming back dead from Vietnam was the low point for me.

When school started again in September, we didn't return to Utah. Returning to BYU as a full-time student would have required financial support from our parents. I didn't want to live on the dole, so I kept my job at the mortuary, enrolled in one class at a college in Los Angeles, and decided to work my way through school. Of course, in 1967 the military draft was full-blown. I was not carrying a full study load, as was required to keep out of the draft, so I knew my name would come up sooner or later. It came up sooner—I received a November letter in the mail from Uncle Sam, summoning me to report.

I had two options for reaching my first principal goal in life, which was to earn a college diploma. Living on a farm for six years during my earlier childhood had persuaded me that the best way to avoid an occupation that involved physical labor was to acquire a college education. Now, I could have avoided the draft altogether as I was married and had a child. Choosing that route would have meant I remained working full-time at the death house or some other type of mind-numbing work while I labored through taking one or two courses per semester at school. Spending five, six, or however many more years to obtain a bachelor's degree was a discouraging thought. My concern was real, since most students who took that path, determined as they may have seemed, didn't complete their education. They got hooked up into work, which turned into a career, and their college graduation goals faded in the distance as the passing years gathered speed.

My second option—irrational to many and unsavory to most—was to enter the army, survive my term, then return and resume full-time study courtesy of Uncle Sam. The GI Bill, with its provision for tuition payment after service, was what had caught my attention as a way to complete college while I was still young. Nothing comes free, though, and this deal had conditions. I had to enter the army, wear a uniform, and probably go to Vietnam before I could collect. My family did not share my logic and tried to dissuade me. I didn't dwell on the impact of leaving my family behind—my selfishness held sway.

I had no dread of army life. I had a disciplined outlook and was confident I could keep in step. Also, I considered myself patriotic; I had been raised to honor my country, and serving in the military was still considered a way of doing so. Besides, I was nineteen years old and invulnerable.

After separating the army recruits from the marines, they herded us out to buses. We piled on and rode to Ft. Lewis, located about an hour south of Seattle. Rolling onto the base, I noticed old World War II–era wooden barracks, open parade grounds with marching troops, and a general feeling of activity. Many more army posts like Ft. Lewis existed around the country. All were generating soldiers for the war.

Our bus stopped in front of one of the barracks. With tentative steps we made our way out the bus door until one of several drill sergeants present stepped forward and yelled at us to hurry up. That was the opening salvo of the roaring and screaming we were to suffer for the next eight weeks. His name was Sergeant Alexander, and I came to respect him. He courted no favorites and treated us all the same—like dirt.

After receiving curt orders from Alexander, with some personal coaching directed to the slow-steppers, we shaped ourselves into a platoon formation and began our military careers.

The sudden immersion in military life was not without shock and accompanying pain. The army was organized to control large numbers of men, and we converted to that system. We started off with a sheep shearing, inoculations, and changing into green uniforms. We lost our individuality; all now appeared the same and moved everywhere in group formations. We became part of the army's planned process to turn diverse individuals into an obedient herd of automatons. That was the army way: break us down to a common denominator and then build us up in the army manner. Our disoriented state helped us achieve that rapid transformation. Whereas a few days before our families and friends had shielded us, we soon lost that comfort and joined a surrogate family—the platoon. We became a part of the Green Machine.

At the processing center, they made us take the army's general aptitude test, the first of several assessments. The testing staff told us the test was designed to assess one's intelligence and aptitude, supposedly to aid the army in filling its many different roles. That was a sensible story, but nobody bought it since we had already heard the sergeant in Seattle tell us we were all destined to carry a rifle in Vietnam. They separated about forty of us out after the test and informed us we could take the officer candidate test, since we had all scored high on our aptitude tests. Most of us in that group took the test; I found it not difficult. Then, while we were still seated in a room, a young sergeant walked in who would change my life.

He was a recruiter for the army's special forces, the Green Berets. As far as appearance, they could not have picked a better man. He was built like Adonis and his khaki uniform was perfectly tailored. He wore spit-shined black paratrooper boots, and his green beret fit smartly on his head—much nicer than those ridiculous bus driver hats worn by the regular army.

In a calm, no-nonsense manner, he told us we were eligible to take the special forces qualifying test. He went on to say that those who passed could volunteer for special forces training after completing advanced individual training and parachute training. He warned us that most would fail the rigorous training, but if somehow we did make the grade, we would likely end up in Vietnam. He tempered that by adding our training would take at least a year before we earned the beret, and once deployed to a unit, we would serve with professional soldiers.

That was the part that caught my interest. I had already heard I was headed for Vietnam, so training for a year first and then serving with professional soldiers seemed practical. I already knew something about the Green Berets from reading news about the war. I had even read the novel *The Green Berets*, by Robin Moore. As a result, I was practically recruitment-ready. The army hooked me with no difficulty. At the least, I figured the salary would improve. My starting wage was ninety-six dollars a month. After airborne training, as a parachutist I would earn an extra fifty-five dollars a month. That 50 percent pay raise sounded appealing.

A few weeks prior to reporting for duty, I spoke with my older brother. He was already in the army and was attending helicopter flight school. He gave me some advice on army life, and then told me that whatever I did, not to end up in the infantry. He brought up a story or two about half-trained infantrymen being led into ambush down jungle trails by green lieutenants. I recalled those disquieting stories as I mulled over what to do.

About twenty of us took the special forces test. I found it much more difficult than the officer candidate test. It was a different type of test: no multiple choice or true/false questions. It was subjective, with questions asking what you would do in a certain situation or scenario—a test that called for thinking. To my surprise, I did well. With hardly a look at the risks, I took a leap of faith and signed on the dotted line.

The first step was to complete my basic army training. I spent the next eight weeks learning soldiering fundamentals. The physical training (PT) and discipline was not difficult for me. I was in good condition from a lifetime of active sports and was used to obeying orders.

I did have to make some psychological adjustments to army life, however. I embraced a strict daily schedule. They told me when to wake up and when to go to sleep (that was easy; it was when they turned the lights out every night). I lived in tight, no-privacy quarters with strangers, a few of whom I would just as soon have never met.

There were other challenges that most civilians were not ready to face.

For instance, on my first night in the barracks bay, an open room housing about forty of us, I had the top bunk and an eighteen-year-old high school dropout had the bunk below mine. I went in to shower, and returned five minutes later to discover my wallet empty. I had started out in the army with thirty dollars, and it was gone on my first day. I suspected the punk, but he said he knew nothing. Not that it mattered much, because we were restricted and I would have no chance to spend a dime for eight weeks.

To control and direct a mass of soldiers requires a plan. The army introduced us to organization and chain of command. Our training company, numbering almost two hundred men, was divided into four platoons, and each fifty-man platoon contained four squads.

In charge of our platoon was Sergeant Alexander. He had too many people to supervise. But we had trainee leadership too. That was the army's way of developing leadership early by delegating some of the supervisory authority needed to handle such a disparate group of men. Alexander picked a platoon leader and four squad leaders from the trainees soon after the first day. Obviously, no background or suitability checks were made for these assignments.

Alexander named me a squad leader. That appointment was not based on my leadership aptitude or superb military bearing. Rather, it was based on my ability to organize my footlocker according to army standard on the first try and to demonstrate a correct about-face movement. Several of the men had not yet mastered standing at attention, let alone making a precise drill movement.

As a squad leader, I became responsible for the twelve men in my squad. I ensured they were up and ready for morning formations, dressed properly in the uniform of the day, and had neatly made their beds. Dealing with most of my squad members was not difficult since all of us were just trying to get through the training together. But I had two men who could not seem to get it right.

One man, though amiable, was slow-witted. A Canadian, he had failed the test to enter the Canadian army and so had come south to join us. Our army required no testing; the Green Machine took anyone with a pulse. He tried his best, but he had a difficulty getting with the program. I spent an inordinate amount of time spoon-feeding the army way to him.

He sometimes had problems putting on his uniform. Often, he would look at me with his open countenance while I helped correct his dress before morning inspection. Repeated mistakes in buttoning his shirt and putting on his equipment belt became frustrating. I reminded him every day he had to shower and shave—a new requirement for him. The army training manuals, supposedly written for a sixth grader's comprehension, proved difficult for him.

He improved little over the eight-week course, but he made it through the training. He went on to the infantry, of course, as the infantry didn't care how well one could read. I still have our platoon photo, taken just before graduation, and there he is: standing in the last row, wearing that helpless expression on his face and his helmet on backward.

My other concern, Vinnie, was a disciplinary trial and obviously a product of irresponsible breeding. He was likely the punk who emptied my wallet on that first night in the barracks. Emotionally stunted, he was a shifty-eyed little sneak with body odor and a serious acne problem. He was an early life lesson for me: one usually can't pick one's coworkers.

I heard Vinnie had joined the army to avoid a prison term for car theft in Seattle. He hated authority, especially army authority. Although sullen, he followed instructions from the army training cadre (drill sergeants). But he was antagonistic and disagreed with or ignored almost everything I said. I knew the problem—what little authority I had stemmed from the corporal stripes pinned onto my left sleeve. He felt he needn't listen to me, as I was also just a trainee.

His continual screwups were costing me though, as I was made an example when punishment was handed out—made to do extra push-ups or walk around the parade field with my rifle held over my head until I could "get my people squared away." It was classic negative reinforcement, a preferred army tactic to shape us into a group that acted as one. Sometimes our whole squad would be put in the push-up position for one of Vinnie's transgressions—the squad couldn't stand him either.

By the third week of training, I had reached my limit with Vinnie. I tried talking with him, explaining we were just trying to get through the training. I tried threats, saying I would go to Sergeant Alexander about it. I even tried pleading. Nothing worked, so I did go to Alexander one evening after I had again suffered that day for Vinnie screwing up.

Alexander did not have any sympathy for me. He told me discipline was the key to making the army function, and that a breakdown in discipline by one member of the team was costly to all. He concluded his little pep talk with a wink and a nod, telling me Vinnie needed to be taken to the woodshed. What could I do? Violence was out of the question.

Thankfully, two nights later the platoon took care of my problem. It seemed everybody had suffered enough from Vinnie. He was caught in the act stealing from his bunkmate. That night, almost everybody in the platoon rose at two in the morning, awakened by the fire watchman (every night the men took turns pulling "fire watch" shifts), and crept over to the sleeping Vinnie. There they held a blanket party—military parlance for holding a sleeping man in his bed and delivering a thrashing. They left him mewling in his bunk.

The next morning, Vinnie was up with the rest of us and didn't exhibit any outward signs of abuse. But he was quiet and meek for the remainder of training, and I never had any more trouble from him.

The army indoctrinated us to prepare for war. That was not difficult since the bloody 1968 Tet (Vietnamese New Year) offensive started during our third week in training. The United States was at war, and the army's purpose was to support national policy. None of us came into the army wholly realizing what that purpose demanded. It meant killing others, not as an abstract thought, but for real.

So the army tried to change our mind-set to accept that prospect and to prepare for it. There was nothing masked about it. When we marched or ran in formation, we always sang songs; they usually pertained to Vietnam or to some guy named Jody who was stealing our girl back home. Weapons training focused on the fact our targets were Vietnamese. Bayonet drill was especially personal. The trainers yelled out, "What is the spirit of the bayonet?"

"To kill!" we screamed back.

But there was no real change in our mind-set because, as I was to find out, war is a concept that can really be understood only after experiencing it.

When World War II started, men were beating down the doors to get into the military. Not so with Vietnam or Korea, the first of our wars to stop communist aggression. Ninety percent of those in my basic training company were draftees, and I would say most were not enthusiastic about serving in the army or going to Vietnam.

I heard word that our company had at least two desertions—unofficially, of course, since our training staff didn't want to spread that kind of news around. We squad leaders shared a room just down the hall from the company's orderly room (administrative office), and in the evenings we sometimes crouched in our doorway and listened in on one of the sergeants, he being fond of talking shop on the telephone. He chatted about a soldier in another platoon who kept wetting the bed at night. The bed wetter staunchly endured the shame just to get out of the army. It was army gossip, but entertaining, nonetheless.

One evening, after spending the day on the range, we were sitting on our footlockers cleaning our rifles when we heard a gunshot. We all ran outside to find the problem. Up on the second floor, there was a commotion: yelling, door pounding, a door splintering, and then a scuffle. Soon, four sergeants came outside carrying one of the trainees. He appeared unconscious and bore signs of a beating.

We soon overheard what had occurred from the blabbermouth sergeant in the orderly room. It seemed the recruit had stolen two or three live rounds on the rifle range that day, locked himself in his barracks room, and fired off a round (he was a squad leader, no less, and shared a room with two others). Whether he had tried to shoot himself and missed, or just fired one off as a cry for help, we never knew. I was sure he received a beating because the cadre had explaining and paperwork to do in order to answer how someone managed to take live ammunition from the range.

I was catching a glimpse of what some people were willing to do to avoid unwanted obligations. We never saw that soldier again either.

While basic training was an eight-week-long introduction to common army life—military fundamentals, discipline, drill—it was not about teaching us skills. It was about changing us, getting us tuned in to the army's wavelength. And if one got his mind right and followed the drill, basic training was not difficult.

Our next rung up the army ladder was learning a military skill. Unlike what we had been told on the first day, and to the relief of many, everybody was not sent to the infantry, though about a third of us were. As I was to learn later, the army required about nine soldiers in auxiliary roles to support one infantryman.

As for me, since I had volunteered for special forces, the army sent me for eight weeks of airborne infantry training at Ft. Gordon, Georgia, to be followed by the three-week parachutist training course at Ft. Benning, Georgia.

2

Earning the Green Beret

Fighting on foot and meeting the enemy face-to-face were skills I learned at infantry school. It was an eight-week course, but otherwise shared only a few similarities to basic training. We did lots of PT, range-firing of various weapons, forced marches, barracks cleaning, and boot polishing. But infantry school demanded a serious shift in attitude. Inside, we knew we were all training to go to Vietnam as infantry—no cooks, clerks, or mechanics littered our ranks.

The infantry was the tip of the army spear. Making up less than 10 percent of the army's ranks, the infantry's purpose was to kill the enemy by direct contact. It also did most of the army's dying. Our course was total immersion, with the purpose of teaching us handiness in killing and how to avoid being killed. The training became more focused, centered on infantry weapons, patrolling, tactical movement, and land navigation. We learned the infantry's version of the "3 R's," which were "shoot, scoot, and communicate."

The training cadre spent a lot of time overriding our basic emotional responses: those learned while living in a safe American environment. At the same time they enhanced our instincts to survive in a kill-or-be-killed environment. They pounded survival into our heads daily. The army wanted us to change our normal social limitations against violence and awaken the savage within us, implant in each soldier a fighting spirit, make killing another human being seem normal.

That regimen sounds harmful and extreme, but it made sense and saved many American lives. Besides, the North Vietnamese were receiving that same survival training. Why should we skimp?

I didn't dwell on thoughts of killing or being killed. It was not the time or the place to be philosophical. Rather, I concentrated on learning the job as best I could, imagining that becoming proficient in infantry skills would keep me alive later. Silly, I know, but killing and death were still abstract concepts to me, and I'm sure to all the others. After all, it is always someone else who dies, isn't it?

In my letters home, I didn't elaborate on the dark nature of our training. No need to upset anyone.

Not that anyone sat around at night honing his bayonet and talking about killing Vietnamese, though we did learn to dehumanize them by calling them gooks, dinks, or slopes. We paid close attention to the training and assimilated our infantry skills—no one dozed off during those classes. Our training cadres were Vietnam veterans for the most part, so we received some of the lessons they had learned in jungle combat. When we got to Vietnam, the training kicked in and no one had trouble pulling a trigger when needed.

Army doctrine still subscribed to conventional warfare tactics—set-piece battles won by superior firepower—which did not fit in Vietnam, where the enemy avoided large scale battles unless it suited them. We did have some training specific to Vietnam, such as a mock-up of a Vietnamese hamlet that we practiced assaulting, learning to search for tunnels and hidden weapons caches. As we were to find out though, the preparation we received for battle in Vietnam was not sufficient. Nothing much was offered about the Vietnamese culture, or to prepare us for the weather, diseases, and the jungle. And, of course, unlike our shooting at paper targets on the firing range, nothing could prepare us for the stand-up, shoot-back targets we would find in Vietnam.

At infantry school we often slept in the woods, unlike at basic training, where only a couple of nights were spent outside. I was a former Boy Scout, had spent many nights camping out as a youth, and knew my way around a pup tent. Of course, at Ft. Gordon, it was different: no nights spent sitting around a campfire telling ghost stories and roasting marshmallows. Then again, it was interesting to watch how some of the others, those who had never slept on the ground, learned to adapt. The mosquitos were thick in that swampy, snake-infested training ground near the Savannah River.

For nourishment during field training, they fed us C-rations. This canned food came in several varieties, all unpleasant, with the ham and lima beans taking honors for vileness. Most of us carried small bottles of Tabasco sauce in the forlorn hope that mixing it in would kill the foul taste of our meals. To this day, I still can't stand the smell of Tabasco. Each meal also had some kind of dessert, such as pound cake, peaches, or applesauce. That was edible, if only for the sugar.

The best item in the rations was the cigarettes. Each meal came with a packet of four. I didn't smoke, but I saved mine because by the second day in the field, all the smokers—and there were many—had run out of cigarettes. It was callous, I know, but despite cries of outrage, I traded my daily cigarettes for desserts and never settled for less; they had their addictions, and I had mine. My favorite was canned peaches, and I usually got it.

Infantry school in Georgia was my first encounter with racial tension. I had had very little contact with blacks while growing up. There were none in my school until I got to high school, where we had only a handful. In basic training, we had just two black men in our platoon of fifty.

It was different at infantry school—at least one-third of the company was black. In the first week of training there were several black-white fistfights, usually over some perceived slight, hastily spoken words, or other such nonsense. The training staff did nothing to counsel us about fighting.

Amazingly, by the second week we were all good buddies. We found out we all had more in common than we knew. The training regimen took care of any outward prejudices, as we were all together aboard the same boat headed for the same port.

On April 4, 1968, Martin Luther King Jr. was murdered in Memphis, Tennessee. Riots occurred in many US cities, and the army restricted all soldiers to their bases. At Ft. Gordon, there was a strained atmosphere, but no incidents occurred and the training continued.

Robert Kennedy was assassinated on June 5, 1968, my first day of airborne training at Ft. Benning, Georgia. This was my third stop in the army, and I began to wonder what social catastrophe would happen next. Major events, like the Tet offensive, the King assassination, and the Kennedy assassination, had each occurred near the beginning of an aspect of my training.

Residing on an army base in a restrictive training mode kept all of us occupied, safe in the army's cocoon. While we knew what was happening outside, we were insulated from most of the social issues erupting throughout 1968 America.

Parachute school is much touted in the army. Walking around with jump wings pinned on the chest identifies a soldier as one who is self-confident, aggressive, and afraid of nothing—at least not afraid to jump from an airplane. Since World War II, airborne soldiers have enjoyed a reputation as being a cut above regular "leg" infantry. That reputation is current, even though today one is likely to see many women soldiers and other noninfantry soldiers wearing wings. A large percentage of the students at jump school, especially commissioned officers, go through it to punch their career tickets and wear the wings. Regardless, all who wear them have earned them, as no one gets wings without jumping out the door of an aircraft in flight.

Jump school is three weeks in length, but could be done in a week. Learning the basic principles and techniques was not difficult, but our training class consisted of four hundred men. It takes time to run that many people through all the different training drills. Also, PT is important to airborne and takes up a couple of hours daily. With the school's reputation for ruggedness, I was surprised how many students showed up for jump school in poor condition, but two-thirds of the students made it through.

By the third week, "jump week," we were all itching to get up in the air. In 1968, the jump school still used C-119 aircraft to jump. They were twin-engine flying boxcars of Korean War vintage, old and slow, but easy enough for forty troops to jump from.

We did our first two jumps from the C-119s "Hollywood" style, with no equipment. We made our next two jumps, carrying heavy rucksacks and weapons, from the more modern C-130s, which carried about sixty troops. For our fifth and last jump, we became the first class to jump out of the C-141, a big jet transport that could push about 150 of us out the doors.

That was a real thrill. The propeller-driven aircraft were slower, so the "prop blast" and noise we encountered on exiting a plane were not unpleasant. That changed with the C-141. When they opened the jump doors, the scream of the jets was distracting, even though the pilot had throttled down to just above stall speed to allow us to safely jump out. Upon exiting, the wind just grabbed me, and I had a sensation of being almost sucked out.

On the way down, I remember thinking, "And I'm getting paid extra to do this!" Jumping was pure pleasure. Later on, when I was in special forces, we made all our jumps at night carrying full equipment and weapons. That took all the fun out of it.

Standing in front of a C-119 "Flying Boxcar" at jump school, May 1968.

Wearing jump wings on my chest, I went home on leave, with orders to report to the Special Forces Training Group in three weeks' time. I had now been in the army six months and had completed about half of my training, but the most difficult half remained. In anticipation of trying for special forces, I had read up on what I could about the unit, which had taken on a leading role in the Vietnam War.

In 1961, President John Kennedy visited Ft. Bragg to inspect the Eighty-Second Airborne Division and other conventional troops. He also inspected the special forces and liked what he saw. It seemed he was a student of military affairs and had a particular interest in counterinsurgency operations—the methods of defeating guerrilla movements—which were then sprouting in various parts of the world, including Vietnam. In the Green Berets, he had the ideal unit to carry out missions in the communist-sponsored "wars of liberation." He also approved the adoption of the green beret as the official headgear of all special forces troops—much to the dismay of the conventional army brass, who wanted all the army to dress, as well as fight, the same way.

The first Green Berets arrived in Vietnam in 1956, and each year, the number of special forces military advisors in Vietnam steadily increased. Their responsibility was to train various native tribes (the Montagnards) into a credible anticommunist threat. They were successful in that mission, so much so that there were not enough Green Berets to fill the need. Originally, anyone wishing to join special forces had to be an NCO (non-commissioned officer) with at least four years in service. To increase the number of Green Berets available for Vietnam, the army opened up volunteering to the lower ranks, which allowed buck privates like me to apply.

With my wife and infant son in tow, I drove cross-country from Seattle to Fayetteville, North Carolina, home of Ft. Bragg and the special forces. We rented accommodations just outside Fayetteville in a trailer park full of military families.

I was experiencing my first time living in the South outside of a military base, and it was different. The steamy hot weather and strange foods, such as grits and okra, were only some of the differences I had to face.

The low-key but open racism was another. I remember driving in North Carolina, nearing Fayetteville, and about fifteen miles from town, I passed a large billboard that pictured a night rider on a rearing stallion, in full KKK regalia. A banner proclaimed, "Welcome to Cumberland County:

You Are Entering Klan Country." Underneath the billboard, a man sat in a parked car, apparently guarding the sign. Just outside Fayetteville, I passed by a motel named Colored Motel.

This was mid-1968, and although I knew about racism and had heard about segregation, I had never seen them. I didn't realize racism was still thriving in the open. It all gave me a better understanding of the civil rights struggles of blacks in the early 1960s. I didn't see any "colored" water fountains, like my mother experienced in Louisiana when she lived there briefly during World War II, but I did notice some businesses that welcomed or catered to only one race or the other.

Later during my time at Fayetteville, I needed to repair a dented fender on my car. I drove around and checked repair prices at three different body shops and went with the cheapest, which happened to be black-owned. He did a good job, and when I paid him and picked up my car, he made an effort to thank me for "going out of my way" and bringing him business. Self-consciously, I told him I wasn't trying to make a statement—I just went with the low bid.

With my fortified self-confidence after doing so well thus far in the army, I looked forward to start my pursuit of a Green Beret. The training was divided into three phases: selection, MOS (military occupational skill) qualification, and collective training.

Phase one existed to select the best and weed out the others: the weak and uncommitted. Those selected advanced to the second phase, during which they learned one of the five military specialties in special forces: operations and intelligence, medical, weapons, engineers, or communications. That training varied in length from eight weeks for weapons to fifty-seven weeks for medical.

In the final phase, the newly trained students joined together in twelve-man "A" teams (the special forces operational detachment) to demonstrate their expertise in skills learned during the first two phases.

After checking in at Special Forces Training Group (SFTG), I was assigned to Company C, one of four companies of about one hundred men each that comprised SFTG. That first day, as we began phase one, we all stood in formation to listen to the colonel's welcoming speech. I noticed that, like at jump school, the ranks were filled with different grades from senior sergeants down to privates like myself—all of us hoping to pass muster and be assigned to one of the special forces groups. It was a little intimidating at first, as the sergeants with their several years of army experience would surely beat out those of us who, basically, had only been in the army since breakfast.

However, we came to realize it was not a competition between ranks, but a struggle by all of us against the system. If we could learn the system, fulfill all the requirements, we were in—all of us. As for me, I was motivated, determined, and in top physical condition. Alas, that would not be enough; more was needed.

Most of us were not prepared for the trial ahead. The army way was to take young men and make them think they were better than they were: willing and able to do anything asked of them. The army accomplished that by getting them together and beating them into submission, knowing that the survivors, the ones who stayed, *would* do anything asked of them.

The physical demands were staggering, what with morning PT, day-long "punishment drills" (such as duck-walking in circles, crouched down with a rifle held over the head, or "walking" in the push-up position), forced marches, and long land-navigation courses conducted day and night at speed.

Regrettably, physical strength alone didn't get anyone through. The constant mental harassment, force-fed every step of the way, made that physical grind even worse. Phase one was designed to see who would take the punishment—those who wouldn't were soon gone.

Our morning formations grew smaller every day as men began dropping out. Quitting favored no rank—all grades were susceptible to the lure of the training cadres' daily offers to end it all by just getting up and walking away. They would say, "How much do you want this? How far are you willing to go, what sacrifice are you willing to make to get it?"

One aspirant in my group, a sergeant who had five years of service and was a graduate of the Army Ranger course, gave me a few tips that helped me. He told me the key to making it through was to keep moving, keep trying, and remember that it would end long before they killed us. He told me, "Pain is required, but the suffering is optional."

His actions illustrated how to acquire the resolution to attain a goal. It's not given to you; you earn it. I learned to drive myself beyond my normal capability through sheer willpower. My body and mind could take much more beyond the point of exhaustion. Get your mind right and the body will follow. I had one instance when I thought about quitting, but by looking around and observing others suffering just like me, yet hanging on, helped me get through the day.

I was not alone in struggling to make it. During breaks, there was none of the banter or bravado that is usually heard around a group of virile young men; we mostly sat together in quiet self-absorption. Where before our belief in making it through grew out of eagerness and youth, our resolve to do so now originated elsewhere. Adversity and pain truly brought out the best in us.

Private Sizemore could do it all. He was not intimidated by the mental harassment; he just kept knocking out the push-ups without any sign of discomfort. Out in the field he was an ace, one of the best woodsmen I have ever seen. I used him as my personal measuring stick, following in his slipstream because he was cruising along nicely. And then, after we had endured two weeks of the suffering and stood at the halfway point, he told me he was quitting because he couldn't wait to get over to Vietnam. I couldn't believe it. I told him the war would wait for him, as from all accounts it seemed our government was milking it. But he was gone the next day. I hoped he made it.

The selection phase lasted four weeks. The physical and psychological torture was only part of the process. Our personal characters—abilities in judgment, self-discipline, maturity, and thinking on our feet—were important and also subtly tested in the problem-solving field exercises we underwent. Thinking back to the special forces aptitude test I completed on my first day in the army, I understood why it was structured subjectively: they wanted soldiers who could reason, who possessed psychological skills, and who could persuade and influence local cultures to work for our goals. They were looking for resourceful problem-solvers, not knife fighters.

By the end of that first phase, two-thirds of the company had departed. Of those who did not make it, the sergeants went back to their previous units, while the privates were sent off to Vietnam to join airborne infantry units. We survivors closed ranks to fill in the empty spaces and waited to meet with the committee to hear if we had passed. We stood ready to enter the second phase of the training—MOS qualification.

Each of us met with a committee of officers and senior sergeants for a pass/fail signal and then assignment to an MOS course. I was fairly certain I had passed, since I kept up with everyone on the PT and field problems and had not been singled out for any personal "attention" by the cadre. The committee gave out MOS training assignments based on our backgrounds, aptitudes, and most importantly, what special forces needed at that time. Needless to say, the MOS "wish list" we completed beforehand was not a consideration. Since I was a private, I was eligible to train as a medic, a demolitions expert (engineer), a weapons specialist, or a communicator. The operations and intelligence (O&I) field was limited to sergeants only.

Timing is everything, and that was my lucky day. The committee told me that I had passed the first phase—no real drama there—but to my surprise announced that I and two other privates were going to O&I school. When I remarked about the senior sergeant prerequisite, they said we were going in as test cases to see if we could pass the course. If we could handle the curriculum, they would open up future classes to more privates. The plan was to place us as assistant intelligence specialists on the Vietnam "A" teams.

The committee mentioned they had reservations about our ability to pass the course, since we had spent so little time in the army and our level of experience was nil. What's more, our classmates were senior sergeants with ten to fifteen years' experience. As I was leaving, one of the committee told me to bring a sharp pencil to class and have my ears open, because at the blackboard, the instructors usually erased with one hand what they had just written with the other.

During that fall of 1968, attending O&I school was a welcome change from the first phase of Green Beret training. The mental stress was not there, as 80 percent of the course occurred in the classroom. I learned much about military tactics, order of battle, map reading, and intelligence-gathering methods during that eight weeks. It was a lot like attending a college course. We had written tests and homework, reading and writing assignments.

At first, the thirty-six sergeants in the classroom ignored us three privates. I'm sure some of them were miffed that mere privates could enter and breathe the atmosphere formerly reserved for those who had paid their dues. That indifference changed soon enough, though, when they realized we were not a threat to take over their jobs. Besides, we three did very well in the course.

On the bulletin board outside our classroom, someone posted the weekly casualty list published by the *Army Times* newspaper. Reading the names of soldiers killed in Vietnam awakened my awareness of the cost of war. A member of my platoon in basic training and a lieutenant from my infantry school had been killed already, two people I had known just a few months prior. War became more real when someone you knew, who had received training similar to yours, didn't survive.

Academically, we three finished in the top ten—much to the surprise of the committee. I thought that since we had recently been in college, our familiarity with study, homework, and taking good notes were the contributing factors in our success. Some of the older sergeants obviously had not attended a college course or been to any type of schooling in recent years, and they suffered in their studies despite their army experience. About 20 percent of the class did not score high enough to pass.

At Green Beret training, Ft. Bragg, NC, November 1968.

The third phase brought together all who passed their MOS courses for final training in unconventional warfare operations and special forces techniques. For that phase, we were grouped together in twelve-man "A" teams, just like in a real special forces group. Two commissioned officers were on each team, having completed their initial training separately from the enlisted ranks. The teams gave us the opportunity to realistically practice all the skills we had learned in the first two phases.

The five-day survival training portion of the course was the most difficult. One morning, our team stood for a search. All food items were confiscated. The trainers gave an order for us to complete eight missions, each in different locations several miles apart, and then be at a certain location on the fifth day to receive an air drop of food supplies. They told to use our survival training and live off the land during the exercise.

Well, living off the land is possible as long as one can make camp next to a fish-filled stream, set up snares, and wait for game to blunder in to them. Unfortunately, we had to be twelve miles away by the next morning to blow up a bridge. Not much time to sit and wait for the fish to jump or a rabbit to amble by. Each day was the same; we had to walk long distances carrying heavy packs through the Uwharrie National Forest. It became a case of forced fasting. We did catch a very small goat on the second day, one we judged as having strayed too far from its farm. We killed, skinned, and cooked it in no time, had a few bites each, and left nothing but bones behind. The next morning, walking through a meadow, I stumbled upon some wild onions that we all shared—they tasted wonderful. That was it for five days.

With the fasting and long marches, we soon grew tired and weak. We were hungry. Not just ready to eat, mind you, but seriously hungry. It became hard to stay awake at night, when we did most of our walking, so we took to tying our rifles to our belts with parachute cord to keep from dropping them while we walked in our sleep. Our growing fatigue and churning guts brought us to the point that we began to weigh survival more heavily than our mission.

Somehow, we made it, stumbling to our pickup location on the appointed day. We marked out a drop zone in a meadow and radioed in for our promised food, which arrived right on time. It was C-rations, but they had never tasted so good—a welcome change from dead goat and wild onions.

The course climaxed with a ten-day exercise that stressed completing a guerrilla warfare mission. We began by parachuting in at night, establishing contact with the forces on the ground, and training and directing them in guerrilla tactics against the aggressor forces. The exercise was again held in the Uwharrie National Forest, located northwest of Ft. Bragg. It was quite an involved operation, using local people as guerrillas, along with some regular infantry from Ft. Bragg (Eighty-Second Airborne Division) to serve as aggressor forces.

The field exercises were designed to allow all the different MOS specialties to practice what we had learned. We had medics working on the "wounded and sick," engineers blowing bridges, radiomen keeping communications going, and weapons specialists conducting training for the guerrillas. As for me, I spent time interviewing local "spies," taking photos and developing the film by hand, and planning raids and ambushes.

Graduation day was a welcome event for the proud few of us who succeeded in running the Green Beret qualification gauntlet. I had been in the army for almost a year, all of it in training. The army's wait to collect on its investment in me was over.

3

On to Vietnam

If asked to relate their first sensory recollection of Vietnam, I imagine many veterans would answer the same as me—it was the smell. Our Boeing 707 jet landed at Cam Ranh Bay at about noon. As we taxied down the runway, many stood up, trying to get an early peek at the war. We stopped, ground crew rolled up a staircase, and a stewardess swung open the door.

Those seated in front, the officers, got it first, and then it quickly reached out. I was physically assaulted by a wall of odorous humidity, as if someone had thrown a hot, stinking wet towel in my face. We had been warned about the heat, and it was staggering, but the stench was unlike anything I had ever experienced. During my life I had already encountered many odors one at a time: decomposing corpses, musty basements, cattle pens in summer, decayed fish, rotting corn, and dirty diapers. Mix all that together and add a side order of burning diesel oil in that dank, 90 percent humidity, and you have a nauseating stink. It was open sewage and rotting vegetation simmering in tropical heat.

As I was to find out, America had brought everything to Vietnam except flush toilets. The privies were fifty-five-gallon oil drums cut down and placed under toilet-seat-clad wooden planks in wood shacks with tin roofs. When full, the barrels were pulled out, primed with diesel oil, and set on fire. The oily, crappy smoke permeated every corner of every American installation. As there were 540,000 military in Vietnam when

I arrived in March 1969, those unfortunates detailed to do the burning were kept busy.

Ears up and eyes wide open, we stiff-walked down the metal staircase off the plane, all gazing and gawking as if we had just landed on an alien planet—which we had. Buses with steel-mesh-covered windows carried us on the short ride to the in-processing center. True to form, the army showed its ability to quickly tag and bag large numbers of troops: they shunted us around in groups like steers at a cattle yard.

In one large room, we sat sweat-soaked on long wooden benches beneath overwhelmed electric fans while a young second lieutenant stood to deliver a briefing. "Welcome to Vietnam. I am Lieutenant Hunt, and I will give your administrative briefing." He paused to rearrange his notes. "While at Cam Ranh Bay awaiting your unit orders, you will not leave the base. You are restricted to your quarters, the mess hall, and the recreational center. You each will receive a directive on what to do in case of enemy attack."

He droned on, dictating a list of dos and don'ts, and reminded us we were there for a year's tour of duty, 365 days. He spoke with all the enthusiasm of a man reading off a grocery list, while we sat, bored and sweltering in the heat. I heard one soldier behind me mutter, "Only 363 days and a wakeup more."

Everyone had arrived in Vietnam as replacements, and although several had previously been told to which units they would report, those plans were subject to change. Several soldiers had their orders altered and ended up going to different units. It all depended on where the army had an immediate need.

For those who thought they were destined for a good unit or a good location, news of change came hard. Some locales in Vietnam were much nicer than others, or rather, less nasty. For instance, any unit stationed in a coastal town would live better than, say, a unit posted in the Mekong Delta, an area underwater for several months of the year. Obviously, the amount of enemy activity in an area also had a bearing on its desirability.

Since the vast majority of the replacements were not going to an infantry unit, I didn't see the big deal about their assignment concerns. Most of them wouldn't be in danger—the only real issue. Besides, we were all getting the same combat pay: an extra sixty-five dollars a month.

I may have been biased, but I had a problem tolerating soldiers working in an air-conditioned office on a large, protected base, with their swimming pools, pizza parlors, and nightly movies, all getting the same pay as an infantryman spending his days humping a rucksack and looking for trouble in the jungle.

Two other Green Berets arrived on the same flight. The three of us stood out from the others due to our different headgear, and we were given some deference at Cam Ranh Bay. No meaningless work details for us. There was no change in our orders. Unlike some who waited days for assignment, a truck picked us up the following morning for the two-hour ride to Nha Trang, headquarters location of the Fifth Special Forces Group.

Riding in the back of an open truck through the countryside gave me a first glimpse of Vietnam. I saw hopeless poverty, squalor, and filth. The thatch shacks, water buffalo pulling plows, outhouse smell, and lack of basics such as electricity and water were all alien to me. It was the third world at its worst—at war.

Arriving at Nha Trang, a former beach resort town when the French ruled, we slowly motored through the crowded streets. Everywhere, street children begged for handouts. The government buildings, all French colonial style with that distinctive, faded orange color, appeared pleasant despite their decay. Of course, the open sewer stench was ever present.

We passed by three young women walking along, wearing the *ao dai*. It was the national dress, featuring a tight-fitting tunic slit down the sides and worn over pantaloons. Beautiful and exotic, the *ao dai* "covered everything but hid nothing."

Then, as we turned a corner, I saw a woman with hiked-up pantaloons squatting and relieving herself on the edge of the street. My culture shock was complete.

We stopped to check in at the Fifth Special Forces Group replacement depot, located a mile down the road from headquarters. We came under rocket attack that first night in Nha Trang.

The target was the airbase located adjacent to our compound. Rockets aimed at the airfield but falling short, into our compound, were our

27

concern. Several of them did, since we were on the outside perimeter, and the rockets used by the enemy were not very accurate.

I was awakened at three in the morning by booming explosions. We all sprang up to run outside to bunkers located by the perimeter fence, only twenty yards from our barracks. Bob Johnson, one of my classmates from O&I school, was right behind me, but tripped over a metal stake anchoring an antenna guywire. He sprawled, clutching his ankle and called out to me. I ran back and helped him hop into the bunker while we waited out the short-lived barrage. His ankle was torn up, and we checked him into the army hospital early that morning. He had sheared his ankle tendons. To his disbelief, the doctors ordered him home for surgery and rehabilitation—his tour was over after four days. In misery, the poor fool apologized for screwing up and abandoning me. We all thought he was lucky, but he seemed genuinely sorry to miss the war.

In the meantime, mine was just beginning.

The special forces came to Vietnam to train and lead mercenary paramilitary forces against the Viet Cong and North Vietnamese Army (NVA). These forces were recruited from Vietnam's minority groups, mainly the Montagnards, mountain tribesmen we affectionately called Yards. This program began in an effort to secure Vietnam's central highlands, the Yards' traditional homeland, from infiltration by the Viet Cong and NVA.

Illiterate hunter-gatherers for the most part, the Montagnards are a tribal society spread throughout the mountainous regions of Southeast Asia. Their culture is centered on the village. Vietnam held over twenty-five tribes, each speaking a different language indecipherable to those from other tribes. Their varied languages were quite basic and contained only a few thousand words. Any word relating to something developed in the industrial age or later was borrowed from the French or the Americans. Somewhat migratory, they practiced slash and burn agriculture and were superb hunters, killing and eating anything in the jungle. They traditionally moved on to a new area when the land and game gave out, but the war had put a stop to that.

Life in a Yard village was quite primitive. I stayed near a typical village,

Ba To. The population numbered about 250 souls. Ba To was situated in a valley offering arable land next to a river. Extended families of ten to as many as twenty lived in longhouses that featured shared space with no privacy. In a communal venture, Ba To's men built rudimentary homes with thatched roofs and woven bamboo walls over rough-wood plank flooring set four to six feet above the ground on supporting posts. When at home, families sat on the floors to work and eat, and slept either on floor mats or hammocks. Food was cooked outside over small open fires. Besides providing food, the river offered drinking water, bathing, and toilet facilities.

Short and stout, Yards were a sturdy race who spent their lives in hard work. Predictably, that type of lifestyle accounted for a life expectancy of only about fifty years. The men possessed great stamina, as they lived by hunting, climbing the steep-sided slopes of the central highlands in search of game. As for the women, I remember one young wife of about fourteen who gave birth in her hut in the morning and that afternoon was out in the vegetable patch working, her newborn babe strapped to her chest. These were hardy people.

Special forces stepped into that picture and began to recruit Yards, initially as militia to defend their villages from the Viet Cong. That was not a problem for the Yards; they were willing to shoot any Vietnamese, regardless of political leanings. The Yards loved the Green Berets because we treated them as fellow soldiers despite their limitations. Best of all, we armed and paid them. The Yards developed into good soldiers.

Fighting camps were established in strategic locales near the borders with Laos and Cambodia to monitor and interdict enemy infiltration along the Ho Chi Minh Trail—North Vietnam's vast transportation network.

It was North Vietnam's construction and maintenance of the trail, a feat of engineering that equaled the Egyptian pyramids—not in stature, but in scope and effort—that was responsible for the US Army emplacing three thousand Green Berets in Vietnam by the time I arrived. It wasn't just a trail; it was a six-hundred-mile-long, intricate network hidden under jungle canopy that brought troops, supplies, and arms via trucks, bicycles, and boats from North Vietnam to South Vietnam by way of Laos and Cambodia.

A myriad of routes branched out from the main north-south trail and ran into South Vietnam along river valleys that led to the population centers near the coast. When I flew along the Laos border on reconnaissance missions, I could see much of the trail system. Bomb craters and blasted trees from the countless raids clearly pointed out sections of road. My experiences on and above the trail helped me comprehend the NVA's determination and commitment in that war. It was in those strategic valley choke points that special forces fighting camps were built—altogether almost ninety. Ba To, the village to which I was assigned, was one of those camps.

4

Camp Ba To

The French army's stronghold at Ba To was overrun and wiped out during their time in Vietnam. Our special forces built a new camp over the French ruins in 1965. Ba To was a small district town straddling Highway 24, which originated at the coast and ran west eighty miles to Dak To, a town near the Laotian border. The Viet Cong destroyed that road during their war with the French, who had depended on roads for resupply. Not having a road didn't deter us; unlike the French, we had plenty of air support and didn't need roads.

Our site was a typical special forces camp: protected from ground assault with barbed wire, fortified bunkers, and interconnecting trenches. We were well armed. The heaviest weapons, two 105mm howitzers, could fire a thirty-five-pound shell out seven miles. Our camp had three trench lines. We twelve Green Berets had the innermost perimeter, and militia manned the two outer perimeters. Our outermost trench line had dozens of bunkers. Reaching at least seventy-five yards beyond the outermost perimeter were concertina and other barbed wire defenses.

The camp was sited at a point where two rivers joined in a Y. Consequently, we had protective water on three sides of the camp. Ba To village was just across the river to our west, beside the remains of a bombed-out bridge. Next to town, we had built a small, fortified outpost, garrisoned by thirty of our Yards.

Inside the camp, our twelve-man, special forces "A" detachment oversaw a force of four hundred Yard militia, divided into three companies with an added combat reconnaissance platoon of thirty men. Many of these mercenaries had families who lived in Ba To village.

Working alongside us was a Vietnamese army special forces team of twelve—our counterparts in training the Yards. Our mission was to lead our mercenary militia on combat operations.

NVA infiltrating from Laos on the Ho Chi Minh trail moved through our area on their way to coastal cities, and we were tasked to find and stop them. To accomplish that, we had at least one of our companies patrolling in the field at all times. The twelve members of our "A" team also rotated in the field with the Yards; we sent two Green Berets out with each patrol.

For their service, we housed and fed our Yards, and paid them each a salary of about thirty to forty dollars a month—very high wages for the times.

Our Vietnam patrol walks were modest by distance, but grueling when taking into account the terrain in the central highlands. While not unusually high, the slopes were steep, often requiring us to pull our way up by clutching trees and vines. Going downhill was worse, requiring the same tree-clutching to avoid sliding. The constant threat of sudden contact with NVA, the difficulty in keeping track of our exact location (necessary when calling for help), the heat, and the constant fight with the jungle vegetation all added to the obvious stress of ground combat in Vietnam. The neutral jungle favored neither side, and the NVA suffered similar difficulties as we.

As for me, I did well in the jungle. I found its closeness a reassuring concealment. The landscape featured triple-canopy jungle on the slopes from top to bottom. From the air, the jungle appeared calming, with its cushion-like roundness, and beautiful, displaying countless shades of green.

On the ground it was another story. The thickest vegetation was at ground level, and then thinned as it rose. Triple-canopy jungle commonly has thick brush, vines, and small trees that reach a twenty-foot height. Above that, reaching to seventy feet, are medium-sized trees. The largest hardwood trees feature trunks five feet in diameter and towering well over one hundred feet. Vines, such as rattan, wait-a-minute, and tangle foot knitted all the lower vegetation together. Bamboo thickets added a final touch to the green perdition.

Much of the vegetation was unfriendly, and grasping anything often resulted in cuts, which quickly turned septic. For that reason I usually wore a thin aviator glove on my left hand for protection while my bare right hand held my rifle. Elephant grass covered many of the open, treeless areas and grew four to eight feet in height. The grass offered us no respite from the jungle. It matured into a strong, thick thatch and was tough to get through. Worse than paper cuts, the leaves' razor-sharp edges cut up any exposed skin—another reason to wear gloves. Bamboo thickets were much stronger, sometimes impenetrable, but at least they didn't slice you to pieces going through.

Seemingly all vegetation was leech-infested, and that went for the water too. Only about two inches long and as thin as dried spaghetti, leeches would grow to a size larger than your middle finger once they were attached to your skin and sucking blood. When taking a break on patrol, we would sit down with our rucks on and lean back against trees. Within seconds you could see leeches moving toward you with their tail-to-head movement resembling miniature Slinky toys. We had insect spray in squeeze bottles that stopped them in their tracks, but once on you and attached, it took minor surgery to get them detached without leaving their heads buried in your flesh. Despite stiff competition from the heat, mosquitos, red ants, snakes, and plant life, leeches reigned supreme as our worst jungle malady.

Vietnam has two seasons—hot dry and hot wet. During the wet season, the monsoon rains could dump several inches of rain per hour. At the least, it clouded up and rained every day at about four or five in the afternoon. One advantage of walking under the triple canopy was that the noise and drenching of a real downpour was muted. The vegetation layers filtered the rainwater so that it hit the ground as drizzle. Walking in the wet was cooler, but the rain made the ground slippery. The nights were the worst; lying down and trying to sleep when soaking wet was as miserable as it sounds.

We planned our patrols for five-day outings. Five days measured the extent of our food, ammunition, and endurance. Unless we ran into a lengthy, unplanned incident, we were not resupplied in the field. We carried water enough only for one or two days, but water was always available from the many streams we crossed. Just fill up your canteen, drop in an iodine tablet, and you were good to go. If we could find them, we squeezed limes into the water to kill the awful iodine taste.

We ate rations made in Okinawa for our Yards: dehydrated rice in a plastic bag, supplemented by dried shrimp, fish, or beef, dried greens, and hot peppers. We could prepare it on the go by opening the bag, mixing in peppers to taste, and adding water. Then we closed the bag, put it in a thigh pocket, and kept on walking. Thirty minutes later it was ready to eat. The amount of rice was large, and one bag would easily last all day and into the next. It was not the best food, but we preferred it to the heavy, revolting C-rations. Our food needs were small, and we managed a five-day patrol on two or three bags of rice apiece, supplemented by a few cans of fruit and some chocolate bars.

Fatigue was our most limiting factor. The first day out wasn't bad, but by the third day, I was feeling the pain. The legs and feet felt it first—continually going up the steep slopes, pulling myself through the vines and thick brush, then working down, side-stepping to avoid the tendency to slip. Some of the terrain we walked was suitable only for those with cloven hooves.

Five days of fighting the jungle, terrain, heat, rain, and insects, along with the stress from the constant threat of danger, crummy food, and fitful sleep, all combined to wear down my ability to remain alert. Not being alert brought on carelessness. How could I remain wary if I was preoccupied with my aching feet and those biting red ants crawling down my neck?

We typically stayed off the well-beaten trails, unless the jungle was just too thick to move through quietly. Sometimes we traveled in the streambeds. Finding a well-used path, we would often set up an ambush and wait for trouble to appear. We had few problems with booby traps, as our area was a transit zone for fresh NVA who didn't know the land and were passing through toward the east.

In the late afternoon, just before dark, we crawled into the thickest jungle we could find to establish our overnight position. We wriggled up a slope so no one could get close to us without detection, and then laid up tightly packed together, hanging in nylon hammocks slung between trees.

We didn't resemble American troops in the field. We dressed in tiger stripes, uniquely marked uniforms made in Okinawa for our militia. Our weapon was the CAR-15, basically an M-16 automatic rifle with a shorter barrel and a steel sliding stock to reduce its length. We carried twenty extra magazines with another three hundred to four hundred boxed rounds in our rucksacks. Our rucksacks were the indigenous style, smaller than US Army–issue. Inside, besides the extra ammo, I carried a spare battery for the PRC-25 radio, a one-pound block of C-4 plastic explosive or a claymore mine, a nylon hammock, some parachute cord, a poncho and poncho liner, an extra pair of socks, two bags of rice, and a few cans of C-ration fruit—preferably peaches, but I wouldn't throw away the applesauce.

My equipment belt, held up by a shoulder harness, carried most of my ammo and two fragmentation grenades. For signaling, I carried two smoke grenades, a signaling mirror, and a pen-flare gun that could fire a small flare through the jungle canopy. Also on the belt were four water canteens, two first-aid bandages, and a marine KA-BAR knife. Unlike our rucks, the harness belt was never taken off.

Other miscellaneous baggage included morphine curettes, pills for various ills, iodine tablets for treating our drinking water, map, compasses (one lensatic and one on the wrist), a snap-link, and a twenty-foot length of nylon rope. We wore jungle boots, a short-brimmed floppy hat, and an olive drab cravat around the neck to help soak up the sweat. We carried everything we needed, nothing we did not. Altogether, our fully loaded weight added up to between thirty-five and forty-five pounds—most of it ammunition. That doesn't seem like much, but five days of humping it up and down in those jungled mountains seemed to increase the load every day.

Our adversary in the central highlands was the NVA: North Vietnamese Army soldiers, whom we called Charlie. By the time I arrived in Vietnam in early 1969, the South Vietnamese communist insurgents, called the Viet

Cong, had ceased to be a factor in the war. They had virtually destroyed themselves during their unsuccessful 1968 Tet Offensive. From then until the war ended, the conflict was almost entirely an NVA affair.

We respected the NVA's fighting qualities. They were brave, resourceful, and well disciplined. Nearly all of the NVA we encountered had walked much of the three-hundred-mile-long route to our area from North Vietnam. Charlie fought against us without the support of air power or artillery; in the meantime he endured all the shells and bombs we laid on him. Most remarkably, he lived in that jungle every day without relief—no one-year tours and then home for him. It was victory or death, whichever came first.

Combat was a whole new experience for all of us in Vietnam. Like everyone else there, I had my own images of what fighting would be like, based on reading books about previous wars and watching war movies. Imagine my surprise when actual combat did not follow my visualizations. *The Sands of Iwo Jima*, *Pork Chop Hill*, and the rest of the movies didn't accurately cover real war at all.

Also disappointing, my previous training didn't prepare me that well either. Training—playing at war—can't deliver the stark realism of life and death in a firefight. To be shot at and missed is frightening, a truly white-knuckle, frozen-nerve moment.

More than anything, it is the noise that is intimidating. The crack of a supersonic chunk of lead passing nearby, accompanied by the other incoming and outgoing shooting, electrifies you. Add to it the blast and shocks from high explosives, whether grenades, mortars, artillery, rockets, or bombs, and your adrenaline-charged senses are incredibly heightened— you are in a primeval state.

During a firefight, I felt I was wearing horse blinders and could see only directly ahead. The noise from the shooting drove me to take cover, willing myself to shrink. Explosions, even those occurring a safe distance away, caused a momentary shock to the nerves. Relying on training was the savior, since I didn't have to think much—just fire, reload, and fire some more. After the shooting stopped, I found it difficult to resume for a bit. I had to wait until the adrenaline subsided.

After experiencing fighting for the first time and surviving it, I found it easier to go out again—the unknown had become known—but fear in combat never leaves. It just wasn't anything one could get used to. The suddenness of the small-unit actions we encountered made them difficult to predict and arrange. There were scant signs that would aid us in calculating our threat on any given day. Enemy contact most often came as a rude surprise. While on patrol, we moved in a constant state of anxious alert, because the outcome of an action was often dependent upon which side saw the other first. As a result, paranoia was not always bad, because it could help you keep an edge. Sometimes that edge was a nice advantage.

On patrol one day during the monsoon season, we were walking along a trail in the pouring rain when our point man came upon an NVA point man walking toward us. The two men were less than ten yards apart when they made visual contact. Our point man was alert and shot first. We deployed quickly and moved forward, winners that day. It was not a situation in which we had lengthy prior warning or a chance to brace ourselves for a firefight. This was not a war for real estate and there was no "front"—no Siegfried Line or defended beaches to assault. There were just the vast areas outside our bases to travel in search of the enemy.

In the central highlands, ours was a close-contact, jungle war. While aircraft and artillery played critical roles, tanks did not. Our combat was principally an infantryman's business, and our actions tended to be on a small scale.

That being said, the size and importance of an action was no measurement of its personal viciousness. A big operation that demanded great resources and attracted the media may have been just a yawner for some of those involved, while the little, forgotten patrol became a real horror show. My worst patrol involved our unit ambushing an NVA squad on a riverbank and then spending two hours cowering under fire from three snipers hidden on the ridgeline across the river. Any movement on our part brought bullets from the unseen enemy. Pinned, I felt helpless. They shot us up some before we could get Huey gunships to come to the rescue.

As for heroism, the size of the action also made no difference. In any case, most heroism in combat went unseen and unrewarded. For that matter, just moving forward against enemy fire was heroic.

We rotated our patrols with regularity, and each of us usually went on a three- to five-day patrol about once every two weeks. Those of us remaining in camp worked on the responsibilities associated with keeping the camp and its nearby village secure. Much of our time was spent training our Yards and running the battalion-sized unit and the fort that contained it. The "A" team members also spent time cross-training each other in our individual specialties. I was the intelligence specialist, but spent time learning the science of firing an 81mm mortar and working with explosives.

Life in Camp Ba To was not idyllic, but we kept busy and time streamed by. Evenings in camp found us in the team house, our gathering place, furnished with wooden picnic tables. We ate there, played cards or read, and wrote our letters.

Receiving letters from home was a major event. My wife wrote to me almost every day, bless her soul, and a stack of letters arriving on our supply chopper was a frequent delivery. Letters from home provided escape from war. They offered a chance to place the war off to one side for a few moments and return home vicariously through a loved one's words.

We slept in two-man bunkers fashioned out of cave-like CONEX shipping containers. Dark and damp, they were not homey, but provided for a protected sleep.

When in camp, we often joined the Yards on late afternoons to bathe in the river. The cool, clear, smooth-flowing water was waist deep for most of the year. Bathing was a daily village event. Just about everyone from the Montagnard village came to the river's edge, stripped down to newborn-naked—men, women, kids, and grandmas too—and with one hand strategically covering their privates, jumped in the water to cool off. If they were not washing their water buffalo upstream from us, we jumped in too, though modestly wearing shorts. When floating in the cool water, we could almost forget where we were. The Yards laughed, splashed, and made bathing an enjoyable event—childlike, really.

We took care not to gaze at the naked girls. In the Yard culture, looking at a girl for more than a few seconds meant you had serious intentions and needed to go and speak with her parents to make arrangements. The Yards condoned no prostitution or fooling around. Young girls married at thirteen or fourteen years of age and appeared worn-out by thirty, disease, childbearing, and hard work taking heavy payment. No problem though, as we were not sorely tempted. A favorite pastime among the Yards, especially the women, was to chew the addictive betel nut. They carried wads of it in their mouths all day long, pausing every few minutes to spit out a red stream. It left teeth, gums, and lips all stained a bright red—when smiling, their mouths resembled open wounds. Then again, betel was reputed to fight bad breath.

Our team medics often conducted medical patrols in the villages and hamlets surrounding our camp. Those medics represented the only medical care the Yards had a chance to encounter, and so the entire village came out whenever we showed up. As well as they could, the medics treated the sick, who suffered from every ailment known to man. Those of us tagging along played with the kids, handed out candy, and generally shared in the festive mood our visits produced. The Yards showed their respect for us by dressing in their finest clothes for their visit to the "doctor."

While it may have seemed that life within the assumed protective zone afforded by our camp was secure enough, there was a war going on, and sometimes that condition came forth in vivid terms. In the middle of the wet season, a storm marched in one day, dragging rainclouds that nearly touched the ground. From our camp, we could scarcely see the hundred yards across the river to the village. It was perfect weather for Charlie, and he attacked that night without warning.

The sound of exploding mortar rounds awakened me in the early morning darkness. Grabbing my rifle and web belt loaded with ammo and grenades, I scooted from my bedroom bunker down the trench line to my duty station. It was pouring rain, and that canceled any chance of air support coming to help; we would have to survive the attack on our own.

Every member of the team manned an assigned position during an attack. The weapons men handled our 81mm mortar, and the team's top sergeant and our commander manned the tactical operations center (TOC), which was our fortified communications center. My post was the .50-caliber heavy machine gun mounted in a protected tower on the roof of the TOC.

The tower was the highest position in camp and gave me a clear view of our entire perimeter. As one would expect, since I could see everything outside our perimeter, anyone out there could also see me. I realized my position was a prime target, it being one of the few structures above ground level. I also knew my concrete-and-sandbagged position would not withstand being hit by any of the rocket-propelled grenades that Charlie used so proficiently. But one can't think of those risks when the bell rings.

My responsibility was to fight off any ground attack against the camp, but also to keep an eye on our own lines to ensure our troops were all shooting in the correct direction—*out* at the attackers and not *in* at us. Among ourselves, we knew the enemy had infiltrated our camp. We believed that perhaps 5 percent of our mercenary forces were spies or NVA sympathizers.

Up in my tower, my first quick survey told me we were not under ground attack since no firing was coming out of our perimeter bunkers. The incoming mortar fire had also ceased. When I took a second, more thorough check around, I heard, rather than saw, where the main attack was focused.

Directly across the river from us was a small outpost. It was manned by a platoon of Yards, thirty men, who were armed only with rifles. I could hear sporadic shooting there but could not see anything through the curtain of rain. I called on my field phone to the TOC below me and told Sergeant Pettigrew, our team sergeant, what I could hear but not see. He told me to support the outpost with fire from my machine gun, as the Yards should all be crouched in their bunkers and not exposed to my fire.

I began firing the machine gun in the direction of the outpost. I knew exactly in which direction it lay—only about two hundred yards away—but I couldn't see it. So I just hosed down the area and hoped it would keep the NVA pinned down. I could not tell what effect, if any, I was having as I continued firing in three- to five-round bursts.

Before long, I had gone through five cans of ammo, each containing a hundred-round belt. I was standing ankle deep in spent shell casings and links. My hearing gone, I only felt Pettigrew's tap on my shoulder. I had been unable to hear him calling me on the phone with an order to cease firing. We heard nothing from across the river.

At first light, a group of us spread out and waded across the river to the outpost. Standing outside the protective concertina wire, we called out and received no answer. I looked around but could see no evidence that my firing the .50 caliber had done any damage—or hit anything, for that matter. The four fortified bunkers, each anchoring a corner of the perimeter, seemed empty. Two barbed wire gates allowed entry into the post: one in front for daily use, and a smaller gate located on the opposite side of the perimeter. The front gate was closed and secured from the inside. We discovered the back gate standing open and entered.

We found our Yards inside. They were all dead; most of them had been shot as they lay sleeping in their bunkers. Some had managed to get out of their hammocks and into the trench, but were killed before they got more than a few feet. We counted twenty-eight dead, which meant two were missing.

We knew what had happened. The mortar attack on our camp had been a diversion meant to keep the Americans' heads down while the NVA took the outpost. The two missing Yards, turncoats who were probably on guard duty at the time, opened the back gate so the NVA could enter. The sporadic firing I had heard had been the NVA slaughtering our platoon.

We waded back across to our camp as the wailing started in the Yard village. The NVA made many new widows that day. In our camp, we examined the area to account for any damage from the night's mortaring. We noted little, but our engineer found something that commanded all our immediate attention.

All of our bunkers and fortifications had overhead cover to protect against mortar attacks. Commonly, a plywood cover was erected two or three feet above a bunker. On top of the plywood, we placed sandbags three deep. That was supposed to cause a mortar round to explode above the bunker, dissipating its blast somewhat before it struck the bunker's fortified roof.

Our diesel and gasoline storage site had this plywood-and-sandbag cover protecting it from overhead attack. Inside, we found an unexploded 82mm mortar shell. A round—a dud one, to our good fortune—had penetrated three layers of sandbags and lodged in the top of a fifty-five-gallon barrel full of diesel oil. A barrel located in the midst of ten other full barrels.

My "A" team at Camp Ba To, August 1969. I'm in
the back row, second from the right.

Main street of the Montagnard village at Ba To, September 1969.

Posing on my machine gun at Ba To, August 1969.

Taking a break on patrol near Ba To, December 1969

At company headquarters in Da Nang, December 1969.

5

Hasty Ambushes

Our fighting was often a one-sided affair. The missions of the two warring sides influenced that fact. The NVA, except for small detachments placed to maintain way stations and act as guides, were just passing through. They ran the gauntlet from Laos through our zone to destinations near the coast. As a result, they infrequently planned and executed operations against us, although random rocket and mortar attacks on our base served to remind us they were out there. The ground attack on our outpost was an anomaly, conducted to terrorize our Montagnards, not to overrun and destroy us.

In contrast, the American strategy was to go out and find enemy units. Neither adversary normally knew the location of the other in the jungle, but we were always expecting contact while the NVA was not. They were on a journey; we were on a hunt.

Our Yards were superb woodsmen whose stealth was their strong point. They were second-rate marksmen, but an M-16 rifle fired on full automatic at short, jungle range can make up for accuracy shortcomings.

One of our tested tactics was to find a trail that bore signs of foot traffic, set up in ambush, and wait. Neither side knew when contact would come, but when it did, the American side typically saw the enemy first and got off the first shots—which made all the difference.

Camp Ba To had a large area of operations to cover, so we sent patrols out in different directions in our search for Charlie. One day, our camp medic, Rich Carmody, and I were out with a combat reconnaissance platoon (CRP) in an area we suspected had NVA activity. At one point, we walked along the edge of a small river flowing down a narrow valley. Lieutenant Phu Van Loc, the Vietnamese special forces leader, halted the file and told us, "This is a good place to set an ambush. NVA will walk along this river."

I looked around but didn't notice anything good about the place. It was a flat, straight stretch of river, with thick brush growing to the edge of a sand and gravel shoreline that extended twenty yards out to the water. From the edge we were on, the brush stretched back about thirty yards before starting up a slope. We had good concealment but no protective cover. We could only lie down and hide in the bushes. Since we had no line of sight in that position, we wouldn't see any enemy until they were right in front of us.

I looked at Carmody, and he just rolled his eyes at me, "Hey, at least Phu is finally making some kind of a decision, silly as it is. Let him play at it."

We didn't comment to Phu on his pointless plan. Instead, we sat down in the bushes with the rest of the CRP. It was a good time to eat some rice, anyway.

Not more than five minutes passed. I was just starting to spoon out some rice when I glanced up at the sound of a scrape on the river gravel right in front of me. Through the bushes I caught a glimpse of someone walking by. He was wearing NVA green. I was reaching for my rifle when our entire line opened fire. I quickly lay flat and started shooting where I had seen the flash of green uniform. Someone else had obviously seen something too, but through the thick bushes I didn't think we really knew what we were shooting at. I know I didn't. It soon ended, not because we had run out of targets—we never really had any—but because some of our Yards had run into the open looking for bodies to loot. They wanted to get the enemy's weapons, as our bounty on each gun was almost a month's salary.

Lieutenant Phu had made a lucky guess with his ambush. Four NVA were down. Not ten feet away and right in front of where I had been lounging, one lay facedown in the sandy gravel, seemingly dead. I approached and noticed he had been shot in the lower back. A Yard brushed by me to check on him. He roughly turned the body over, and the NVA groaned in pain.

Surprised at finding him alive, the Yard raised his rifle to dispatch the wounded man. I snatched at his rifle and pushed it away—I wanted a prisoner. The Yard gave me an ugly look with his wild eyes. For just a second, I thought he was thinking about shooting me. Clearly, his bloodlust was up. But he quickly cooled down and consoled himself with grabbing the man's rifle.

Two other NVA were sprawled lifeless on their backs. Drag marks and streaks of blood in the sand led us to a fourth soldier lying in the bushes. He had crawled away to hide despite having been shot in the chest and legs. I radioed in a contact report and requested a chopper to pick up two wounded enemy captives.

Our interpreter, Mr. Bob, questioned the soldier with the chest wound. The man gurgled that he was part of a battalion that had just traveled down from North Vietnam. He and several others had become lost an hour earlier after missing a fork in the trail. Their company commander, a lieutenant (the one whom I had just saved from execution), had come back to get them and lead them to their group.

I led Mr. Bob to my captive lieutenant, who had been shot in his kidneys and was in serious pain. Mr. Bob tried talking with him. He said nothing and just kept staring at me with a hateful look on his face. As the chopper descended to pick him up, I leaned down low to ask another question in the seconds I had left with him. For an answer, he gathered what remaining strength he had and spit in my face. You had to admire his spirit.

Later on in that patrol, Carmody wrenched his knee climbing down a steep embankment. He tried limping on, but his condition quickly became worrisome and he could not continue. We had to call for a chopper to take him.

Our problem was the absence of a decent landing zone. We were in thick jungle with no clearing nearby. A Huey chopper was sixty feet long and had a fifty-foot wingspan; we needed an open space at least that size.

We did find an area that was quite small but would serve if we knocked down three trees. The trees were about fifty feet tall and had trunks one foot in diameter, but a claymore mine with its one and a half pounds of C-4 explosive could cut down a tree of that size. We spent over an hour blowing up the trees and hacking away the small stuff before we had room for a chopper to land. Our landing site looked like a green cylinder from above. The pilot slowly descended the green shaft we had provided; those lifesaving Huey pilots could fly in the jungle.

We put Carmody aboard and the Huey lifted straight up, clipping some trees near the top. I was looking up at the chopper when a branch hit me on top of my head. I wasn't hurt much, and we moved on.

That night we were sleeping in our hammocks, all tightly packed together in a thicket, when a circling aircraft woke me up. My radio squawked out my call sign. It was Spectre, a C-130 gunship, looking for us. I had been unable to make a night radio call due to our bad location, so my camp had asked for help in finding me. It was a good feeling to have that kind of support.

When our patrol returned to camp, our team sergeant chewed on me for not getting on the Huey with Carmody—our policy was never to go out alone with the Yards. He said it wasn't our lack of trust with them so much; more so, who would call for help on the radio, our lifeline, if I was unable? That explained why the Yards had taken such good care of me on our return to camp—and I had thought they just liked me.

A jolt to my naiveté on the validity of our war came four months before the end of my tour. The blow was delivered by Pettigrew, our team sergeant. One of our patrols had gone out without any US advisors and had run into an ambush. They suffered several casualties. Since none of us were out there with them, the Yards were unable to call for air support or medical evacuation and came dragging in, carrying their dead and wounded.

I mentioned to Pettigrew that I should have been out there with them. He abruptly said, "You weren't out there because this war is all a waste. We don't need any more Americans to die in Vietnam."

He was a career man and had been a mentor to me and the others. To suddenly hear how he really felt about America's involvement in Vietnam was surprising. However, he was on his third tour and had seen the war for what it had become: endless. Later, I would understand his mind-set.

Of course, that didn't stop him from sending us out when our turns came up. He went out too, taking his chances with the rest of us.

During a later patrol, Jerry Jensen and I went out with fifteen Yards from the CRP to look at a valley located near our boundary with the American Division's operational area. Based on some sightings made by air reconnaissance, the area was suspected to have substantial NVA activity.

While on patrol, we preferred to be within range of our camp artillery at all times. Air support was usually available but sometimes not timely, and no one wanted to wait around for help when under fire. On this patrol, our area of interest was outside the range of our own artillery, so we had made arrangements to call on the American Division if we needed support. The artillery located at Firebase San Juan Hill was within range.

Having spent a day and a half quietly wending our way to our target area without contact, we escaped the triple canopy to a narrow, grass-covered plateau overlooking a valley. We crouched, hidden in the elephant grass at the edge of the plateau, which dropped about five hundred feet down a steep, jungled escarpment into the flat valley. Our vantage point offered a panoramic view of our target area not often found in the jungle.

The valley, about three hundred yards wide, stretched from left to right for some length, at least eight hundred yards. Fallow rice paddies covered the length of its floor. Visible terracing on the lower slopes indicated previous farmers had used all the available land and taken the trouble to coax more arable land out of the hillsides. Only wild rice and weeds grew now. A fast-moving stream, about twenty feet wide, flowed down the middle of the valley from left to right. It was a rare day without rain, and sunlight sparkled off the water flashing against the rocks in the stream. It was a beautiful valley, and peaceful-looking.

Although we did not notice any structures, the wide, well-used trail that paralleled our side of the stream commanded attention. While we hunkered in the tall grass, watching, two NVA soldiers filed into view from the left. Armed with AK-47s, they wore the NVA green uniform with green, cloth-covered, plastic sun helmets shading their heads. They followed the trail off to our right without stopping, and fifteen minutes later entered tree cover at the far end of the valley. It was the middle of the day, and two enemy soldiers had just walked along in the open as if they were safe, secure, and back in Hanoi. That wasn't acceptable behavior in our area, so we decided to drop below and ambush the trail.

We angled off to our left and navigated down the ridge. The route was fairly easy and we soon neared the bottom. Stopping just short of a terraced paddy, we remained in tree cover while taking a closer look at the situation.

Leaving Jensen and most of the patrol there, Minh, our point man, Mr. Bob, our interpreter, and two other Yards accompanied me to find a likely ambush spot. Since the ridge protruded in a manner that narrowed the valley, we kept to the left, staying in tree cover above the small, terraced paddies.

Soon we arrived at the extent of the ridge's bulge, leaving us a mere twenty yards from the stream and twenty feet above the trail. The ridge then began receding back to our left. In effect, we were sitting at a choke point in the valley. From our height, we could see the trail lead off to the left for a couple of hundred yards before vanishing in the trees, and likewise almost a half mile off to our right.

The terraced rice paddy situated just below us was a perfect site to set an ambush. Crouching behind the three-foot-high paddy dike gave us cover and concealment from which we could watch for targets in both directions. Our escape route was the same path we had come down.

One of the Yards scurried off to link with the others and guide them to us while we started setting up. Carved into the side of the ridge, the paddy was a level, elongated patch of ground about thirty yards long and five yards deep. Long unused by farmers, weeds and bushes had taken over the paddy bed. Jensen deployed the men while I radioed in our situation and position.

I contacted the San Juan Hill fire direction center and coordinated with them to make a prearranged fire plan and have artillery ready to support us if needed. Firebase San Juan Hill was located on a mountaintop about six miles away, and its battery of six 105mm howitzers was well within range of our little valley. Meanwhile, we had spread out along the entire length of our paddy dike and so had fields of fire in both directions.

With a watcher on either end, we opened for business and lay in wait for someone to come along.

Our first customers were two Yard women. They appeared from the left, carrying bundles and chattering away. They passed by. Our Yards couldn't understand a word they said, which was not surprising given the different Montagnard dialects.

When the women were halfway down the trail toward the tree line on the right, they passed by a single NVA soldier headed in our direction. He was still over a quarter mile away. I used my binoculars to get a close look and got a surprise.

The soldier was a woman. She was carrying a rucksack on her back but was unarmed. I thought she must be a courier, and I made an instant decision that we would capture her.

Mr. Bob asked for the binoculars. He looked at the woman and then started chattering to the Yards. They became quite animated. I took another look with the glasses and saw the reason for their interest. The closer she came, the better looking she appeared. Trim in her NVA fatigues, with long black hair spilling underneath her sun helmet, she was beautiful, the more so given where we were.

I picked out the three Yards closest to the trail and gave them the nod to snatch her when she walked by. Their task was simple: wait for her to pass, jump five feet or so from the paddy dike to the trail, and grab her. The three chosen for the job giggled like lottery winners while the rest of the gang sat around to watch the show, eyes gleaming.

She was just thirty yards from us when Jensen alerted me with a hiss and pointed. Another soldier was on the trail and heading toward us from the treeline on the far right. I took a peek through the glasses: an NVA in full uniform and carrying a rifle. I motioned to everyone and canceled the plan to seize the woman. She passed by without a glance in our direction. I could see her rucksack was lightly loaded—she was a courier for sure, and it was her lucky day.

The Yards were deflated at the turn of events, but grew serious when we looked again at the trail and saw we now had three NVA walking toward us. We would take them out instead.

I watched the three walk closer. All three had AK-47 rifles slung across their chests. The NVA were disciplined soldiers, and one visible characteristic of that was their tactical movement on the march. Those three were spaced at least fifteen yards apart. Unlike some American troops, there was no bunching up, smoking, or joking with one another when they moved.

We had to make some quick adjustments since their spacing caused them to extend outside our coverage. I put Minh, usually a decent shot, on the far left with several others. They would shoot the point man when he was directly in front of the left side of our line. Jensen and a squad of Yards would target the middle man. The rest of us would have our sights on the trail man, who would be about forty yards away when we fired. As the enemy drew closer, we braced ourselves for contact.

I was proud of the CRP that day. Those men were very experienced and, for Yards, well disciplined, so they knew how to keep down and stay quiet when springing an ambush. I left it to Minh to open up when the lead man passed directly by him, and he pulled it off perfectly. As he rose to fire, the entire line did likewise. Everyone was told to fire single shots, but I heard several fully automatic, magazine-emptying riffs. No matter. The three NVA walking along a trail beside a stream that day never had a chance against the storm of lead that hit them. All three went down immediately and stayed down.

With a shout, most of the Yards were jumping down from the dike and scampering to the fallen NVA—there were weapons to collect. I left two Yards in place as lookouts while I hustled out with Mr. Bob to check on the trailing man.

He was lying face up at the edge of the stream, half in, his legs in the water. As I approached, an NVA corpse floated past me facedown, only to snag on some nearby rocks. I knelt to search the body of the man I had fired upon. Two holes in his chest oozed blood. I looked at him and thought he was already dead, his unblinking eyes vacantly gazing at the sky. But then his mouth moved and he said something I couldn't quite hear, not that I would have understood it anyway. His head slowly swiveled toward me. He gently turned his eyes and stared right at me. I was looking in those eyes when the life ran out of them.

I didn't dwell on it, not then, because sudden shots by an AK-47 firing from the treeline to our right interrupted our activity. It was one … two …

three shots, and then an entire magazine on full automatic. We were out of range and didn't hear the bullets impact anywhere, but it got our notice.

We were gathering ourselves to leave when the long, automatic rip of a light machine gun, most likely a Soviet RPD, spurred us to instant action. Automatic weapons fire always commanded attention. Likely we had killed the lead element of a larger unit, which was now deploying to take us on.

Without any farewell or adieu, we melted into the woods behind the paddy. As fast as we could, we took the same course up the slope that had brought us down. We reached the top in a hurry—unobserved by NVA, I believed—and sat in the thick elephant grass to catch our breaths and have a look below.

It was an amazing sight, and the only one like it I was ever to witness. A large group of NVA was spread out below us and advancing toward our ambush position. Jensen tried counting them—there had to have been well over fifty, but who could tally with accuracy in that moment?—while I got on the radio. I advised the artillery on San Juan Hill that we had stirred up an ant's nest in the shape of a company-size unit and caught them in the open. Although they couldn't see what I was looking at, I was sure the men on the guns at San Juan Hill were beside themselves at our report. Having enemy in the open was a cannon cocker's dream. I made minor adjustments to the original map coordinates I had previously given and told them to send some rounds out.

I had heard the Americal Division had undistinguished infantry, and I was to have some experience with that later, but as for their artillery, it was the best I ever saw. They sent in a ranging round that, incredibly, whistled in and landed smack in the middle of the NVA herd. I roared into the radio for them to fire for effect with everything they had. Behind me, several of the Yards were jumping up and down and cheering—they had never seen a sight like it either.

San Juan Hill's six tubes sent artillery rounds crashing in fast and furious, and soon the valley floor was partly obscured by the quick light flashes and dirty gray smoke of the explosions. We sat up there on that plateau in relative safety and watched the show, captivated. I have no idea how much damage the artillery did—I can't remember how many I reported, but I did give a requisite large body count to the artillery fire direction center. It was an educated guess, as none of us were about to go back down there to count bodies. But I thanked the artillery for their fine work and put away my priceless radio.

Having a radio was an instant power trip. It was twenty pounds of salvation. With that radio in hand, I could summon great forces to help us. Did we need food, ammo, reinforcements? Did we need fast medical attention? Did we need more firepower? I could have it delivered pronto. My tech-challenged Montagnards, being not that far removed from the Stone Age, were in total awe of its capacities, as was I. With just a word, I could unleash a hail of high explosives on a target of my choosing: delivered silently via artillery, screaming in from a Phantom jet, or noisy and deadly from circling gunships. It wasn't a mere radio; it was a proclamation of capability and magnitude, and a source of professional satisfaction.

6

With the Old Guard

Firebase San Juan Hill, home base of the Fourth Battalion, Third Infantry Regiment (the Old Guard), was located on a hilltop fifteen miles south of Ba To. The unit was part of the Americal Division, cobbled together from several infantry brigades and formed in 1967. The Old Guard was the division's most famous unit, but not its most effective.

San Juan Hill was the closest American unit to our camp. We kept liaison with them to exchange intelligence on NVA movement through our adjoining areas of responsibility. At their request for a meeting, I accompanied Lieutenant Donaldson and Sergeant Pettigrew to San Juan Hill to meet with their operations staff.

On a previous visit to our camp, the Americal had seemed impressed by our Yard force and with the amount of NVA contact we had in our area. In our clashes with the NVA we had reported killing ten of them to every loss our camp suffered. They found it notable because their statistics were not nearly as respectable, yet we both operated in a similar area. Counting bodies was a peculiarity of the war and an inexact effort due to the nature of combat. Since we were not liberating real estate, the army graded performance in Vietnam on numbers, particularly the body count. Americal's operations officer didn't give us a definite figure, but we deduced San Juan Hill was reporting a one-to-one kill ratio, at best.

The operations officer was telling us sugar-coated nonsense, and we both knew it; one of us just wouldn't admit it. We figured Charlie was hammering them.

Their typical operational procedure was to airlift a company-sized unit out to a location on a search and destroy mission. Both of our bases were located in "free-fire zones," meaning that we could shoot at anyone we saw and destroy anything we found. Landing in noisy choppers, consolidating, and then setting out gave any nearby NVA ample time to pinpoint them and move out of the way. It was no wonder they were ineffective in the field. They had all the stealth of a Macy's Thanksgiving Day parade.

Our strategy was to sneak around nimbly, few in number and lightly loaded. An American infantry company with its one hundred or so soldiers burdened with heavy packs didn't enjoy the advantage of speed or surprise. Instead, it operated from a position of strength, arduously tramping around as if to say, *Here we are, come and get us.* Of course, the NVA would only come and get them when it wanted. Theirs was a different nature of war, a war of booby traps, sniping, nighttime mortaring, and long walks in the sun.

I don't remember who brought up the idea, but before we left San Juan Hill, we had agreed to support a company already in the field. We talked it up and settled on providing a squad from our reconnaissance platoon that would walk point for the Americal company. Pettigrew graciously volunteered me to lead this first foray on a combined arms operation.

Two days later, six Yards and I were picked up at Camp Ba To and helicoptered out to join Company B. It was late afternoon and they had just stopped to camp overnight on a treeless, plateaued hilltop. The chosen spot was an old location where previous patrols had camped on earlier days, leaving their defensive foxholes behind. With us came hot food, mail, and water.

Company B had been in the field for fifteen days and was showing signs of wear and fatigue. Thus far in its search and destroy mission, the company had been sniped at daily, triggered two booby traps, and mortared for three nights, suffering six wounded. They had yet to see an enemy soldier.

I met with the company commander, Captain Hagen, and his platoon leaders to go over a game plan. Meanwhile, the company mortars plotted their night defensive concentrations and sent out a few ranging rounds around our position. Then San Juan Hill sent over a couple of artillery rounds to help plot their planned defensive concentrations for the night. These nightly defensive measures, useful in case of a ground attack, seemed comforting to the troops. But I thought the noise would bring every NVA within miles to pay a visit. It certainly provided the enemy our exact location if they wished to mortar us.

I had a chance to speak candidly with Hagen after his staff went back to their positions.

"I haven't worked with GI's before. What kind of troops do you have?"

"This is my second tour. I was in the Ninth Division in '67, down in the delta." He paused to let me digest his combat credentials. "These troops aren't as good as the Ninth. My lieutenants are fresh out of officer candidate school, and the most senior has only a year in the army. Except for two, my sergeants are all recently out of sergeant's school, shake and bakes, and they all have only a year on too. My men are draftees who smoke too much dope and spend their time avoiding danger and counting the days until they're gone. No one wants to die over here." Hagen's chin was on his chest as he spoke. Then he looked up briefly and said, "I took a round in the chest in the delta—I don't want to die here either."

I didn't have a ready reply to that admission, so I just nodded my head and kept quiet. Perhaps my silence was unsettling, because he continued, trying to justify his situation.

"I can't blame anyone; it's the system. We come out for thirty-day patrols and then rotate back to San Juan for a two-week stand down to provide firebase security. Then it's back out for another thirty day go-round. We don't see the NVA often. They snipe at us a lot, and the mortaring and booby traps are murder. Our casualty rate is over 10 percent and we rarely get any confirmed kills. Morale sucks."

In my brief time there, I had observed his men were not cut from the same cloth as the soldiers I served with. They just shuffled around inside the perimeter with little spirit and no apparent motivation. Hagen seemed cynical and burned out. I was thinking part of their problem might have been leadership. By the next day, I had my confirmation.

After my gloomy chat with Hagen, my Yards and I found places to bed down for the night. There were no trees to tie up our hammocks, so we found some previously dug foxholes in which to lie down under cover. It was a strange feeling to be surrounded by one hundred men. My first night sleeping in a hole was peaceful—no rainfall and we weren't mortared.

I had a learning curve with the Americal, and it started straight off. I had wanted to get going at first light, but it seemed to take forever to get the infantry underway. Hagen had another leaders' meeting, and then people slowly rose out of their holes and started repacking their rucksacks. Each soldier carried much more gear than we did, at least sixty pounds each. They walked along like beasts of burden with their huge packs. Many had items hanging off to make noise and get caught in vines.

I had brought along our ace point man, Minh, and he led the way off the plateau. The company followed us, keeping thirty yards back from our rear man.

Later that day, some idiot was playing his tape deck. From the patrol's point, at least fifty yards up the trail, I heard Jimi Hendrix singing "Purple Haze." I stopped the procession and walked back along the file until I found him. I didn't bother complaining to the music man's sergeant; if he found no problem with the noise, hearing otherwise from me wouldn't help. But Jimi quickly shut down after I gave him a hiss and a dirty look.

With their huge rucks slowing the procession, the men had trouble getting through the brush and vines on the steep slopes. I heard a lot of struggling, falling down, and cursing—too much noise by far.

I had advised Captain Hagen that we could find the NVA only if they did not know our location. That night, I convinced him to waive the nightly defensive artillery ranging and the helicopter resupply and to assemble close together in the thick jungle on a hillside. He set out several three-man listening posts around our site for early warning, and we passed the night quietly. It looked like Hagen was getting with the program.

Minh led us out again early the next morning. At first we kept off the numerous trails, but the noise from the lumbering men breaking branches and falling down behind us forced us onto the trails. Moving up one narrow V-shaped draw through the thick jungle, we suddenly made out the shapes of several log-reinforced bunkers dug into the steep hillsides above each side of the trail—we had walked into a prepared ambush zone.

Although abandoned, the bunkers seemed ready for use. Since they were there to protect something, we kept moving up the draw to the top of the ridge. On top was the ever-present, high-speed NVA trail, well maintained and well tramped with footprints from the NVA's rubber-soled canvas shoes. Following the steep, downhill-sloping ridgeline, we crept toward the flat ground ahead.

My Yards, inscrutable and seemingly relaxed to that point, picked up a subtle sign from Minh on point and became alert, looking and listening with rifles at the ready. Third in line and about fifteen yards away, I saw Minh drop to a knee. I gave a hand signal to those behind, and we all reacted the same way. I peered ahead through the thinning vegetation and saw an NVA walk on the trail toward us.

When the NVA was no more than ten yards away, Minh rose and emptied his M-16 on full automatic. I stood up and watched the soldier turn around and sprint out of sight. A veil of falling, shot-up leaves dropped onto the trail like bits of tossed salad. Every one of Minh's twenty rounds had missed high.

We gave immediate chase. I called Captain Hagen on the squad radio and told him what was happening. He was about a hundred yards behind and would want to know what the shooting was about.

As we rounded a bend in the trail, we could see there were three NVA, all running together for their lives. They dropped into a bunker located next to the trail. We quickly covered the bunker and Vanh, our interpreter, called out to the NVA to surrender. For an answer, one of them stuck his rifle out and fired off several rounds. Our reply was to lob two grenades into the bunker.

We pulled the three bodies out of the bunker, along with three AK-47 rifles. By then, the infantry had come forward. Some of the men came up to look at the bodies—likely the first enemy dead they had seen, as I saw cameras come out.

Fifty yards farther along the trail, the jungle opened up into a narrow valley. I noticed a small hamlet ahead, surrounded by patches of rice, vegetables, and banana groves.

While he seemed willing, Hagen was not saying much, and he was hesitant to make any decisions. His lieutenants stood by waiting for orders, content to just shepherd their individual platoons. When Hagen came to me and asked, "What do you think?" I figured it out. He was slipping off his tactician's rucksack and trying to put it on my back—waiting for me to show the way. That made me a little nervous. I had only recently turned twenty-one and was a mere buck sergeant with less than two years in the army. We had a hundred men sitting down waiting for direction, and we needed to press on.

I knew what we should do, but I wanted to express it to Hagen in a manner that would involve input from him. Make it seem he was calling the shots. After all, he was the captain making the big bucks.

"*Dai uy* (Vietnamese for "captain"), that was an NVA outpost we ran over. Ahead is a hamlet and a valley growing food for them. If we go out there to look, they could be waiting in ambush—most likely in those trees beyond the huts. They know we're here, but we don't know where they are or how many they are. They have the advantage."

He was quick to pick up on my line of thought and said, "We could back off, go around them, and come up from behind."

I kept up the exchange. "If we deployed half our men here to keep Charlie occupied, we could sneak away unnoticed with the other half."

We tossed ideas around and decided on a deception. Hagen sent two platoons, half of the company, to search the now abandoned village and remain overnight there. They would call in choppers for a late afternoon food drop, register mortar and artillery defensive fires, and make it look like the whole company was camping for the night. Meanwhile, the remainder of us would quietly slip away in a different direction.

After studying the map, we plotted a new course. Our two platoons reversed and went back up the trail we had come in on, and then headed out in another direction. By early afternoon we had found another high-speed trail on a ridgetop and were moving toward our target valley.

Our hike had been rapid, and the men were stumbling, bushed and wheezing, when the jungle abruptly ended and turned into elephant grass. We stood for a moment at the edge of the trees, catching our breaths. Our position gave us a view through the tall grass to a large, slightly downhill-sloping plateau, stretching nearly treeless for at least a thousand yards to our right and straight ahead. We wove through the elephant grass and had not moved more than two hundred yards when a Yard behind me suddenly hissed and pointed. Through the interpreter, I heard, "The trees are moving."

I looked right and finally saw what he was pointing at. It did seem that small trees, colored a different shade of green, were moving through the grass. I brought out my binoculars and soon spotted what weren't trees, but NVA with cut shrubs attached to their helmets. They had camouflaged themselves before moving. Due to the tall grass, all I could see were bobbing heads. They were at least six hundred yards to our right and moving parallel with us.

"Down!" I ordered. The infantry surprised me with how fast they hit the ground. They had not seen what I had, but they knew from my excitement that something was going on.

Hagen scurried forward, and I showed him where to look with his binoculars. By then, the first platoon leader, who had been counting the "trees," advised us he tallied over twenty-five NVA. Anticipation flowed through the company at our windfall—we had found at least a platoon of NVA in the open.

Hagen started up again, "What do you think?"

"We're outside rifle range, so we need help," I said. "We're beyond your artillery at San Juan too, but could your mortars back at the village do any good?"

Hagen was already thinking ahead of me and got on his tactical radio. He found an air force forward air controller (FAC) in the air only ten minutes away. The FAC advised he could guide in two Phantom jets loaded with "snake and nape" (250-pound low drag bombs and 500-pound napalm canisters). That was the help we needed.

From our vantage point above the enemy, I saw they appeared to be heading in the direction of a deep jungle ravine located about three hundred yards in front of them.

"*Dai uy*, the NVA are headed to that ravine ahead. If you can stay and coordinate the air strike, I could take one platoon and set up an ambush above that ravine. You have the only radio to talk with FAC, but we can talk on our squad radio."

Hagen gave me one platoon, keeping the remaining platoon. We dropped our rucksacks and were off and running, crouching in the grass to keep hidden. Wading through the elephant grass at speed was exhausting, and I called for a short breather just before we were out of the dense mess.

We saw the FAC circling overhead. It had found the plateau, but was trying to locate the NVA, who had gone flat in the grass at its approach. I had a signal mirror and used it to try to signal our presence to the FAC. Since I couldn't speak with the pilot, I didn't want him to see us and think we were the enemy. I also asked Hagen to advise the FAC about our presence.

The FAC must have seen my mirror flash, because he suddenly swooped down from his thousand-foot altitude straight at us. I was terrified: was he lining us up for a rocket shot? He was armed only with white phosphorous smoke rockets, but they would cause casualties if they exploded near us.

I yelled into my radio, "FAC is diving on us, call him off!"

The platoon and my Yards all hit the ground in transfixed panic. He pulled up and flew low over us, probably having a chuckle. We had just survived a sight usually reserved for the enemy.

Hagen coordinated well with the FAC, and after two marking rockets were fired near where the NVA had gone to ground, he told the FAC to have the Phantoms drop ordnance over the smoke. Once the marking rockets landed, the NVA knew what was coming next; they were hightailing it to get away from the smoke before the jets arrived and dropped their bombs.

We didn't wait around to watch the show, instead moving on along the top of the ravine to find a spot where we could set up in a line and see to the bottom. Nobody needed to warn the men about carelessness or vigilance; their alertness had quickened to become a survival trait.

Two Phantoms swooped in and made a pass, each dropping bombs. Hagen contacted me and said it looked effective, although he couldn't tell from the distance and the smoke. I asked him to wait at his location and attempt to spot any NVA after the smoke cleared while we set up our reception party.

We found a good spot for an ambush, one that gave us some cover and also afforded a partial view through the jungle to the bottom of the ravine located about a hundred yards below us. Through breaks in the trees, we could see it had a small stream running along its gravelly bottom and a trail alongside the stream.

We had only to wait about thirty minutes before one of the Yards caught a glimpse of someone moving on the trail. Soon we saw more movement. Although they were often obscured by the trees, we spotted many NVA. Some of them were carrying bodies, while others were helping the walking wounded.

At a word, everyone opened up on the NVA file. The Americal machine gunners fired long bursts from their M-60s up and down the line, and our three grenadiers were firing grenades as fast as they could reload. The noise of the shooting was deafening, and it all seemed to be outgoing. We continued for several minutes, long after we ceased to observe movement below.

After a reasonable interval, half the platoon and my Yards descended to kick and count the bodies. Although it sounds grisly, the higher-ups kept a scorecard and would want to know. An hour later they came back up the slope and reported they had found twelve bodies and twenty rucksacks full of rice—many leaking grains out of bullet and shrapnel holes. The Yards had found only a few weapons. Obviously, several NVA had escaped our ambush.

After returning to Hagen and his platoon, we went over the situation and decided against walking out in the elephant grass to find and count any bodies lying there. The shrapnel-shredded rucksacks we had found in the ravine attested to the bombs doing damage, and we needed to get out of the area since we didn't know the enemy situation.

While the infantrymen sat around in animated conversation—I could see they had been invigorated by having the upper hand for once—Hagen reported the body count to San Juan Hill, adding an optimistic estimation of NVA bombing casualties. I sat in the elephant grass and ate my rice out of a plastic bag.

The next day, we consolidated the company and moved in another direction to keep the NVA guessing. They knew we were in the area, but where, exactly? We had no contact during the day, but I noted that the Americal troops were moving better. They were more quiet, alert, and quickly got up after rest breaks to press on. They had become ardent hunters.

That afternoon Hagen decided to have the choppers bring in food and water, as well as some ammo to replenish the third platoon after their shootout in the ravine; all had been firing on full automatic and put an impressive amount of lead down the ravine. When I commented on it, their lieutenant explained they didn't often get a chance to fire at visible targets and so had taken full advantage of the opportunity.

I recommended taking my Yards, along with one platoon, and setting out an ambush that night at a likely spot where two large trails intersected at a stream, located about a half mile from our position. A night ambush was unpopular with infantry in Vietnam—who wanted to stay awake all night lying in an exposed position? Yet everybody in the company wanted to go out on that ambush. Hagen could hardly believe the transformation in his men—the worm had turned for them.

We completed our five days with the American, and I was ready to return to Ba To for a shower and some decent food. I felt sorry for Company B, since they had ten days to go before leaving the jungle. And I was relieved I wasn't assigned to an infantry unit. Their regimen and lack of success in the field had spawned a despairing atmosphere that coursed through the entire unit like some contagious virus.

I needed to get back to my unit, to that different atmosphere. At Camp Ba To, we all realized the United States wasn't doing all it could to win the war, but we tried our best to do our part. I think the Yards had something to do with keeping our spirits up. They were not concerned with geopolitical realities; they were fighting against their enemy, the Vietnamese. Whether the Vietnamese came from the north or south made no difference to them. They knew someday we would leave Vietnam, and they told us, "Leave us your guns when you go."

As the American resupply choppers landed at our position and started unloading hot chow and clean uniforms, Captain Hagen thanked me for our help, telling me his men had learned much from the Yards. It had been a role reversal—American soldiers learning from the Montagnards. As I climbed aboard their chopper with my Yards for our ride to Ba To, I noticed they were having ice cream in the field that evening.

7

It's Just Luck in the End

Our camp did not exist in a vacuum. We received reports of enemy activity, and as our detachment's intelligence specialist, I was responsible for collating all the information we received, whether by observations on the ground, in the air, from other units, or our many informants. All the data was analyzed, and from that I developed reports that gave summaries of our enemy's situation. Since I saw every piece of information that came into camp, I was aware of what we *supposed* the NVA was doing, and where. We used that intelligence to help us decide where to send patrols.

In response to information we received concerning a suspected NVA base camp, Jerry Jensen, one of our weapons sergeants, and I led the CRP out on a rainy day to find it. NVA used base camps as way stations or resting spots in their infiltration through our area. Since an overflight of the area had seen nothing due to the triple canopy cover, our objective was to go in at ground level and scout a part of our operational area that had not been looked at before.

We left camp at about three in the morning, wading across the river in the dark. We always left before dawn so as not to attract attention. Likewise, when notifying our militia they were going out on patrol, we alerted them just one day before the event and never told them where or in what direction we would go, knowing NVA informers lived in camp and in the village.

We moved away from the village and its tended farms and rice paddies. Our area of operations was located in a "free-fire zone," and so our villagers were only allowed to farm the land close by: up to a mile from our camp. The intent was to deny food to the NVA. Beyond our camp, yet still in the valley, existed many rice paddies, orchards, and a few small hamlets long abandoned and grown fallow due to the war. Whenever walking through those areas, we helped ourselves to any orphaned limes and bananas we could find to reinforce our meager rice rations. Our situation characterized much of the central highlands during the war: small villages with their supporting crops grouped around protective garrisons, while huge tracts of good, arable land lay abandoned.

A stream running down one of the feeder ravines to our valley became our access to the hills. We waded uphill in the stream for a half mile, and then, after pausing to pick off the leeches, pushed into the jungle. Our route led us through bamboo thickets, which slowed us down and forced us to work around them in spots. The day was spent traversing the sides of ravines that all sloped down into the same long valley. An easier route would have been to walk up the valley floor, or to trek along the top of the high ridge running parallel to the valley. But those areas would have guaranteed we come in contact with NVA, and we wanted to arrive at our target area unannounced and unexpected.

Late that afternoon, we found some convenient bamboo thickets on a slope that we nestled into for our overnight position. For night defense, we positioned two claymore mines, one above and one below us, placed snugly against large trees to keep the back blast away from us. It had rained all day, and it never let up through the night.

We awoke as it was getting light. The weather had worsened. Being socked in with fog and drizzle was worrisome, since any air support we might need could not get down to us. Air support was always our trump card when fighting Charlie, and we had lost it. The NVA were now fighting us on an equal basis—until the weather broke.

We pushed on toward our objective, taking it slow and quiet. The Yards, raised in the jungle as hunters, could move through it like ghosts. In walking with them I had learned some of their methods: go slowly, carefully placing each footstep to avoid breaking twigs or slipping; stop and listen every few yards; place feet sideways when climbing the steep slopes. As we moved on, the weather got worse, and although we felt only a steady drizzle under the green shelter, the sound of the downpour striking the canopy above was resounding.

A couple of hours later we came upon a large trail on the spine of a ridge we had been traversing. The spot at which we came onto the trail was only about ten yards from the top of a connecting, perpendicular ridge. Our point man, Minh, turned right and crept up to the top, where the trail intersected with another, even larger trail that ran along the spine of the perpendicular ridge. We followed Minh. At the juncture of the two trails stood a rudimentary open hut. Minh tiptoed toward it. I was third in line, and was just coming into view of the hut when Minh bent down, kicked out with his foot and then fired two rounds. Inside had lain two NVA: trail watchers, sleeping on the job. Minh had kicked them awake and shot them dead.

Minh's shots placed us in a precarious situation. We set out perimeter security and crouched down to study the map and find a way out.

I expected a rapid response to our gunshots, but after thirty minutes, nothing had happened. Gunshots by themselves might not raise the alarm, as Minh had fired only two shots. Charlie often used gunshots to signal or to take potshots at any monkeys or other game that got close enough to supplement the cook pot. And sounds sometimes did not travel far in triple canopy. My real fear was that someone would come walking down the trail, as it was well tramped.

We decided to get back into the thick stuff and keep moving. Finding two trail watchers asleep in the middle of the day was a lucky break that could only have been due to the miserable weather. We cleaned up the area of any trace of our presence and dragged the two bodies into the brush with us, dumping them off in a bamboo thicket.

In the early afternoon we stumbled onto the NVA encampment. We inched down a steep slope, hanging on to trees and bushes to keep from sliding in the rain. At the bottom, we straightaway entered a huge, open area, hidden from above by the triple canopy. With considerable effort, Charlie had clear-cut all the brush, vines, and small trees. The larger trees, those creating the second and third canopies, were left standing. The lower branches on all trees had been cut to a height of fifteen feet. From the air, the place was just jungle. On the ground, we stood in a huge natural cathedral, with living trees serving as columns to hold up the green ceiling.

Underneath, huts for cooking and storage stood spaced apart. Located all around and modified to serve as sleeping areas were vines strung between trees, placed to drape a covering poncho and spaced just right to hang hammocks—there were well over a hundred. A stream ran through the middle of the camp, then swerved sharply to one edge of the clearing and flowed along at the foot of a twenty-foot-tall limestone cliff at the hillside's edge. Against the cliff, the NVA had dug out pools in the stream for bathing. A large unit could stop to rest and remain safely hidden.

Again, luck had looked our way. The camp was empty, although it appeared well used and well kept. It was impressive and frightening. We plotted its location as well as we could for future reference, picked a new direction, and moved out smartly without looking back.

The weather cleared the next day, along with our hopefulness. We had narrowly avoided two possible disasters on the previous day and were anticipating better fortune. Jensen and I hoped we would get a chance to dry out, for those two days of soaking had produced tender feet and jock itch. The rain and the jungle never seemed to bother the Yards; if they had ailments, they suffered in silence.

On leaving the NVA way station, we had turned at a ninety-degree direction from our route into it, and we took pains to hide our route of march. Our two trailing men ensured we did not leave behind telltale broken branches, bent grass, or easily spotted footprints to advertise our presence and heading.

By noon, two ridgelines and about two miles separated us from the way station. We resumed our search mode. Our route led up a steep-sided gully with a stream bed that flowed at its bottom. The stream was wide and rocky, but the numerous sandy spots along it made the going fairly easy. As usual, I was third in line, with Minh on point. In the thick jungle, we kept at least five yards apart, widening that gap in more open areas.

We progressed up the stream's right side in silence. Minh was almost fifteen yards ahead of me and the second Yard ten. For some reason I paused and looked to my right, at the gully's side. Something looked different to me. Then I noticed what appeared to be rudimentary steps that had been hewn into the rock and dirt wall. I looked up the steps to the gully's top, about twenty feet above me, and standing there was an NVA soldier. He was dressed in the NVA green uniform, wearing his sun helmet, with his rifle slung across his chest. He must have been looking behind, because he was just starting to turn and face in our direction.

I fired my rifle from the hip on full automatic and loosed the entire magazine at him in my adrenaline-fueled haste. He went down and lay still. Without thinking I ran up the steps while reloading, slipping twice and banging a knee in my rush. The other members of the patrol were right behind me.

At the top of the gully, we fanned out. Before us lay a small hamlet, maybe ten thatch huts and a few animal pens, all under cleared triple canopy. More NVA were there; we started receiving fire from the huts about fifty yards in front of us. We advanced on line, crouching and firing as we moved.

I was advancing with the others, firing my CAR-15 from the hip, when I received a blow to my stomach and a burning pain in my right forearm. It felt as if someone had pounded my stomach with a baseball bat and then stabbed me with a red hot nail in my right forearm. I was hit.

Well, there were no heroics for Marky boy; he collapsed behind a rocky outcropping and quit. In an instant I became survival-centered—my little skirmish was over.

While I lay there, sniveling and panting, I checked myself out. The blow to the stomach had been a rifle bullet hitting the steel sliding-stock of my CAR-15. It had ricocheted off the stock into my right forearm. I saw the rifle stock was bent, but it had possibly saved my life, as otherwise I would have been gut-shot. I pulled up my shirtsleeve and saw where the bullet had gone into my forearm. It wasn't bleeding much, but it burned.

The NVA ran off in the face of the Yard onslaught, and the firing ceased. While the Yards tended to their searching and looting, Jensen came over to check me out. I showed him the bent stock and my forearm. He grabbed my arm and looked closely at the wound.

"I think I can see the bullet."

I looked and dabbed lightly at the wound with a bandage to clean off some of the blood. Yes, I could just see a glint of metal embedded in the muscle. We got the Yard medic to come over—he had been busy chasing after chickens. He and Jensen took hold of my arm and squeezed the wound until the bullet dislodged, like popping a big pimple. The bleeding started in earnest. I tried not to whimper too noticeably from the fiery pain.

We looked at the bullet, just a battered chunk of lead. Jensen looked around and said, "It must have hit the rocks in front of you and shattered."

Whatever. I was glad to be left holding a stinging arm rather than laid out with a stomach wound. I was in shock. Not from the wound, mind you, because it was nothing serious, but from the abrupt awareness that I was not bulletproof. It's always someone else that gets it. For civilians, the misbelief we are immortal dwindles due to life's episodes through the years. In that one afternoon, I lost my illusion all at once. I also knew that possessing all the skill in the world would not get me through war unscathed. It required something else—luck.

Jensen got on the radio and called in our contact report, mentioning my slight wound. Minor though it was, to prevent infection we were ordered to find a landing zone and prepare for medical evacuation. The closest likely landing zone we had seen all day was at least an hour behind us. Fortunately, I could walk, and after burning all the huts and destroying the food stores, we moved off to the landing zone we had passed earlier.

The chopper found us at a small clearing we marked with smoke. Jensen and I climbed aboard and waved goodbye to our Yards—abandoned to make their way back to Ba To alone. I wasn't too worried about their safety. Since they had no Americans (thus no radio and no support) with them, they would make their way back without enemy contact, barring some misfortune. They came in safely two days later.

As we gained altitude, my anxieties receded in the cool air with the soothing motion and sound of the Huey. I thought about the several near misses we had had on that patrol: running into NVA sleeping on duty, bumping into a deserted way station, getting the drop on the NVA at the gully, and my ricochet break. Altogether, we had enjoyed a string of good luck. I had two more months to go in Vietnam, and thinking about it, I knew I had become self-absorbed. The army had taken a shot at killing me and missed; I deserved to go home.

8

Aftermath

I did not get "short-timer's fever" until I was down to my last three weeks in Vietnam. I was helping unload supplies from an air force cargo plane at Ba To, and I exchanged pleasantries with the crew chief. When chatting with fellow military, the subject of how much time one had left in Vietnam always came up. It was a form of one-upmanship to have less time remaining in-country than the other. I told him three weeks, and he looked at me with envy. Other than the time-drag I had endured during my first month, my time in Vietnam sped by. Keeping busy was the key.

Although I kept active and enthusiastic about my work up until the end, my beliefs had changed. I went to Vietnam with a vague idea of "winning," but that frame of mind shifted soon enough. It wasn't due to enemy contacts, because from my perspective we were having our way and winning in combat. Rather, the change came from seeing the lack of commitment by the Vietnamese soldiers I dealt with and our army's restricted efforts due to political priorities. We were at war; we were killing and being killed. Yet we were not trying to defeat the enemy. My obligation to the war and its purported goals lessened and was replaced by self-centered considerations—I wanted to survive and go home.

I realized my war was over when I began processing out of the Fifth Special Forces Group in Nha Trang two days before leaving Vietnam. I had to walk a mile along a dirt road to the headquarters building from the repo depot. I checked in with the group sergeant major. He took one look at my dusty boots, gave me a dressing down, and told me to get out, clean up, and then come back when I was presentable.

I had lived through combat and had just come in from an "A" camp. I felt deserving of the credit that serving and surviving should have accorded me, and expected some slack for it. That was my mistake. He was far removed from the war: just a parade ground martinet dressing down a common soldier.

Vietnam was a central point in my life, and so it remains. Coming home, I made the shift from war to peace without distress—no recurring flashbacks, nightmares, or night sweats to note. Some veterans returned to America to wander without purpose, rudderless. I knew what I wanted and went right back to school after my discharge.

And tried not to look back. In Vietnam I had learned to trust men with my life, but after returning home it became clear I didn't really know those men. Contact was soon lost—not that I would ever forget them.

What was discomfiting was the distance between veterans and civilians at home. I never encountered any abuse from the antiwar crowd, but then no one ever shook my hand and thanked me for my service either. I met indifference. While the war was still very real to me friends, and even family members seemed uninterested in what had happened to me. Someone would say, "Glad you're back! Are you going to the big game on Saturday?"

Thinking about it, I realize it wasn't them; it was me. I was still decompressing, and it took some time for me to understand Vietnam couldn't mean anything to them since they hadn't been there. Their concerns revolved around different issues: getting those braces for Junior, trying for that promotion, how to get the neighbor to curb his dog.

It wasn't that no one supported the war. I would have understood that. It was the fact that no one talked about it—just ignore the war and it will go away. Everyone was involved in living their lives and couldn't be bothered with concern about faraway Vietnam. Evidently they already knew the real story of the war from having listened to Walter Cronkite on the evening news. I recognized that I had changed, that I was different from those who had not shared what I had seen and endured in Vietnam.

I needed to get over it and I did; it just took some time. My second son was born six months before I came home. We drove back to Ft. Bragg from Seattle so I could serve out the last six months of my enlistment. Kevin was teething, and spent the entire five-day trip crying and fussing. His older brother was fine, but my wife had to pry my rigid grip off the steering wheel at the end of each day.

Speaking as a veteran, the reason why Vietnam remains in our consciousness is that the experience made those of us who survived it, better. Don't misread me. I'm not arguing for war as a self-improvement treatment. I realize that the war's trauma damaged many combat veterans physically and mentally. Still, war's trauma supported rather than weakened us in the end.

My time in the army, and especially my year in Vietnam, has been a source of strength to me throughout my life. Living in fear of death made us better. We climbed to the top of the mountain and made it back down, and that increased our self-confidence, self-image, and ability to deal with adversity. After a war experience, we mourn our losses but have a greater appreciation for life and look at life from a changed perspective. We have learned not to sweat the small stuff, because after surviving combat, it's all small stuff.

My life as a soldier was over. I left it behind, unforgotten, and continued on with life.

PART TWO

Finding a Career in the City of Angels

9

Career Prep 101

Re-enrolling at Brigham Young University was an experience far different from my first go-round in 1966. My first year had featured me as a young kid far away from home, at a big school, and trying to juggle an active social life with the university's study demands. My work habits were untrained and mediocre. I had hardly cracked a book in high school, and my placement on academic probation after my first semester proved it.

This time I entered school with a focus I had not had before. I wanted to get in, get a diploma, and get a job. Three years of army life had seasoned me, and I was ready to hit the books.

As a veteran, I was eligible for GI Bill education assistance, and that helped me make a smooth transition from the army. I felt I had earned every penny I received. That benefit allowed me to concentrate on school without having to work. Returning to school, my major concerns were twofold: how soon could I graduate and what field of study would I choose?

I entered school with a desire to be a teacher. I envisioned myself teaching PE and history, maybe coaching a little—generally hanging out at a high school and running around in shorts at the gym all day. That notion withered once I started looking at job opportunities posted on the employment board at school.

There was a glut of teachers in 1971. Few jobs were available, and those open all seemed to offer low pay and poor location. I saw openings for jobs such as a junior high school teacher in Rock Springs, Wyoming, for $8,000 a year (Wyoming? The wind never stops blowing), or inner-city Los Angeles (I could see myself teaching apathetic kids inside a run-down classroom while gangbangers were stealing my tires in the parking lot).

When I first dreamed of teaching, I was young, unemployed, uninformed, and didn't realize that teachers were not paid a decent wage for their efforts. Later, after spending three years on meager army pay, I had a changed perspective. I wasn't looking to be wealthy—earnings above the poverty line would suffice. I was at a fork in the trail, and I needed to pick a direction in which to move forward.

A friend helped me make a decision on which way to go at the start of the spring semester. He was majoring in zoology with aspirations to become a forest ranger. I was whining to him one day about the teacher employment situation, and he recommended a class he had just finished, Law Enforcement 101. He told me the class had been interesting.

By a timely coincidence, I had just finished reading *The New Centurions* by Joseph Wambaugh, a book about the Los Angeles Police Department. I found the book intriguing. It was responsible for my emerging awareness of law enforcement. One persuasive dynamic in the mix: my army experience had roused a different spirit in me, one that sought some action and adventure in life. I had joined a National Guard special forces unit near BYU just because the unit went out and conducted a parachute jump every month during weekend drill. A career in law enforcement might feed that newfound need. My family supported the idea. I signed up for that course and never looked back at teaching.

Dave Saunders had been with the San Diego Police Department, and he was at BYU working on his master's degree in criminal justice. He taught my first law enforcement course. He had stories for every topic we discussed, and he must have loved the work. His enthusiasm soon infected me. I, too, desired a job where I couldn't wait to go to work every day. I changed my major to criminal justice and began looking forward to a career in police work.

Then, just a few weeks before semester's end, Saunders abruptly left school and took a job as a special agent with the Drug Enforcement Administration (DEA). Saunders skipping out of academia to become a federal narcotics agent at first chance caught my interest and got me looking at federal jobs too. Working as a patrol officer in a large city looked interesting, but after researching the DEA, the international scope and specialized work of a narcotics agent became more appealing.

I began my job search a few months before graduation in May 1972. I focused on obtaining a job as a federal narcotics agent with the DEA. To that end, I took the federal civil service exam. Scoring high was important as positions were awarded starting at the top of the list. The test was fairly difficult, and I scored an eighty-eight out of one hundred. Thanks to my army service and the Purple Heart I received in Vietnam, I gained ten additional points.

The DEA office in Salt Lake City conducted an oral interview. I sat before a panel of three special agents, and we had a discussion based on their questions about my background, objectives in life, and reasons for wanting to work in narcotics. They asked me several questions about my service in Vietnam; the war was winding down but still served as an important current event.

At the end of the interview, the agent in charge, Harry Saltillo, told me something that I retained and used myself years later when I sat in his chair and interviewed potential agents. "When we as a panel are deciding whether to pass or fail an applicant, we ask ourselves one question—would we want to work alongside you? The answer in your case is yes, we would want you working with us."

Looking at my pleased expression, he tempered it. "Your score is very high, but there is a backlog of applicants already cleared. I would guess you'll have to wait at least a year to get hired."

"That's disappointing. I graduate in three months, and I'll need a job then."

"Let me give you some sound advice." Saltillo had my attention. "You have some life experience but no 'street' experience. Working as a policeman would give you that, and make you more valuable to DEA when we hire you."

I was nodding in agreement.

"Now, don't go and work for some small department in a dinky town.

Go to a big city with big-city problems and get a well-rounded education in crime. Besides, big departments are always looking for new officers."

"That sounds good to me. But I don't have a department in mind; can you give me a recommendation?"

"Glad to. I've been working in this business for many years all around the country, and I believe the Los Angeles Police Department is the best police force in the country."

The LAPD actively recruited officers from around the country, and it had an accelerated application program for those who lived outside the Los Angeles area. I drove down to Los Angeles from Utah over a three-day weekend to put my name in the hat. In three days I underwent a physical fitness test, a written examination, and scrutiny before an interview panel. I also took my first Rorshach ink blot test.

The head shrink conducting the test asked me what I saw in brief glimpses at different ink blots and why I saw them that way. Supposedly he was examining my personality characteristics and emotional functioning—trying to determine my "normalcy." LAPD gave this test to every applicant in an attempt to ferret out those with thought disorders. Police work sometimes attracted applicants who believed a police officer commission came with unlimited authority, supported by a gun and badge. That misconception attracted some unsavory types: thugs, bullies, control freaks, and psychopaths.

I found the test to be almost laughable though, as anyone other than a drooling idiot could couch his responses favorably and seem normal for a few moments in that formal atmosphere. All he had to do was say those demons and monsters he really saw in the ink were butterflies and flowers. As far as the test's validity, I thought the process not far removed from reading tea leaves or tarot cards to determine suitability for the job. In any case, later on I found myself working with a few officers whose personalities caused me to think they had somehow slipped through the ink-blot net.

A final test remained before each applicant returned to the interview panel and received his rating. The majority of applicants, and certainly all of the Vietnam veterans, underwent a polygraph (lie detector) examination. Polygraphs were not as widely used in application procedures during that time as they are today. The LAPD, however, used the test for one primary reason: identifying those who had used illegal drugs. The LAPD chief, Ed

Davis, was unwavering in his decision that anyone who had used an illegal drug, especially marijuana, would never wear the blue uniform of a Los Angeles police officer. Of course most everyone supposed that all Vietnam veterans had spent their time over there stoned. That preconception didn't bother me. I had never even seen marijuana before.

I waited in a room with five or six other applicants from out of town, including two current New York City policemen who had traveled to apply with the LAPD. They had already finished their polygraphs. I gathered from overhearing their comments that one of them had failed the drug use question.

Then they called my name to meet with the interview panel, bypassing the polygraph station. The chairman of the panel explained they felt confident waiving the test since I was a Mormon and had served in the Green Berets. As I was graduating at the end of May, they offered me a slot in a police academy class starting in early June. I told them I would be there.

I enjoyed my last two months of classes at BYU and looked forward to moving to Los Angeles right after commencement exercises. My final law enforcement course was in criminal investigations. I found it stimulating despite the instructor. Professor Johnston was a retired FBI agent and the head of the criminal justice department at school. As I was to recognize later, he was old-school FBI, always dressed in a white shirt and school tie and wearing the ever-present brown wingtip shoes. Our problem with him was that he spoke the way he dressed—in a no-nonsense monotone that carried no interest. He was tightly wrapped, serious about everything. And we all know that dullness is often a consequence of seriousness. However, to his credit, he did encourage a lively discussion in class based on the excellent textbook; perhaps that was to avoid having to speak.

Our class was small, numbering about twenty students, all majoring in law enforcement. We got to know one another fairly well due to our classroom discourse and common career goals. That is, all except for one student. His name was Richard McCoy. He always sat in the back in the corner seat—the closest man to the door. He was anonymous looking, quiet to a fault, and barely noticed. He may as well have been part of the furniture. I recollect him because of a conversation we had just after I returned from Los Angeles and my interview with the LAPD in March 1972.

It was at the end of class, and I was standing at the exit chatting with another student about my monthly National Guard duty and parachuting. McCoy, who usually bolted from the room at class's end, had been delayed by something; maybe he dropped a pen or fumbled with his books. At any rate, he overheard my remarks as he was passing. Surprisingly, he entered the conversation and mentioned he was a helicopter pilot in the National Guard, as well as an avid parachutist. He and I had an animated chat for the next few moments. He was also a Vietnam veteran and said he had transported Green Berets while there. I don't remember talking with him again after that incident, but I always thought he was a person who had more to him than met the eye.

As it turned out he did too, because on April 7, 1972, instead of coming to class, Richard McCoy was out hijacking a commercial airplane.

Prior to the 1970s, there were no security measures on commercial aircraft. People got on board without having their checked luggage, carry-ons, or persons searched. Occasional disasters occurred due to bombs in baggage exploding, usually arranged to collect insurance. But most airplane hijackings were politically motivated, hijackers demanding to be flown to Cuba or some Middle East country. In the late 1960s, pilots flying routes in the southeast United States feared to hear the demand from an armed fanatic, "Take this plane to Cuba."

Some concern existed within the airline industry about the rising problem, but changes were slow to occur since loss of life was rare. Pilots met hijacker demands and the incident was soon over. That all changed when the ransoming of passengers for cash started. The infamous D. B. Cooper event, the only hijacking never solved, occurred in November 1971 when he parachuted from the rear door of a Boeing 727 with $200,000 in cash. That incident spawned a series of copycat crimes in 1972, about fifteen in number. One of them featured Richard McCoy.

I heard about the hijacking after it happened because it occurred over Utah on a United Airlines flight out of Denver to Salt Lake City. A few days later, Professor Johnston sheepishly announced in class that one of our classmates had been arrested for hijacking the plane and jumping out of it over Utah, carrying $500,000 in cash. Only a few students had ever noticed McCoy in class, so it wasn't as disruptive as one may imagine and was quickly forgotten. But I remembered him—I knew then he had not been just bragging to me that day when he mentioned he was a devoted parachutist.

In the end, he was convicted and sentenced to forty-five years in prison. Less than two years later, he broke out of a Pennsylvania federal prison in a dramatic escape. A few months afterward, he was killed in a shoot-out with FBI agents after they tracked him to his residence in Virginia.

10

The Academy

"Keep knocking them out! You vermin are going to keep doing push-ups until *I* get tired. I see some of you are lying down and resting. All right, maggots, hit the hill! Sprint! Sprint! The last two to get back will be sorry they showed up today!"

Officer Arnado and the other five officers who conducted physical training, or PT, were standing among us. Arnado—profane, rough and tumble—had most likely been a tormenter of the weak while growing up. But out on the PT field, the bully was in his element. Fifty-five recruits lurched to their feet and attempted sprinting to a low hill about one hundred yards away. Once to the top, we turned around and ran back down onto the grass and to Arnado, each of us determined not to be last. Groaning for air, we hit the grass on command and starting doing sit-ups. By then we had been on the PT field for over two hours.

It was Friday, "Black Friday," at end of the first week of LAPD Academy class number 6-72. We had heard rumors about Black Friday being difficult, but the reality of it came hard. It brought me memories of my army training, and I saw that day for what it was—an exercise to separate the weak and uninspired from those motivated and focused. LAPD was culling the candidate herd. The way I saw it, the academy cadre spent the first week looking us over and feeling us out and then on Friday put us to the test. I'm sure they had already spotted some who would get up and walk off.

That day, six candidates did get up and leave. Others, perhaps thinking the torture was only a one-day thing, managed to hang on for a while. Then the continued arduous physical training wore them out, and they too called it quits. When we graduated five months later, fewer than half of us, only twenty-six, would proceed to wear the blue uniform.

Two weeks before that Friday, I had just graduated from college. I had been on the school rugby team, and I was in good physical condition. That fitness did not save me from pain and fatigue, but compared to some of the others who showed up soft for training, I had it easy. My best asset was my mental approach. I had encountered plenty of physical and mental stress in the army, and I recognized the academy's version for what it was: just another thing. Endure, and it would end.

The LAPD Academy was the finest training facility I ever attended. It wasn't the buildings; it was the instructors. All of them were dedicated professionals. Our instructors made every class and every subject meaningful, relevant, and interesting. Regardless of the subject, the common strain woven into every class was officer safety. The subtle, continuous mantra was that as police officers, we were shepherds of the community flock, but to remember the wolves in sheep's clothing out there waiting to get us. We trained to be ready in an instant for deadly scenario changes. After completing the academy, those who found harmless events that suddenly turned hazardous appreciated the training—training, of course, based on lessons learned from previous encounters costing officer lives.

My class picture at the LAPD academy, October 1972.
I'm fourth from the left on the back row.

Receiving my award from Chief Davis, October 1972.

Graduation day at LAPD academy. I'm standing on far right.

LAPD recruiting drive in Los Angeles, 1973. I'm seated left

Integrated into the grueling PT schedule was self-defense training. We learned that many in the public did not respect our authority nor fear the badge and gun we carried. I've had people tell me, "Put that gun away. I know you can't shoot me." And they were correct.

The police baton could get the point across, though, and we learned to carry and apply it with confidence. We also learned techniques such as the bar arm control and C clamp. Those were control methods we used that choked resisting suspects into submission. The C clamp was a dangerous hold as it could easily render someone unconscious. To get it right and know how much pressure to apply, we practiced on each other, under orders to apply pressure until our partners passed out. Some, when getting choked, panicked at the discomfort. I remember one candidate struggling and crying out for his mother. It wasn't a pretty sight.

Some recruits had never been in a fistfight or been hit in the face. We boxed, which was helpful in that regard, but combat wrestling was the real training lesson. It helped us get the feel of being in a street fight. The object was to use any means necessary to get your man down on the ground and handcuffed—no biting or eye gouging, but anything else that worked was fine. As we were to find out, there were no rules of conduct on the street. Putting a person under control who didn't want to be controlled was not that easy. Sometimes we needed to use the sheer weight of two or three recruits to force one person down. Endurance was the key; the man with more stamina won.

During my five months in training, my family rented an apartment in Van Nuys, and I commuted every day to the academy, located in the hills of Elysian Park just across the street from Dodger Stadium. After class each day, I returned to the apartment, did my homework, and collapsed in bed. Those five months were not much fun for my family.

The five-month curriculum featured a full program presenting all aspects of police work, and it passed by quickly. The first three months, presented to us in concert with stress and pain on the PT field, trained us in skills we needed to serve and survive on the streets. During the fourth month, we were sent to one of the seventeen city police divisions for some on-the-job training. Our fifth month found us back at the academy where we fine-tuned our new skills in a more pleasant atmosphere. Even the rabid Officer Arnado showed a semihuman side.

Graduation day was a formal affair with the chief and members of the city council attending. My parents and family attended as well. I was honored as the class outstanding graduate. As part of that tradition, I received a Smith & Wesson revolver from the city for my efforts. I felt I would need it where I was going.

11

Wearing a Blue Uniform

I reported to work at Southwest Division for roll call on a Monday morning at seven. At the roll call assembly, the lieutenant serving as watch commander called roll and spoke about the previous day's crimes and happenings, giving us instructions on what to look for during our shift. We stood while he conducted a perfunctory uniform inspection and then closed the meeting with a reminder, "Get some felony arrests today; it's the end of the month and our numbers are down."

It was the numbers game, something I would always have to contend with in public service. We broke to check out a car and hit the street. My car, a new '72 AMC Matador, was still hot and the seats warm after being brought in by the night crew just moments before.

The division was situated in south central Los Angeles, a high crime-rate area. Unlike my new blue uniform and shiny badge, our faded building was twenty years old, built before the armored bastions in favor today. The office walls painted in that basic police-station bilious green went well with the depressing government-gray lockers and metal desks provided for our use. The front door, for walk-in citizen use, was always open, and visitors always found two officers on duty behind the long front desk.

Twenty patrol cars deployed during the day shift, with an added five cars working evenings and nights. No car left the division parking lot without carrying two officers. The residents living in the division were about ninety per cent black, with a small number of Hispanics and Asians. A few white widows rounded out the population. The white widows had lived there with their families since the end of World War II when the area's population was mostly white. Eventually they were unable to afford to move when white flight occurred in the late fifties and early sixties.

Along with the whites, businesses also left the neighborhood, but the University of Southern California stayed—a beautiful school sited adjacent to the Los Angeles Coliseum and the sports arena in the northeast corner of the division—all surrounded by urban blight. The division's major commercial avenues, bustling during the forties and fifties, featured pawn shops, run-down motels, liquor stores, and fast food spots scattered among unoccupied buildings and vacant lots displaying weeds, dirt, and broken concrete. The numerous liquor stores were hangouts for the drunks and layabouts and always had a group of men lounging around outside. Very few grocery stores or banks existed within the division's boundaries. Several of the many empty storefronts had become churches. A saying on the street went, "He couldn't find a job so he opened a church."

Tim Riley was my training officer, and I would work as his partner for the next seven months until I finished my probationary period. Tall and rangy, he was easygoing and even-tempered. Unlike a typical police officer, he rode a Harley-Davidson Sportster to work and lived in Venice, an open-minded, free-spirited beach community in west Los Angeles. I liked him right away.

As it was my first day, he spent time going over some rules of the road with me. Riley was driving, which meant I as passenger would be responsible for keeping our log—accounting for every minute of the shift, writing all the reports—and wielding the shotgun if needed. We carried a 12 gauge pump shotgun locked onto the car floor by the front seat. Exiting a highly visible black-and-white police car and loudly racking a shell into the chamber was an immediate attention-grabber. That simple action had a way of quelling tense situations; it caused people to pause and reflect.

Riley spent a couple of hours driving around the division explaining the crime situation and getting me familiar with our boundaries and some of the notable trouble spots: motels, liquor stores, bars, and apartment buildings.

South Central Los Angeles has been incorrectly referred to as a black ghetto. South Chicago or the Bronx it was not—no concentrations of high-rise, low-income housing. Instead, it was early suburbia grown old. However, not all the houses and buildings were run-down nor were all residents poverty-stricken. Most of the dwellings were single-family houses with yards, driveways, and garages. Built in the forties and fifties, many of the houses were kept up with decent paint and mown lawns, usually indicating owner occupation. But others, usually rentals, were ramshackle litter boxes. The dreary, faded stucco apartment complexes were usually not taller than four stories, offering less chance of an earthquake's shakedown. Most residents were employed, but a significant number lived either on some kind of government dole, by criminal enterprise, or both. It was not white-collar crime, just theft and drug dealing. Most of the homes could have been located in any typical lower middle-class neighborhood except for one distinguishing attachment: antiburglar bars present on most ground-floor windows and doors.

We stopped at an auto repair shop on Sixtieth and Western Avenue, known to chop up stolen cars for parts. Two former convicts ran the shop. We found four low-rider cars parked in the back: '63 and '64 Chevy Impalas with hydraulic lifters to lower the cars to the ground when parked. Old Impalas were the street machines of choice among gangbangers in south LA. The cars all sported trunk lids with punched-out locks—an indication the car had suffered a break-in. I asked one of the owners why he didn't replace the locks. He told me a punched lock indicated that nothing of value was in the trunk, so why waste money and invite another break-in by repairing it? We checked the license plates against the documented registrations but found nothing amiss.

After, we drove a few blocks north on Western and stopped to check out a motel. It was what we called a "No-Tell Motel," used by prostitutes, drug dealers, and other reptiles, with rooms let by the hour. Riley explained we needed to make frequent unannounced visits to keep some businesses on their better behavior—suppressing crime through high visibility.

We drove by some of the many liquor stores in the division, drifting along slowly while giving everyone the look-over for something out of order. The drunken layabouts and aimless loiterers, those not dozing off, gave us the dirty eye right back, fortified from drinking long sips out of their paper bags. Riley explained that once a month or so, we would organize a three-car posse (for protection in numbers) and stop to check out every person on the premises—we always found a few with outstanding arrest warrants.

I learned we always kept our car windows rolled down, even in winter, so we could hear what was happening on the street. It was with eyes frequently itching that we drove around in LA's approximation of fresh air. Riley told me if we had to chase someone on foot, not an uncommon occurrence, then the passenger officer bailed out and ran while the driver stayed with the car and circled around to try to cut off the suspect—this to stay near the car radio, our only link to help. The constant radio traffic was distracting, as every car in our division was on the same frequency. Riley explained I would soon learn to juggle a conversation with him as well as listen for our call sign—3A91.

On the day shift, we averaged about fifteen to twenty radio calls for service, while the evening crews usually handled twenty-five calls or more. The night watch, lasting from just before midnight to 7:00 a.m., featured radio calls tapering off to almost nothing after 3:00 a.m. Night watch was a fairly popular shift and had plenty of volunteers since they could cruise around snooping without being tied to the radio all night. Better them than me, and they could have it, because I wanted to live on the same time schedule as normal people.

Riley asked, "Are you hungry yet?"

"Yeah, I could eat. But I haven't seen us pass any place where I would want to eat."

"You won't either, because we haven't a single safe eating spot in the whole division. We have to get permission to leave the division and go up to Wilshire Division to eat. Tacos or a burger?"

We had tacos. It was my opener on a long journey in law enforcement, spending my lunch break wolfing down a "gut bomb."

In between our radio service calls, we cruised the streets, never parking, always moving forward like sharks while we trawled for trouble. A low-rider Chevy passed by as we waited for a red light on Crenshaw. We saw four youths inside, and four heads missile-locked on us as they drove by. Riley turned to follow them, advising, "Keep your eyes on the side, see if they pitch anything out of the car. Did you notice the blue scarves on their heads? They're Crips. Now, let's see how far they can go without committing a traffic violation."

Our neighborhood was home to the Crips. It was 1972, and the Crips were fast becoming a serious nuisance. Besides dealing drugs, they were also into home invasions, burglaries, and armed robberies. Their weapons evolved from cheap pistols and sawed-off shotguns to Uzis and MAC-10s.

It didn't take me long to understand the situation in south LA. The prevalence of drugs, alongside the area's hopelessness and lack of jobs, made joining the drug trade hard to turn down.

We followed them north on Crenshaw for about three minutes before the car made a sharp left turn on Sixty-Third Street. "See that? They couldn't go a mile without screwing up." Riley chuckled. "Turning in front of an oncoming car and no left turn signal—looks like we get to shake them down."

The Chevy was slow to respond when Riley turned on his red lights, but pulled over and parked. I gave the license number to dispatch to run for a record while Riley quipped, "This is not about a turn signal, of course. We just want to see if they are carrying guns."

We got everybody out of the car and onto the sidewalk, where we had them kneel down with their hands clasped behind their heads. Having been through the ordeal before, they knew how to assume the position. I searched them one by one while Riley stood watch. They were unarmed. I took down their names and addresses while Riley peeked around in the car. We found nothing and sent them on their way with a warning.

Later that afternoon, we had thirty minutes until the end of the watch. Our car's patrol area was one of the farthest from the station, so Riley started north, driving to time it so we arrived at the station right at four. Some cars were shameless and resorted to circling the station near quitting time so as to punch out on the dot.

In the middle of some forgotten conversation between us, the radio sounded out three loud beeps, warning everyone a hot call was coming out. "All units in the vicinity and 3A91, a 211 in progress with shots fired at the store, 6214 South Vermont Avenue. Unit 3A91, handle code three."

A "211" was the penal code section for robbery—in this case with shots already fired. "Code three" indicated it was an emergency and we were to go with red lights and siren to the location. The store was located less than a mile away.

The first thing Riley did was stop the car and turn it off. I looked at him in confusion. He calmly pulled the key out of the ignition and reached down to unlock the shotgun rack by my knees. Both officers usually carried keys, but only one set had been available that day. He gave me a patronizing look and then started the car, telling me to handle the shotgun as we raced around the corner to Vermont Avenue.

Riley turned off the siren before we drew close. As we approached, we could see our location was a small mom-and-pop store, situated between a Laundromat and a closed storefront church. We pulled up about thirty feet from the front door. Riley had his door open and was waiting for me as I struggled with my exit, banging the barrel into the side of the door as I pulled the gun from the floor mount. I guess you could say I was nervous—the radio dispatcher had spilled the news there was an armed robbery in progress and someone was already shooting.

Looking down first to clear the gun barrel, I looked up at the store's front door while jacking a round into the chamber and saw a man run out with a gun in his right hand. I didn't say anything or think anything. I just stood behind the open car door, brought the shotgun up, and started to tighten my finger on the trigger. Riley's shouting brought me back from the brink. "Hold off! Hold off! It's the owner!"

I eased off and looked over the sights at my target. He was Asian, and he was wearing a green apron. Riley calmly told the man to lay his gun on the sidewalk and back away, which he did. I tried to decompress after nearly shooting an innocent man. The owner led us inside his small store.

Lying on the floor in front of the cash register was one of South Central LA's standard robbers, apparently sent down from central casting: young black male wearing high-heeled half boots, flared burgundy polyester pants, a long-collared, long-sleeved polyester shirt, and a woolen watch cap pulled down over his Afro hair style. I bent over and picked up a cheap .32-caliber, nickel-plated revolver out of the blood puddle spreading beside him.

The owner told us he had been in the back stocking shelves when he noticed two young men enter the store. He was hidden behind a stack of cereal boxes and they didn't notice him. One stood near the doorway and the other pulled out a gun and grabbed the owner's wife, pulling her from behind the register and placing his gun against her head. He told her to empty the cash register. She didn't struggle but did as told, opening the register drawer. At that, the owner pulled out his own gun, a Colt .357 magnum, from under his apron. He took careful aim and shot the man holding the gun. He then snapped one off at the lookout, who bolted out the door with the first shot.

Taking notes, I was amazed at the man's story. Perhaps his wife would later question his tactics, such as shooting at someone holding a gun to her head, but one look at her stoicism had me doubting it. Unless she was in shock, she appeared as hardcore as he.

The owner's shot had hit the would-be robber just under his left armpit, and he looked bad. Riley called for an ambulance as other patrol cars rolled up to assist. I got a partial description of the other man, the lookout, from the owner, as his wife wasn't talking much. Patrol cars fanned out to try to spot him. Other officers walked to adjacent buildings, looking for possible witnesses. I stayed close to the bandit and waited for the ambulance to arrive, watching him bleed on the floor.

The ambulance arrived within ten minutes. The attendants placed the robber onto a gurney and rolled him past the gathering crowd and into the back of the ambulance. The crook had yet to show any signs of life other than an occasional eyelid flicker. I got in the back with him, and we raced off toward the hospital just as the detectives arrived to begin their investigation.

I looked the bandit over and noticed the track marks on the inside of his elbow. "Looks like he's a junkie," I mused.

The attendant was bent over the man and working on him. Looking up as we pulled in to the hospital, he said, "Yeah, but not anymore. He just died."

With no one alive for me to guard, Riley picked me up at the hospital and we returned to the station to write up the reports. That was the thing with police work: every arrest or major event demanded several hours of report writing. Using a pencil, we hand-printed all our reports in capital letters.

As we left for the day, Riley teased, "Too bad he died on you—you lost a felony arrest on your first day on the job. The lieutenant won't like it either; numbers are down." To his good credit, Riley never chided me for my blunder with the shotgun, an action that could have turned my first day on the job into my last.

My opening day at work had been an education. I saw the poverty, hopelessness, and violence that saturated most of that part of the city. From what I gathered, drug use was a major factor in many of the crimes that ravaged the neighborhoods. The heroin junkie killed while robbing a store showed me how things were in South Central Los Angeles. I would have no trouble staying alert on the job.

After the major drama on that first day at work, I was hoping my second day would be less of a spectacle. It was one of those rare days featuring rain, and it came down hard. Rainfall had a tendency to paralyze LA traffic. Rain falling on smog-saturated, oil-slickened roads turned them slippery, resulting in traffic collisions. En route to our first radio call, we passed a liquor store and I noticed no one lounging around. Riley explained, "The rummies are staying inside today. They'll collect at some abandoned house to stay dry while they drink."

We pulled up at a house Riley knew well. It was owned by one of the division's widows, living alone on monthly social security. She invited us in for coffee. Mrs. Sharpton must have been at least eighty years old. She was skin and bones—a human husk—but she was very much alive. Her living room featured the clutter of a lifetime spent acquiring dust collectors. She was partial to tiny ceramic bunnies. Located next to the unused fireplace stood a narrow bookshelf holding a few dozen bodice-ripper paperbacks. She was pleased to see Riley, as he evidently was her favorite officer.

She had called saying someone was trying to break into her house, so we made a show of conducting a security check before leaving. That seemed to please her, as all she really wanted was some company. We didn't mind spending a few moments with her. Riley explained she had moved into the house after World War II when it was newly built, and in recent years rarely ventured out. The LAPD had become one of her main sources of human interaction.

Radio traffic was light that day. The city seemed to pause for relief and ride out the street-cleansing weather. The normal foot traffic was absent. Street gutters were full of water, and we had to hydroplane through a few intersections. Few cars coursed the streets, thankfully, but of those out in traffic, many drove at their worst. We saw cars blowing through red lights, displacing great waves of water with their speed, and generally driving stupid, as if the rain would hide their violations.

I was driving. It was my first time, and surprisingly so since the instructors at the academy had told us we wouldn't get behind the wheel for months—we should be content just riding in the front seat.

A car in front of us suddenly made a wicked maneuver, cutting to the right in front of another, and then making a sharp, braking right turn, nearly causing a collision. It looked like someone had almost missed his turn. I decided it was maybe time to write my first traffic ticket. I informed Riley of my intentions as I turned on the red lights and pulled the car over. He gave me a raised-eyebrow look, but said nothing.

We had to get out of the car into the rain to put on our yellow raincoats, so our wool uniforms were soaked straight off. Our wool hats had clear plastic slipcovers, and we put them on to complete our ridiculous ensemble. In the driving rain, I turned my collar up as I walked to the driver's-side window. Riley halted at the right rear.

The car was a white Cadillac with a man driving and a woman passenger. He didn't want to open his window, but I persuaded him to lower it enough to hand me his driver's license and registration. Before I could even start to tell him the subject of our meeting, he started on me. "I know you. You see a black man in a Cadillac and you have to pull him over."

"No, sir, you're wrong about that. Look about you. This is a black neighborhood. And there are quite a few Caddies around too. I didn't stop you because of your color or your car. I stopped you because you were driving recklessly."

In our brief exchange, he had failed the attitude test. We all know about the letter of the law. He had violated traffic laws and was subject to receiving a citation. And then there is the spirit of the law, which would allow me to factor in justifying points, such as the weather, before deciding what to do. His lack of remorse and laying the blame on me for the pullover helped me decide what to do. Rain running down the back of my neck didn't help his cause either.

From the look of their body language, he must have been having an argument with his wife, was losing, and now chose to take his frustrations out on me. She just sat there with that stony look on her face, waiting for me to leave so she could continue their fight.

Writing a ticket in that rain was a one-time-only experience for me. Trying to fill in the blanks of a citation was absurd. Back in the car and soaking wet, Riley told me to head for the station so we could dry off and change clothes. His patience and poise with me was remarkable. He mentioned in an offhand way, "Now you know why we don't make traffic stops in the rain."

Later that afternoon, the rain slacked. We drove to answer a call on Denker Street. South Central Los Angeles, like many of the communities in LA, had both good and bad neighborhoods. Denker was in the worst of the bad. Decades past their prime, the shabby, single-family homes bordered by littered, weedy yards revealed it was an area without hope, just a bleak existence. Our call was for a "415 dispute," usually meaning a fight or at least a threatening argument had come from the house in question.

We parked one house over from the given address and walked up to the door. A woman let us in and started to complain about her boyfriend, who then walked into the room. A tall man with no shirt to cover his rippling muscles and prison tattoos, he stood listening. Behind him on the wall, I saw the two hanging photos found in most homes in South Central LA in those days: John F. Kennedy and Martin Luther King Jr. Riley left me with the woman and led the boyfriend into the kitchen—we separated them so they couldn't get their stories in sync and so one wouldn't butt in on the other's tale.

The woman divulged they were not married, a common circumstance in domestic clashes. He had been slapping her around and then pointed a gun at her. Riley came in and said the man had no identification. I told him about the gun issue and went out to the car to call in the name given by the man. There was no record of the name. When asked about the gun, the man walked to the couch, pulled it out from under the seat cushion, and gave it to Riley.

At that point our sergeant pulled up and walked in to join the conversation. He decided we should take the man to the station for fingerprints to determine his identity. Riley got in the backseat with him, and I drove us to the station.

An identity check revealed his true identity. Riley told me to book the man as he was an ex-convict with a gun—a felony in California. I let the man out of the interview room and told him to come with me down the hall. He knew his way around police stations and so asked me what was going on. As we stood in the hallway just outside the booking room, I told him I was arresting him on a felony charge. He said, "No, you ain't," and in a flash swung a roundhouse fist at me.

I ducked and went in and tackled him. Being a former high school wrestler, I knew how to take people down. He was large; I was small. I was trying to turn his thrashing body over and get his hands behind him to cuff his wrists when the house fell on me. It seemed every officer in the station piled on, all trying to get some hits or kicks on the man to control him. Since I was at the bottom of the pile with the intended target, I was catching about half of the licks.

We finally cuffed him and placed him in the booking room. I rose and dusted myself off, noting my bruises, bloody nose, and torn uniform. I felt like I had been tied to a whipping pole. Just two days on the job and I was already showing signs of wear and tear.

I felt good about our little brawl though, because it confirmed all the academy training—the "one for all and all for one" principle they tried to instill in us. That day I became a believer in the "us versus them" attitude embraced by most police. When the public sees visions of several police officers ganging up on one person, they often draw a conclusion of police brutality. We didn't see it that way. When someone resists a lawful arrest and attempts to harm an officer, every cop around is going to join in to control that person—this to prevent injury to the officer. There are no one-on-one bouts, tag-team fighting, or Marquess of Queensberry rules allowed in those street fights.

Trying to control or arrest a doped-up crazy was a situation often calling for gang tackling. One Sunday morning we received a call concerning a fight in the street. Riley and I turned the corner, and some idiot was jumping up and down on the roof of a car—totally nude. The car's owner was lying unconscious on the sidewalk next to the car. Mr. Nudist was cranked up on PCP.

Riley observed the situation and called for an ambulance and more help. We stood near the car waiting for help to arrive, watching the nudist continue his rants and jumping. Within five minutes, two other cars arrived, and the six of us got down to business. By then many neighbors had come outside to observe LA's finest in action.

All six of us were needed to get the addle-brained crazy from the car to the ground and under control. On the way, he got in a few good licks, kicking Riley in the stomach, while another officer took a fist in the ear. He was taking our punches and baton strikes well, obviously feeling no pain, but we finally wore him down with our weight and got him handcuffed. The neighbors watched it all as we whaled on him. Since Mr. Nudist had also suffered some bruises, we put him in the ambulance with his victim. It turned out they were next-door neighbors and friends. Who would have thought? As we returned to our cars, most in the audience gave us a round of applause.

Are there police officers who go beyond their mandate to protect and to serve the public? Definitely. I worked with a few of them.

One man, Officer Ruby, was what we called "badge heavy." He thought his badge gave him the power to do what he wanted, and what he wanted to do was harass and thump. To Ruby, almost everyone out there was a suspect. He was the worst of the lot, but there were a handful in our division with similar traits. A racist and a bully, he would confront people on the street, in their houses, or in businesses, and come up with any issue in order to pick a fight—jaywalking, spitting on the street, whatever. He showed no restraint, and no infraction, whether real or imagined, went unpunished. He was a malignant tumor.

The watch commander had trouble finding a partner for Ruby because many of us wouldn't work with him. Black officers definitely would not go out with him. Bad enough that he was trampling citizen rights; he also put his partner in the ring with him when he decided to hassle someone for

Dragon Chaser

sport. I figured that if we all had been in Vietnam together, Ruby would have been fragged by then. His abuse of power angered many of us; he betrayed us and what we were supposed to represent.

It is probable some officers entered the job already self-loaded with Ruby's negative attitude and demeanor, but most did not. More often it grew on them. The many dangerous and damaging aspects of police work eventually wore some officers down, conditioning them to a point they no longer cared or tried to understand. Cynicism and burnout resulted. In all parts of our training, the LAPD academy had instilled idealism, fighting for justice, and serving the public. That idealism did not easily endure the reality on the streets of South Central Los Angeles.

The sordid evil we witnessed and then tried to clean up eventually exacted some toll on everyone in uniform. The violence I sometimes experienced in making arrests was expected; the lies I listened to were not. It seemed everyone we spoke with was lying, and that wore on you. Few witnesses wanted to get involved with us, and others were lying to save themselves. This perception naturally tended to influence our interactions with the good citizens of the neighborhood, and there were many—they were among the victims.

Riley was my mentor in preserving a healthy attitude. One day, we helped break up a fight that escalated. It had started between Officer Ruby and a suspect, instigated by Ruby, most likely. Afterward, I asked Riley, "You have a lot of time working this area. How do you keep from turning like Ruby?"

"The problem with Ruby is he thinks everybody is a criminal or a criminal sympathizer," he said. "This job is to blame for that because we're only called out when something bad happens. We usually only get to meet the victims or the suspects. We never see the rest of the people who live here. So I tell myself that most of the people living here are just fine—which they are."

Riley did have the skill to separate harmless people from those not so. He had spent eight years on the job, four of them in Southwest Division, and he still had the ability to keep a positive viewpoint and not let the sewage we waded in pull him down. There were others like him in the division, and I took my cues from them.

Burglaries were a constant problem in a neighborhood peopled by the haves and the have-nots—those with jobs and those without. Sometimes, the haves were at work while the have-nots burgled their homes. Juvenile burglars were almost as common as adults. They starting out at about age thirteen by skipping out of junior high school to break in and plunder homes. Burglar bars on windows and doors helped keep the casual thieves out, but the determined types could always get in.

Almost every day I had a call to take a burglary report when someone came home and discovered the break-in. The routine was the same, and sad; take down the information from the victim, tally the loss, and perhaps help to put a temporary fix on a broken window or door. All the time knowing that the owner's belongings would never come back. If I could just get my hands on a burglar … I had my chance on a sunny morning in June.

Our call was a "459 in progress," to a home on South Arlington near Florence. That was code for a burglary, and it meant the burglars were still in the house. I drove fast to get there and arrived three minutes later, parking two houses away. We got out and ran to the house, keeping away from the front in case they were watching out the windows. Riley covered the front and I went to the back of the single-story, stucco house.

All the windows and doors were burglar-barred. I found the back door kicked in and standing open—burglar bars mounted on a cheap, flimsy-hinged door were worthless. I yelled out to Riley I had an open door and was going in. I had also alerted the burglars, but I didn't want my partner to not know where I was.

I entered through the kitchen and made my way down a hallway to the front door to let in Riley. I had not seen or heard anything amiss. But stacked in front of the door were various items of loot: a toaster, silverware, silver candlesticks, and other things that could be carried off and pawned.

Riley said, "Another car is just a minute away. Let's wait until they arrive before we start looking. We don't want anyone running out the front door while we're in the bedroom looking under the mattress."

Two cars arrived within seconds of one another. Two officers stayed in the front yard while the other two covered the back. Riley started down the hallway to the kitchen, "I'll look first in the kitchen and work back to you. We'll meet in the bedrooms. They're probably under beds or in the closet."

Poking around the living room revealed nothing. I tiptoed down the hallway. Located before the bathroom was a hall coat closet. I pulled open the door and looked through some hanging coats, seeing nothing. Then I looked up at the shelf. A coat was wadded up, covering most of the shelf. Peeking from underneath the coat was a blue tennis shoe with an ankle attached. I grabbed the shoe and gave a pull, and the kid flew out with arms flapping to land on his back in the hallway. A few seconds later, I heard a clanging of pots and pans and a frightened shriek. Riley had caught another one in a kitchen cabinet. I never did figure out how my kid boosted himself up and wedged onto the shelf, covered up with a coat, and then managed to close the closet door.

One of the assisting officers went next door and interviewed the witness who had phoned in the break-in. We called her type "Gladys Glassnose." Every neighborhood had one: a person who always had her nose to the window checking on the neighborhood, watching who came and went. She had observed the two boys walking around when they should have been in school. They disappeared from her view, but when she heard the back door being kicked in next door, she knew what was happening and made the call for help. They were fourteen-year-old ninth graders from Horace Mann Junior High School.

Like many public schools in south LA, Horace Mann was known as a training ground for burglars, drug dealers, and gangsters. The fenced yard and security guards at the entrance gates tried to keep hoodlums out and students in. Teachers were advised to use an old beater car to commute in, because anything decent was a candidate for theft or vandalism.

At one of my earliest burglary calls on the job, I had met a teacher from Horace Mann. She was the victim. She informed me about the situation in many of the area's schools. In her opinion, Horace Mann featured burned-out teachers standing in front of dispirited and frightened students, an environment that made it near impossible for a decent kid to get an education.

Obviously, cynicism and burnout was not only a problem for police officers. The feeling of hopelessness affected people throughout the area. Too bad they couldn't hang out with Officer Riley.

Homicides occur everywhere in the United States, but their incidence is much higher in the large cities. Los Angeles had a high rate of homicides, the highest in California, and South Central Los Angeles led the way for the city. I responded to at least one a month in my area. Deaths occurred wherever and whenever people mingled and had disagreements. Each death was memorable, some just more so than others.

The Hyde Park Social Club was a lesbian pick-up bar on Hyde Park Boulevard. Located in the lower west side of the division, it was part of my car's patrol area. Most of the action there occurred at night, and we had two or three calls a week. Friday nights were demanding. Inside was peaceful enough, with drinking and bar banter the order of the evening as individuals worked at hooking up with someone. Except that only females were allowed in the private club, it was just a typical LA bar.

It was the outside activity in the small parking lot behind the club that required our frequent presence. Catfights, fender-bender collisions by drunken drivers, and drug overdoses were our invitations to intercede. Heroin, uppers, downers, hallucinogens—all were abused with equal ardor by those seeking some chemical assistance.

I had occasion to go inside the Hyde Park club only once in daylight, but it was a memorable event. On a Sunday morning, Riley and I cleared the station and immediately received a call to go to the club because of an anonymous "unknown disturbance" phone call. It was before 8:00 a.m., and no one was out on the street as we pulled up near the front.

The club was a two-story building with a narrow front, showing only a door and a large window, but extending deep into its lot. A narrow driveway stretched along its left side to the parking area behind the building. We heard nothing as we walked up to the front door, which was standing ajar. I pushed lightly on the door. It opened only a few inches before hitting some heavy object inside. I put both hands on the door and shoved harder. Then my feet slipped out and I was on my knees in the concrete entranceway. I looked down, and saw I had slipped on blood pooling from underneath the door.

Together, Riley and I struggled to push the door wide enough to squeeze inside. A lifeless man lay facedown in the entryway. I checked for a pulse and found none. The body had numerous stab wounds in the back and appeared to have bled out, given the large amount of blood surrounding him. A .357 magnum revolver lay beside the body.

Just beyond the entrance and down the left side stretched a long bar with red leather stools. On the floor about halfway down the bar, leaning back between two stools, was another man. He was obviously hurt but holding a bottle of Jack Daniels to his mouth as he squinted at us. Riley recognized him as the club's bouncer.

I crouched next to him and asked what had happened. "That dude on the floor didn't like losing. He went out, got his gun, and came back to get his money. I heard the shots. Then he shot me in the back. He shouldna done that, so I fixed him good."

"Who was he shooting at and where are they?"

"I guess they still upstairs, I ain't heard nobody come down."

Riley called for an ambulance and assistance and then went upstairs to check while I tended to Bouncer. He looked just like Godfrey Cambridge, a well-known actor at the time, but Bouncer was much larger. I tried to pull him out so I could staunch his wound—he had been shot in the right shoulder blade—but he stayed wedged between two stools. Riley came back and told me there were three dead men upstairs lying around a card table. A game of poker gone bad. I bent down to ask Bouncer the identity of those upstairs but he had passed out by then. After taking a round from a .357 magnum I was surprised he was still alive. I never found out how four men ended up playing poker in a lesbian bar.

Working in South Central LA gave me an education in criminal behavior and a chance to observe what people do to each other, even to those they love. The robberies, burglaries, fraud, rapes, assaults, and homicides were all different and all troubling.

Our least favorite calls to handle were the altercations—what we called a "415" after the penal code citation for disturbing the peace. That was because we didn't know what to expect when we knocked at the door. With the stressful social environment in that depressed area, in-house fighting was common. It didn't take much to set people fighting. The Rams were in Los Angeles during that time, and whenever they lost, we had several calls to go into houses and break up vicious fights among the drunken losers.

Working my first New Year's Eve helped me to stay focused on the potential danger lurking behind those closed front doors. The shooting started before midnight. It was an incredible, area-wide symphony of guns with scary, ripping bursts of automatic rifle fire hitting all the high notes. That night left little doubt in my mind that a gun lay behind every door in my neighborhood. On our shift, every car worked overtime to answer calls—we had dozens of reports to check on shots fired. Many homes suffered bullet hits from celebration shots fired into the air coming down to hit something in the neighborhood. But on the whole it was peaceful—just booze-induced gunfire. We made no arrests and, seized no weapons. No one was hurt. Amazing.

Bar fights and squabbles outside liquor stores were common, but most of our calls to break up fights came from a home—usually a man thumping on a woman. We entered the house, separated them, and tried to mediate. If the man had an outstanding arrest warrant, it provided a quick ending to the altercation. We hauled him off to jail. If the woman showed visible signs of abuse, we likely took the man away on an assault charge. Surprisingly though, a fair number of calls brought us in to rescue the man from taking a beating by the woman—well deserved as it often was. There were plenty of tough women in that neighborhood, and they didn't fight fair.

A 415 call came to us one day from an anonymous caller, likely a neighbor who heard the screams and yells but didn't want to be identified. The untidy, run-down property indicated this was likely the rental housing of an unmarried couple. The day was hot, and although the house windows were open, no sounds alerted us as to the setting inside. We looked around at the neighboring houses but saw no one, although I was sure people were peeking at us from behind curtains. They wanted to see what would happen now that the man had arrived.

Riley told me to wait at the front door while he took a quick look in the back. I stepped onto the front porch. The main door was open behind a closed screen door. Standing there, I heard a muffled gagging noise from within.

Inside was dim but putting my face up against the screen, I made out a frightful sight. A woman was lying on the couch, gagging and struggling, while a man on top of her had his hands around her neck, choking. I pulled open the unlocked screen and rushed in, drawing my baton. Without a word I brought it down on top of his head—a dangerous and prohibited blow. Out cold, he dropped like a stone to the bare linoleum floor. I jumped on his back and was working to get his hands behind to cuff him when my lights went out.

I struggled to sit up. Riley had arrived just in time to see her brain me with a crystal ashtray that had been on the coffee table. I had a small cut on top my head and a headache, but the police hat I was wearing took enough of the blow to save me from serious injury.

As Riley was cuffing her, she scolded me for beating up on her boyfriend. I thought I had saved her life, and she rewarded me for it with a crack on the head. What was that all about? Love is blind. We took them both to jail.

Some of the conflicts we handled turned deadly. One Saturday afternoon we received a "415, man down," call, indicating an unknown type of disturbance had resulted in a casualty. The house was located on Seventieth Street near Crenshaw. Seventieth Street was respectable, its older homes well kept up. As we approached the house, we saw a man lying on the cement front step. We hurried to him. He had been shot in the stomach and was unconscious but breathing. After we called for an ambulance, the wife let us inside. I noticed a .22 rifle leaning against the wall just inside the front door. Riley began questioning the wife while I nosed around to see who else was in the house.

The house was what we called a sleeper. The outside presented just another stucco-sided dwelling like its neighbors, surrounded by a small grass yard. The front door, with the obligatory antiburglar screen door, was equally plain and uninviting. The burglar-barred windows, standard for the area, completed a picture that announced to any potential thieves, "This is just another run-of-the-mill house that doesn't deserve a second glance."

Once inside, the camouflage came off, revealing a residence whose owners had spared no cost in furnishings. The living room had a plush carpet decorated with expensive sofa and chairs, although French provincial covered with clear plastic was a show stopper for me. Bedrooms, baths, living room—the entire house was decorated top to bottom in the owner's image of Versailles. I was French-weary by the time I looked in the garage and found the boy.

He sat on the garage floor and leaned against a cabinet next to his parked bicycle. He was the couple's twelve-year-old son. He had picked up on the tension in the air and sat still. I kneeled down beside him and asked what had happened. Without coaxing he spoke, sensing something was wrong but unsure.

"Mom and Dad went out to lunch. I stayed home and rode around on my bicycle. They came back and Mom called me into the garage. Dad left in the car."

"What did your mother want with you in the garage?" I asked.

"She asked me to get my gun. Dad gave me a .22 rifle for my birthday. We have been out to shoot it a few times already. So I got my gun out. She asked me to load it and show her how to fire it, so I did."

"Why did she do that? His story wasn't sounding good.

"I don't know. I didn't ask her. She just told me to stay in the garage. She looked mad, so I stayed in the garage."

Waiting as ordered, he was polishing his bicycle wheels when the shot came. I advised the boy to remain in the garage when I heard the ambulance arrive.

Riley related the woman's side of the story to me, a story in conflict with that of her son. She had an argument with her abusive husband at a restaurant earlier, and he had embarrassed her in front of friends. When they came home, he dropped her off and went to a drugstore to get a prescription filled. He came right back. In her anger, she had brandished the rifle just to scare him. She did not know it was loaded or even how to fire it, but somehow it accidentally went off and hit him.

A division homicide detective contacted me later to thank me for the timely interview of the son. He mentioned the husband had died on the operating table. As the wife's story differed from that of her son, they were arresting her for premeditated murder. In a knowing tone, the detective said that humiliation was a major motive for murder.

I never found out how the case concluded, but I felt sorry for the son. He had lost a father, and his guileless honesty most likely sent his mother to prison.

Patrolling in South Central LA in our black-and-white vehicles kept us on display. One afternoon in early 1974, my partner and I had finished a burglary call. As we pulled away from the victim's house, I cleared us on the radio just as a call sounded to help an officer needing assistance. The location given was only a few blocks away. I radioed we were responding.

At the intersection of Sixty-Third and South Arlington, I stopped at the stop sign, quickly looked left for oncoming traffic, and started a right turn. As I looked up, a man was standing directly in front of the car. I slammed on the brakes while he lurched backward, falling down onto the street. I had not hit him. He struggled to his feet, talking to me in a slurred voice, and continued crossing the street in a stumble-walk. From my perspective, he was falling-down drunk. Yelling at him to watch where he was going and to stay out of the street, I sped off to the call—an officer needed help and I was close.

That night I was home eating dinner when my sergeant called me from the station. He said to come to the station straightaway and hung up. Not expecting anything, I arrived at the station and was placed in an interview room. These were the soundproofed rooms with one-way windows that we used when interviewing witnesses and suspects. In that room I sat.

Four hours later, two internal affairs investigators came in, introduced themselves, and advised me they were investigating me on a charge of hit and run driving: a felony. Without giving me a chance to catch my breath, they told me they had received an eyewitness account that I hit a man and left him in the street at Sixty-Third and South Arlington. They had also pulled my partner in, the poor bugger, and had been grilling him while I sat on ice, cooling my heels like a felon-in-waiting. My partner had not seen the incident since he had been writing in the log book at the time. The headhunters, as we called them, probably thought he was lying to cover me.

I was guilty until proven otherwise. I spent the next two hours going over the scenario with them several times. They tried to trip me up and catch me changing my statement. It seemed the drunk I had narrowly missed hitting was not a drunk at all, but was suffering from Lou Gehrig's disease. He was trying to make his way home, located four houses away from the intersection where we met. I tried to mitigate my actions by explaining I was traveling to my "officer needs assistance" call. Although

I should have stopped the car, got out, and assisted the man safely off the street, I had not. I felt the officer assistance call had priority due to my assuming the man was drunk. It was a mistake on my part.

The final charge against me was CUBO—conduct unbecoming an officer—and I was nailed for three days without pay. I took the hit quietly, but I was disappointed, especially after my sergeant took me aside later. He advised me that a first-offence CUBO charge resulted only in a letter of reprimand anywhere but in South Central LA. The then-current racial sensitivities required that I, a white officer, receive punishment. It was 1974, and LAPD went out of its way not to scratch the racial animosities festering just under the surface, a wound that was not nearly healed from the Watts riots in the summer of 1965.

Nonetheless, good things happen in bad circumstances. Just two weeks later, I received a letter from the Drug Enforcement Administration offering me a position as a special agent. I had to make up my mind quickly, however, as I was to report to the Los Angeles office in two weeks if I wanted the job.

I probably mulled that decision for all of five minutes before mailing back my acceptance. I had enjoyed my stint with the LAPD and had been proud to wear the blue uniform, but working as a narcotics agent was what I wanted. I had learned much on the streets of Southwest Division that would prove very useful for my career choice. I was confident I would hit the street running with DEA.

12

Learning to Chase a Dragon

My conversion from police officer to special agent was dramatic. Gone was the shiny badge and the blue uniform, along with the black-and-white car with red lights on the roof. Now my uniform was street casual and my car was unmarked and anonymous. My gold badge stayed concealed. No more reacting to radio calls for citizen assistance; I was part of a group of proactive narcotics investigators tracking down LA's major drug dealers.

Police patrol had shown me that illegal drugs played a major role in criminal activity. Now I would see the extent of the problem. Los Angeles in the 1970s, as it sadly remains, was a supermarket with every drug of abuse readily available. Although we worked at seizing many illegal drugs, our primary duty was chasing dragons—going after heroin, one of the most addictive dangerous drugs out there.

Fresh from the ten-week-long DEA Academy in Washington, DC, I reported to the Los Angeles DEA office, located on West Sixth Street, in May 1974. Our office housed eight enforcement groups and attendant support staff. I was assigned to Group Four. Quarters were tight, and our group wedged eight agents into one room. We each had a government-issue gray metal desk, all pushed together in the center of the room to save space, so we sat facing each other in a huddle. That closeness facilitated sharing the two phones provided for the eight of us. Off in a corner, we had one electric typewriter—little used, as most of us hand-wrote our reports for the secretary to type. The place wasn't much, but we didn't spend much time there either. We spent most of our time out working in the city.

My group of baby boomers came of age in the 1960s, leading America in social upheaval, Vietnam protests, and, of course, widespread illegal drug consumption. Humans have always desired to ingest substances that make them feel good, legally or otherwise. And that's the rub, because despite all the clear dangers of drug abuse—health factors, prison risk, violence, expense—feeling good is good enough. When I started enforcing drug laws in 1974, the drug abuse situation in America was running from bad to worse. Outnumbered and surrounded, those in drug law enforcement fought an unwinnable war, but we never ran up the white flag.

With a few exceptions, dope dealers stay low and are careful with whom they deal. It's a high risk, high reward business—huge profits are possible, but the hazard of arrest or having the drugs stolen demands caution.

So how did we find the dealers? We needed someone familiar with the narcotics business and the players, someone already in the business. For us, informants were the best investigative tool in the chest. Ex-dealers made excellent informants, for they knew the enemy personally, having been one. Often labeled "snitches" or "stoolies," we referred to them as "CIs" (confidential informants), and we couldn't operate without them.

Drug investigations most often commenced with a CI pointing out a dealer, someone he knew. The simplest technique entailed having the informant introduce an agent, posing as a buyer, to the crook. The agent then made a small, undercover purchase of dope. That pinned the crook to a narcotics delivery. From there, one or two additional buys were made while we used our investigative means to find and get a fix on the crook's source of supply. A final large order was made, and the crook was arrested upon delivery. Sometimes we also got his source and so could continue up the chain.

Since I was new to the job and learning, I was not given much responsibility. The boss gave me several pending cases to handle. Most were corpse-like; their only living elements were the periodic no-new-leads reports I filed monthly. The others consisted of fugitive cases: arrested dealers who had obtained bail and then taken off. If the fugitive was Mexican, he was definitely in Mexico, so forget it.

My partner, Gary Knudsen, had been on the job for two years. He was one of the senior agents in the office and one of the best. Except for the supervisors, hardly anyone had more than four years on the job. We were all new; I was just the newest. Gary had several informants reporting to him, which meant he had several active investigations going. I helped by writing reports, following up leads, and conducting surveillance. I learned much of the job from him.

Although fewer than half of the agents in the office ever made undercover buys, most everyone dressed the part, affecting an appearance of a man-about-town in 1970s Los Angeles. The idea was to blend in when on the street. Gary was our poster boy. He had stylish long hair and a short beard, and wore tight designer jeans, flared to hide the ankle gun; a collared, cotton, western-style shirt; a short, brown leather jacket to cover the shoulder-holstered .45 automatic; and brown, ankle-high boots—West Hollywood cool.

Likewise, our cars had to blend with our undercover and surveillance roles, so we drove around in many different models. Cars seized from dopers accounted for much of our fleet—if they were not too out of place. When we wanted to impress a crook, we had several seized luxury cars to use. Usually cars were handed out according to seniority. My first car served to represent my position in the office pecking order. I started out with a green, 1970 VW Bug with no air conditioning.

Junior agents got the nod whenever a group needed help on a big case. We normally didn't have anything of our own going on, and we needed seasoning, anyway. I was detailed to help Group Two serve a search warrant. At nine o'clock one evening, I met the search team at the meeting point in a grocery store parking lot near Las Tunas Drive in Temple City. I introduced myself to the three agents already there. The senior agent running the operation was Bob Davies. Overweight and blustery, his high regard for himself was not shared by others. He was known around the office as a sloppy investigator. Someone always had to check his work later, as he didn't pay attention to detail. It showed, since he often missed a loop in back when belting his pants.

He advised us we were to secure a dealer's apartment prior to serving a search warrant. The apartment house was typical Southern California, three-story stucco. We parked in the street out front and walked in a group to a door on the first floor. Davies knocked while I asked, "Shouldn't someone cover the back?"

"Lloyd, your job is to show up, keep up, and shut up. But go ahead, you go cover the back," Davies said, rolling his eyes and getting snarky with the rookie.

I reached the back just in time to see a window screen pop off and a woman start to scramble out a bedroom window. She dropped into the low bushes beneath, crouching. I walked over and presented myself to her. She was embarrassed at being caught but came peacefully as I ushered her to the front. She agreed to open the door at our suggestion. I heard no more advice from Davies after that.

We checked the two-bedroom apartment for anyone else and then sat around on cheap rented furniture in the living room, waiting for the search warrant. Davies was sitting on a couch and noticed a small can of tear gas displayed on the coffee table. His curiosity got the best of him, and he picked the can up and started fiddling with it. It went off, spraying tear gas in the room. The gas smell drove us outside, where we remained until the warrant arrived.

One of the other agents, embarrassed, later apologized for Davies. It was no big deal to me since I didn't have to work with him every day.

Not long after the tear gas incident, I had another skill-building assignment to help out Las Vegas agents in an undercover buy operation in El Monte, a rough and tumble LA suburb. Three agents traveled from Las Vegas to make a buy from two brothers selling heroin. Two other agents and I were tacked on for support.

Norm Haddad was the case agent. He had a reputation as a crack undercover operative based on his exploits when earlier assigned to New York. He was first-generation Lebanese and looked the part of a big-time doper—you would never mistake him for the man.

Haddad's informant had introduced him to the brothers, Emilio and Eduardo Saltillo, in Las Vegas two weeks earlier. He had arranged to come alone to meet the Saltillos at their house in El Monte for a one-pound heroin purchase of $12,000. For safety's sake, we planned he would go in the house, talk, and then go to a nearby supermarket parking lot to make the buy—no side trips or detours. Haddad said the deal would be over within an hour. He had no buy money on him, no gun, and no body wire, thinking he would probably be searched once in the house. He was dressed for the part, looking like a Vegas lounge lizard in his blue polyester suit, black, pointed shoes, and a wide white belt.

Haddad drove a seized green Mercedes and parked in front of the Saltillo house at two o'clock. We kept two cars parked a block away on either side of the house while the others hid around corners, out of sight but ready to respond.

Two hours later, Haddad and the Saltillos piled into Haddad's Benz. He drove to a bar on Valley Boulevard and they all walked inside. I and another agent went in separately to watch, mingling with several early afternoon drinkers. Haddad and the Saltillos sat at the bar drinking tequila shooters, all chummy and appearing to enjoy themselves. I eventually caught Haddad's eye and made a motion toward the men's room, indicating he should come in so we could talk. I went in and waited—Haddad never came in. Twenty minutes later, I went out and spotted them still at the bar, pounding down the shooters.

By six o'clock, we had rotated the inside cover surveillance three times. They finally roused themselves and drove back to the Saltillos' house. We were concerned, since Haddad had not shared anything with us, but assumed they were killing time, waiting for someone to bring the heroin. Dope dealers weren't known for their timeliness. We set up our house surveillance again and waited.

Our concern had worsened by nine o'clock. Haddad was breaking all the undercover rules by not communicating with us. Since he was inside the crooks' house, he was out of our sight—and beyond our protection. The Saltillos were both former convicts, big and ugly, and our imaginations started to wander. Haddad had no buy money, so robbery was out, but why was he in there so long?

I volunteered to get close and try to look inside the house. I slinked through the darkness around the entire house. Every window was covered with curtains or window shades. In the rear, where the bedrooms were, the shades were taped down, allowing no possible view inside. Near a detached garage in the rear was the back door of the house, which opened to the kitchen. The door's upper half was clear glass and I got a peek at the small, lighted kitchen. I had heard or seen nothing that indicated anyone was in the house, yet we knew they were there.

We had no supervisor out with us, so we made our decisions by committee. It was almost ten o'clock and time to find out if Haddad was still healthy. We phoned the El Monte police, and two officers responded to help out. We wanted uniformed officers to knock on the door so the Saltillos would know the police were outside. We placed three agents in hiding, out of sight in the front, while three of us went to the back door.

I was peeking into the back-door window when the officers knocked. In an instant one Saltillo emerged from a hallway, passed by the kitchen, and headed into the living room to answer the door. A second later he ran back, calling that police were at the door. What happened next was confusing, but the Saltillos would not open the door and the police kept pounding and shouting for it to open. The Saltillos yelled out for the police to leave, but of course that would not happen.

Then, at the edge of the hallway that opened onto the kitchen, I saw an outstretched arm wielding a gun. I shouted a warning from my position so the police at the front door would know, and then called to the gunman to drop his weapon and come into the kitchen. He backed up, realizing someone at the back door had him covered. He must have been worried too, because the gun and hand kept darting in and out of view. He yelled he would not surrender. Then I caught sight of another gun in hand that flashed into view and then withdrew behind the wall. Both of the Saltillos had their guns out.

I trained my revolver on the hallway entrance ten feet away, determined to shoot the first person who came out armed. Without any warning or sound, Agent Haddad walked trancelike into my view. He gave one bleary-eyed glance at me and stumbled back out of sight—back with the Saltillos. I had come close to shooting Haddad. At the least the fool could have dropped to the floor out of the line of fire. Having our man barricaded in with two crooks limited our options.

An agent behind me shouted that the SWAT team was ready to enter and that tear gas was coming in sixty seconds if they didn't throw out their guns. That ploy did the trick, and two guns clattered onto the kitchen floor. We kicked open the kitchen door as the Saltillos came out together and lay prone on the floor. Then Haddad came out, dazed, appearing to look for a place to lie down on the crowded floor. Another agent, showing sympathy, led him outside.

The adrenaline rush that comes with near-death experiences soon subsides but, thankfully, I saw Haddad before that happened and clocked him while he was sitting in his car. I was still shaky from the experience when I apologized to him later; perhaps that persuaded him into admitting maybe he had screwed up too.

Our search of the house revealed they had all been in the back cutting heroin: adding milk sugar to change two ounces of brown heroin into one pound. A reluctant Haddad gave us the story later. After drinking away the afternoon at the bar courtesy of Haddad, the crooks confessed they could not produce the promised pound that day, only a measly two ounces. Haddad didn't want to bust them for such a small weight. He told them his customers were not discerning, so they added milk sugar to the two ounces of heroin to make a pound out of it.

I witnessed other undercover messes during my career, but Haddad, the New York star, had shown me the worst. I was fast learning the particulars of narcotics work.

Watching and following crooks—surveillance—was an important skill that I developed early since I spent long hours in the car. That's how we learned a doper's methods and acquaintances. Sitting on a crook's house involved long waits in between the driving tails. One had to find a good point to set up, get comfortable, and remain quiet and alert until he moved.

When following a moving car, the objective was not to lose it in traffic or be seen by the crook. Most of them were looking for a tail, because that was what good crooks did. Mobile surveillance was rather exciting with the constant movement, directing cars here and there to rotate the lead car behind the target. We had to adjust to the target's countersurveillance moves: sudden turns, pulling over and stopping, timing a traffic signal to pass through as it turned red. The tension mounted when we lost the suspect and had to fan out to try to pick him up again.

That strain got the best of me once. I was driving a van while we followed a doper in the San Fernando Valley. We thought he was heading to his source to pick up heroin. He was wary, making several countermoves, and we found it difficult keeping him in sight without alerting him. At one point he turned left against oncoming cars on Ventura Boulevard. We lost him by the time we could turn in the heavy traffic. Five cars were on the team. We drove around for ten minutes before I pulled into a used car lot on a hunch and spotted him hiding in the back among other cars. We set up again. When he moved after a few minutes, someone called on the radio, "Don't lose him again."

Agent Gonzales somehow ended up on the crook's tail—something we tried to avoid. Gonzales was an able agent, but lousy at driving on surveillance. We preferred him to be a trail car, but this time he had ended up on point. He followed with no buffer car between, locked onto the rear of the crook's car. That would burn the deal once the crook made a turn and Gonzales turned with him.

I was tense, caught up in the chase, and voiced my frustrations out loud, calling Gonzales a useless idiot and other assorted terms. Unfortunately, I had forgotten the van was equipped with a radio transmit button on the floor; my foot had been on the button and my entire tirade was transmitted to one and all.

After the mission, somebody told me about my carelessness. Later, Gonzales approached me at the office. I stood up, ready for a deserved thrashing. He simply said, "Mark, you should be more careful when transmitting on the radio. The boss may not like your language." He showed class in his understated remarks to me, class that I had not shown.

While I was getting the hang of the job quite well, I wanted to make my own case. For that, I needed an informant. My first informant was a cast-off. He had made two small cases over a year earlier for another agent in the group, since transferred to San Francisco, but had not produced anything since. Gary told me the man was out of the business and uncooperative, but I wanted to take a try at revitalizing him.

His name was Walter Chapman, and he met with me at a Denny's restaurant near his apartment in Rosemead, appearing cautious. We made some small talk. He was working at a transmission place, going to school nights, and everything was just fine. So he said. But he couldn't give me the company's name and was vague about school. That made me suspicious.

I had been told he was a junkie, but he could have fooled me. He displayed no sleepy-eyed nodding or slurred speech, but was attentive, sat up straight, and gave me coherent answers. Then I asked him if he still snorted heroin. By not saying anything and casting his eyes down at the floor, he answered me.

Chapman wasn't keen to get back in with us, I could tell, but he was having money problems. DEA seemed to be his new best option, since he knew a heroin dealer he could burn.

The dealer's name was Herrera. Before I met him, I conducted some background work—on my own, because not much office assistance was forthcoming to a rookie until he had put together the foundation for a decent case. I checked out Herrera's address and sat watching his house for several hours during the weekend. For wheels, he drove a clean '71 Monte Carlo. He lived in a shabby Hispanic subdivision of stucco, single-family homes just off the south side of Interstate 10 in Ontario. I got a good look at him and noticed he had a wife and at least two kids. He appeared to have a robust trade selling heroin out of his house; I observed several people coming over for in-and-out visits. He had no criminal record and on the surface looked like any other guy.

Chapman and I met with Herrera at a Vons supermarket parking lot in Ontario. We arrived in a Lincoln Continental undercover car bearing Arizona plates and parked next to Herrera's Monte Carlo. Herrera remained sitting behind the wheel as Chapman and I got out and leaned back against the Lincoln while we talked. Two agents hidden nearby in the lot watched us from their cars. We made casual talk, and I recognized right away that the two seemed friendly and had done business before. Strange that Chapman would turn in his friend, but as I was to learn, reward money cut through most bosom ties.

Herrera asked me straight up if I was a cop. I said I was not. It was a lie, but one I could live with. I claimed I was new in town, looking for a heroin source to supply some customers in Phoenix, and wanting to buy kilogram quantity (2.2 pounds). He made arrangements to sell me a one-ounce sample of his best heroin for $800 on the following day.

Working undercover impersonating a drug dealer was a challenge that lent excitement to the job. How an agent looked, talked, and behaved were important, but in the end successful role-playing depended on a few basic principles. You had to school the informant well on the background story he fed the dealer—reducing the lies told about you beforehand reduced the questions a dealer may pose in that first meeting. Keep it simple, as you weren't there to impress the crook.

And it was vital to keep business as the objective. You were not looking to meet any new friends or someone to hang out with; you wanted only a buy-sell association with the crook. It was rather like buying a car: you buy the car or don't, and leave. You don't invite the salesman out to dinner. It was a business transaction, not a coffee klatch. You were never going to earn the crook's trust; after all, you both were conducting a criminal transaction. The sooner completed and done, the better.

Ultimately, the doper's greed would seal the deal. He might not feel comfortable with you or particularly agree with the details of the transaction, but you had the money, and if he wanted some of it, he had to make that leap of faith, override his doubts, and deliver the drugs. Later, after you had arrested him and he was standing there looking at your badge, cuffed, he would always whine, "I knew you were the man."

After making two one-ounce heroin buys from Herrera, it was time to order up a big load and take him down. Herrera would not give me his phone number, so I had to keep Chapman in our deals as a go-between to set up the buys. Herrera didn't trust me, but that was all right; I didn't trust him either.

We had not identified his heroin source. The small amounts I had bought from Herrera had been fronted to him by his supplier. Herrera told me he needed some earnest money out front if I intended to conduct a large transaction. I couldn't do that, of course, but I met him one evening at a supermarket parking lot in West Covina, supposedly for more negotiations, and then surprised him and flashed $20,000. That showed him I was capable of a kilogram buy. Showing the money unannounced reduced the risk of him making a plan to rob me for the cash. Hopefully, ordering a large amount would bring his supplier out in the open.

Surveillance on Herrera began early on the delivery day. Two agents, dressed as highway maintenance workers in coveralls and Day-Glo vests, stood on the edge of Interstate 10, leaning on their shovels and acting as if they were "working" on a sprinkler system. They had a direct view of Herrera's house fifty yards away. His car was parked out front and nothing moved. Our meeting time was set for three o'clock at a 7-Eleven store six blocks away on Grove Avenue. Herrera had informed Hendricks we had to do the transaction quickly as he had plans later that afternoon. I interpreted that to mean he had been ordered by his source to make the sale and get back quick with the money.

Our road workers alerted us when they caught sight of a male Hispanic walking up to Herrera's house just a few moments before three. The paper bag he was carrying could have been his lunch, but we knew better. Five minutes later, Herrera walked out of his house alone, holding a paper bag, and departed in his car. At that point I turned off my portable hand radio and hid it under the seat of the Lincoln. Chapman sat in the passenger seat—like me, nervous.

Herrera pulled in beside my car parked in front of the 7-Eleven. He got into my backseat, sitting behind Chapman. He was carrying the paper bag. Everyone was tense, so we got right to business. Without a word he opened the bag. I turned around to look into it and saw it was full of golf-ball-size pieces wrapped in condoms. The pungent smell of vinegary pickles identified it to me as Mexican brown heroin. My chain-smoking CI remained rigid, staring ahead through the smoke and waiting for the guns to come out.

"I have twenty-five ounces and I need your twenty thousand dollars," Herrera said. I was still looking at him when he patted his waistband and pulled up his shirt to show me the butt of his .45 automatic, adding, "And this is to make sure there is no trouble."

His gun flash was not without cause. We each were holding something of worth, and rip-offs were a concern for us both. He believed I had $20,000 in cash, negotiable anywhere, but he also had something that warranted guarding. Although not legal tender, heroin was very valuable.

An ounce of gold was then trading at $175—an ounce of Mexican heroin sold for $800.

I knew our cover agents were inching closer and poised for my arrest signal, but I was in a fix. I had to get myself and the CI away from the car when they moved in to make the arrest—I felt a shooting on its way. "Don't worry, don't worry, there's no trouble," I said to Herrera while thinking, *Oh, yes, there is trouble.* "I'll get the money from the trunk."

I pressed the trunk release button in the car and the trunk lid popped open—the bust signal. At the same time I opened the car door and scuttled low and away, grabbing for my ankle gun. This was the sticky part of undercover work—the bust. Four agents appeared from nowhere and were on to the car in an instant—probably saving the crook's life with their speed. Herrera didn't have time to draw a breath before his door was wrenched open and he was pulled out and thrown down onto the asphalt. Luckily for him, no one saw the .45 until he was already pancaked on the cement.

A surprise visit to Herrera's house found the source sitting in the living room, drinking coffee and waiting for his money.

13

The Graveyard Case

Every agent had his turn pulling office duty, either on the radio to assist agents in the field or on the phone handling incoming calls forwarded by the receptionist. I had the duty one day in late 1975 and was busy writing a report at my desk when Luna's call came in.

"This is Agent Lloyd speaking. May I help you?"

"Agent Lloyd, my name is Richard Luna, and I'm going to make you a star."

Drug informants came three ways. Most of them were dopers we caught and then flipped to turn on their connections. Survival instincts kicking in, they made deals to save some jail time. Not all dealers flipped. A few hard cases remained loyal, tightlipped, taking the hit alone. Others cooperated to save a girlfriend or wife caught up in the crime, trading his help to keep her out of jail.

At times we recruited CIs. If we spotted someone in a position we needed, we approached and tried to obtain his assistance.

Our third type of CI was the walk-in, the volunteer. They came in all shapes and sizes: the good, the bad, and the worthless.

Luna's tall talk on the telephone piqued my interest, so I made arrangements to meet him in La Habra that evening at a Marie Callender's restaurant. He said he drove a red Ford pickup.

I needed someone to cover me, since I was meeting a stranger. You could call it paranoia; I called it due diligence. My regular partner was not available, so I asked Bob Patrick, my roommate while at the DEA Academy, to come and back me.

When sizing up a potential CI, we always looked at his motivation. Why would he volunteer his services in a business that could prove deadly to him if he was found out? During an undercover drug negotiation, we went to great lengths to protect our undercover agent's true identity. But after the arrest, the doper presumed the informant was in on the deal since he had not been arrested. Later, the defense attorney showed the defendant the CI's written statements, and his suspicions were confirmed—the informant had set him up.

Most informants were mercenary—they knew a dealer and calculated they could make some money after setting up his arrest. A handful were patriotic and wanted to help us clean the streets. Others, the brazen schemers, were active dopers who enlisted our help to rid them of competition.

Far fewer in number but rated as the most zealous and diligent were CIs who came to us to administer their revenge. Richard Luna came seeking vengeance, and he became my best informant.

Bob and I arrived early at Marie Callender's on Whittier Boulevard and sat in his car in the parking lot. We didn't often see one another, so we caught up on things. He mentioned he had put his house on the market.

"What for? You only moved into it last year."

Bob exhaled, rubbed his forehead, and said, "Rita and I are divorcing."

I looked at him. "I'm getting a divorce too."

We sadly shook our heads, both knowing nothing more needed to be said. The LA office was populated by agents either going through a divorce or recovering from one. What was it? Law enforcement in general, and especially narcotics work, was hard on marriages. Anyone coming in without a rock-solid marital relationship was sorely tried. Was it the job? We worked in drug-doused LA on ridiculous schedules: overnights and weekends spent sitting in cars, frequent road trips. Or was it us? Most of us were aggressive type As with egos. If we thought the job at fault, perhaps we just made it that way, shaping our work to rescue us from ourselves.

The era did have an effect on us, though. It was the 1970s—police were not popular, and narcs in particular were shunned. Many of us operated in an almost continuous undercover mode. Besides disguising our true identities from the drug dealers, we often had to do the same for regular citizens we encountered. We portrayed ourselves as someone different when we were gathering information—a probation officer, housing official, real estate salesman—avoiding that narcotics connection. The make-believe identities carried over into our personal lives too. So many people were using illegal narcotics at that time that being linked with drug law enforcement made you someone to avoid. For years after, from force of habit, I'd hesitate when someone asked me what I used to do for a living. "Oh, I worked for the government," was a stock answer.

A man pulled his red pickup in to the lot, took a good look around, and strode into the restaurant without waiting. He walked with a balanced gait, like he was ready to make a run for it if the need arose. Watching him walk, we agreed he had the look—definitely our CI was a Mexican heroin dealer. His appearance was nothing extraordinary. He resembled any day-laborer or roofer. But his bearing tipped us he was wrong.

Bob stayed in the car to watch the outside while I entered the restaurant. Luna was sitting facing the door in a booth near the back, so I slid in across from him and introduced myself. He was fidgeting and anxious, so we passed on preliminaries. I asked him to tell me what he had. He wasted no time in getting on with his story, spitting it out in clipped phrases, still angry.

He had been playing eight ball in a Hollywood pool parlor a few months earlier and met James Ogilvie. Luna categorized Ogilvie as a know-it-all braggart. They played pool together several times and became tolerable friends. One day, Ogilvie, who portrayed himself as an attorney for a big-time hit man in New York, mentioned his client was coming to LA and looking for a good heroin dealer. Luna indicated he could help in that regard, as he knew heroin dealers in Mexico and was willing to make introductions.

Ogilvie introduced Luna to Jaime Vila, his New York contact. A big, raw-boned, and swarthy Puerto Rican, Vila presented an unchanging persona. His black leather jacket was accompanied by a perpetual snarl. He liked to stand leaning forward on his toes when speaking, suggesting a violence barely restrained. Luna did not favor Vila's in-your-face manner, but listened to him nonetheless since he came right out and said he had lost his heroin source and needed someone new. Vila said he wanted fifty kilograms a month to supply his dealers in the Bronx. That was a huge amount of heroin. Despite Vila's dramatics, Luna was impressed, thinking he may be the ticket to the big money. Luna assured Vila he would make arrangements in Mexico for a good source.

Luna got busy and looked up Tony Escalante. He was a medium-level (one to two pounds) heroin dealer working out of Tijuana. Luna had met him a year earlier in Tijuana, as both were in the business. Luna needed Escalante because he had something Luna lacked: a good source. Escalante became excited when informed about the Vila possibilities and agreed to bring his source out from anonymity. This was a bold move as dopers disliked revealing their sources—especially if those sources were good.

Bernardo Romero owned a ranch several miles outside of Los Mochis, Mexico. The altitude and climate were ideal for Romero's primary occupation: growing opium poppies. He was a chemist and known as a one-stop shop for heroin. He grew the opium poppies, processed the opium gum into heroin, and would cut (dilute) the heroin to his customers' purity specifications. Despite the risks, the Vila business opportunity brought Romero out. This was his chance to be a source of supply to New York, home of the largest concentration of heroin junkies in America. He made the trip to LA with Luna and Escalante to meet Vila.

Soon after, Escalante and Luna picked up a kilogram of heroin from Romero in Tijuana, drove it across the border, and delivered it to Vila for $30,000. They returned to Tijuana and gave all the money to Romero; he had promised them a portion of the proceeds after the sale.

The next month, Escalante brought three more kilograms up from Tijuana. Romero followed from Mexico and diluted the heroin at Vila's apartment, turning it into ten kilograms. Luna had no active part in the deal but knew about it. Vila paid $90,000 for the initial three kilograms and then took the diluted ten to New York. There, his dealers retailed the heroin for $1,000 an ounce, grossing about $350,000.

Luna waited a few days and then got on the phone, trying to get his promised share of the money. No one returned his calls, and he never saw any of the money made from those two deals. Vila had his source (Romero) and his smuggler (Escalante). Where did Luna fit in? He didn't. They had cut him out.

Luna allowed the bitter rejection to fester for a couple of weeks. Then he decided it was time for payback and called the DEA.

Luna's story featured a major heroin dealer from New York, a chemist in Mexico who grew his own opium, a border smuggler, and a crooked lawyer. His tale had captured my attention. For starters, I ordered phone records for Vila, Luna, and Ogilvie—all the players with US phones. I wanted to see who and where they were calling.

Vila had been living in Hollywood for only two months, so his records were sparse. I sent off an inquiry to our New York City office listing all his New York calls and asked for the subscriber information. Ogilvie's phone had been disconnected, and he dropped from sight. I waited for phone information from New York and tried to figure out a way to get Luna back into the group.

A brick wall blocked me right away. I had looked up Luna's criminal record, which was substantial, and discovered he was on parole. He had pulled two years in prison at Terminal Island in Los Angeles on a drug trafficking conviction. Had we been playing baseball, I would have said he was stepping up to the plate already carrying a full count. I wasn't disappointed in the lad's character, because it takes a doper to know one. But a visit to Luna's parole officer produced the bad news. No one on federal parole could work as an informant.

The parole officer shrugged his shoulders, held up his palms, and explained his office was trying to rehabilitate the parolee. That wouldn't happen if DEA put him back into the drug trafficking business. There was nothing to gain by arguing, or by advising him that Luna had never left the heroin business. We both knew it was just bureaucracy at work. I couldn't touch Luna for six more months.

I put the Vila case on a convenient shelf and became busy with other cases, which was beneficial because New York did not answer my queries about Vila's New York calls anyway. After waiting four months, I re-sent my New York inquiry. A month later, I received the phone information, along with a short note of apology—my initial report had been misfiled and forgotten.

While I was looking over the New York phone numbers, many of which were related to active drug investigations, George Conway called me to come and see him. Conway supervised Group Six, which was designated as the central tactical group (CENTAC). CENTAC was a new, nationwide program to target major worldwide drug trafficking syndicates. Aiding the initiative was extra funding from headquarters. It was 1976, times were hard, and DEA's budget was skeletal. Our CENTAC, one of several operating around the country, targeted a New York heroin syndicate that used Los Angeles as a source of supply.

Conway welcomed me into his office. We shook hands, his as big as sixteen-ounce boxing gloves. On the wall behind his desk, I caught a glimpse of two photos of him from his days as an offensive lineman with the Philadelphia Eagles. Having gone soft, the big guy still moved on light feet.

"New York just called me about your report on the Vila numbers. Many of his phone calls tie in with our New York heroin case. So what do you have going on?"

"Not much yet. I have info from a CI who is off-limits at the moment, and I just got the phone toll information from New York. I'm going over numbers now, and I'm waiting for more word from New York."

Conway nodded. "Your wait is over. New York recently took down the head of the syndicate they're targeting. They said this guy, Jaime Vila, is the new leader of the gang."

I could see his wheels turning. Then he made his decision. "Mark, here's the deal. We're the CENTAC group, so we have to work this case because it's connected to New York. But you have a CI into Vila, which is important. So you have a choice. You can give me the CI and remain with Group Four, or you can bring your CI over to my group and we'll work this case together. What do you want?"

Was he kidding? "I'll be right over," I said.

Group Six contained several senior agents, and they had spent the last year running down investigative leads for the New York faction of CENTAC. In short, they had been supportive gofers. When I joined his group, Conway assigned Bob Patrick, my academy roommate, to help me with the case.

Bob voiced straightaway that we had better do a good job of it because he knew a few agents in the group had designs on my case. Any misstep on our part would give them an excuse to pirate the case away. It was office-style eminent domain. Conway had cut me slack when he didn't take away my CI. I was still a junior agent. The realization that others coveted my case confirmed that I had a good investigation going. I just needed to finish it. Keeping a wary eye on the office sharks, I joined the group.

A few weeks later, Luna came off parole and I signed him up as an informant. He embraced his new role and started paying off from the start. He had numerous contacts in Tijuana and knew several of the smugglers running drugs over the border. Within a two-month period, he phoned three times. Each call gave me a license plate, vehicle make, and approximate time the car would cross the border. I had only to phone down to customs at San Ysidro and alert them. It was easy pickings; all three were good hits. Luna wouldn't tell me who his Tijuana contacts were, but his information was solid. Those cases gave me the chance to see how Luna worked and check his reliability, but they didn't help advance the case against Vila.

We needed Luna's complete story, so Bob and I spent three days conducting a thorough debriefing. We looked for specific information on the dates, events, and people in the Vila gang. Luna's attention span was limited, so we ran two sessions a day, interviewing him for two or three hours in the morning and then again in the early evening. He was poor on dates, but could remember events well enough.

Once Luna's take on the Vila organization was in hand, we restarted our investigation in earnest. I flew to New York to compare what I had with the New York files. Bob remained in LA to work on locating current addresses and phone numbers for the Vila gang. The New York file on Vila was extensive and dated back over two years. One thing New York didn't have, however, was a live witness who could testify as to Vila's heroin dealings. They knew of several dealers or associates of Vila, but had no one who would talk.

Vila was feared on the streets. He was known as a karate expert and had savaged several who crossed him. He was also suspected of killing at least a dozen people who ran afoul of him. The New York Police Department had an open murder investigation on Vila. They named it the Graveyard Case because he always dumped his victims' bodies in one particular marshy location in Jamaica Bay near Kennedy Airport. Some were shot, some beaten to death.

After reading all the files and talking with investigators, I had a clear picture of Jaime Vila. He was bad, nationwide.

While still in New York, I learned of two incidents that clarified Vila's violence. Bob phoned from LA and said the LAPD had just called him about Vila. The day before, a man named Hector Roiz had been found shot to death in Vila's Mercedes-Benz. The car and body were found on the Highland Avenue freeway on-ramp in Hollywood. Evidence showed Roiz was driving, pulled over to the edge of the ramp, and was shot in the back of the head by an assailant sitting behind him. The .45-caliber slug that killed Roiz passed through his head and continued on to strike the car's keyed ignition, effectively killing the car also. The shooter couldn't push the body out of the car and drive on as planned, but had to get out and walk away, abandoning the car. I'm not making this up; it was a case of bad luck turning worse.

That same day, I also received a call from Detective O'Leary, a homicide investigator for the New York Police Department, asking if I was interested in talking to a shooting victim—a rarity in the Vila case because the victim had survived the hit.

Bennie Escobar, a heroin distributor in the Vila gang, lost a kilogram of heroin to robbery. He duly reported the loss to his boss, one of Vila's lieutenants. The next day, as he walked down the dark hallway of his apartment building in the Bronx, three unknown men appeared out of the gloom and emptied their pistols into him. Nine bullets hit Escobar and he was left sprawled on the hallway floor.

I visited him in the hospital, but he knew nothing about Vila's Los Angeles operations. He would survive to become an ace witness in New York's murder case against Vila.

On returning to LA, I looked at what Bob had accomplished in my absence. He had not been idle. He had found Vila's new apartment in Hollywood and also located the apartment of Vila's chief minions, the Castillos. Twin brothers Robert and Albert Castillo were Vila's slow-witted boyhood friends from Puerto Rico. Luna had mentioned the Castillos helped Romero cut the heroin and then carried the dope to New York. Bob had opened pen registers on both the Vila and Castillo places. Pen registers listed incoming and outgoing calls, giving the numbers called, dates, times, and length of call—valuable in following the group's activities and opening up new leads.

Bob was a solid partner in our case. His analytical mind served him well as an investigator. Street enforcement work was not his strong suit, but he fit in well with what we were doing: analyzing bits of information to piece together the people and events in the Vila heroin gang. Always flying under the radar with no big personality, no flash and dash attitude, Bob brought a dependability to his work that management often overlooked, distracted by all the other shiny articles in the office—the self-promoting attention-getters. We worked well together, our mutual marital problems not often mentioned. We found it easier to concentrate on an undertaking promising better success.

Luna's information was good, but his pen was out of ink. We had his story, had verified all that we could, but he had been cut out by Vila and Escalante early on. He was of no further use until we needed him to testify at trial.

We sat on the outside without an inside man to give a peek at what Vila was doing. This was not a typical buy-bust investigation. Not a case that involved an informant setting up a dealer for an initial buy to tie him in, then ordering up a large load and taking him down. Rather, this case was a long-term conspiracy investigation. With no drug buys, at the trial there would be no show-and-tell. We wouldn't have a load of heroin to show the jury, nor a chemist's report on the quality of the heroin. This had to be a historical case, putting together evidence of Vila's criminal acts from the past. Our investigation crawled for six months.

To make that historical conspiracy case stick, circumstantial evidence, verified by a live witness, had to show the jury beyond a reasonable doubt that Vila was, in fact, a heroin dealer. We didn't have that live witness. I needed something to jump-start the case and get it active. We needed another witness besides Luna, someone who could give us contemporary testimony on Vila's crimes.

Deliverance came one fine day when LAPD Sergeant Piastro telephoned me at the office.

"Lloyd, I got a guy here who says he was Vila's attorney, and he wants to talk."

No one ever confused James Ogilvie with a real attorney. A licensed, albeit penniless lawyer who never made a living in law, Ogilvie fancied himself as legal counsel for gangsters. His inspiration must have come from watching *The Godfather*. Fantasy aside, his mistake was becoming actively involved in crime instead of just lending advice to his criminal associates. He caught a conviction for pandering in early 1976, which got him disbarred in California. That was one reason he had dropped off the radar screen at the beginning of our investigation. He was facing trial on perjury charges in two weeks. Sure of his conviction and subsequent prison sentence, he decided to call and make a deal. Contentious and conniving, Ogilvie was a total loser. But he knew the Vila organization inside out and proved to be the witness who could tie it together—heroin deals, murders, and all.

Bob and I earned our pay the hard way when debriefing Ogilvie. What a load. In getting his story down on paper we had to overcome two major hurdles: his unpredictable, irritating personality and his reluctance to come clean. The man seemed bipolar; his moods took us along on a roller-coaster ride of highs and lows. His speed-talking prattle would fly along, then sputter and cut out, replaced by morose, single-syllable comments. We often had to force him to speak, his words emerging wearing our fingernail marks. He was one of those people who often prefaced a remark with, "To be truthful," as if they are dishonest by nature and are just making an exception for you. I hated that.

Ogilvie's interview-avoidance tactic was nothing new. His deal with the prosecutor required full cooperation in order to earn consideration at his sentencing. Like many others, he thought he could fake assistance by giving just enough information to appear helpful, but without saying anything damaging. It was cooperation without involvement. We had seen that act before and called him on it, but it was no easy task unearthing the truth. He wasn't a born liar, as there is no such person. Lying is an art, and Ogilvie's skill at it exhibited careful study and a keen devotion.

We accompanied Ogilvie all the way, shambling along with him step by step on an arduous journey in reaching true disclosure. With him it was similar to the five stages of death theory about what terminal patients go through: he was in denial, became angry, tried to bargain, slid into depression, and at last accepted it.

His acceptance came on the second day of our long sessions. Head held low, hesitant, he took a deep breath, exhaled, then looked up and paused, steeling himself to let it go. We had waited him out. He was transformed from the mumbling maniac to someone wanting to get the story out, becoming fearful of keeping it in. His confessions gushed like a mountain spring.

Ogilvie gave us the whole story, everything we needed. He had witnessed Vila receiving large loads of heroin from Romero and Escalante in person, and had been at the Castillos' apartment when Romero cut loads of heroin to triple the output. While Ogilvie was at Vila's apartment one night, Vila came in with Albert Castillo. They were both spattered with blood, and Vila blurted how he had just shot Roiz on the freeway. Ogilvie related information about Vila committing two other local murders as well.

Ogilvie had given us all we needed to finish the case. We scrambled to gather circumstantial evidence to support his statements. We needed corroboration since we knew that, standing alone, his personality would not win over any jury.

Once Ogilvie was onboard, our prospects brightened. Based on his information, we had new leads to run down. It was still slow work putting together the bits and pieces of the case, and we still hoped to catch Vila in possession of a big load. With Ogilvie's revelations, we used our pen register material and discreet surveillance to try to make that happen. Meanwhile, however, the case had been open almost a year, and upper management had become impatient for something to happen.

A phone tip from Ogilvie ushered in the final act. He advised us Vila had ordered a shipment of 154 pounds of heroin, and it was due to arrive any day. Pen register information confirmed increased phone traffic between Vila and Romero in Los Mochis and Vila and Escalante in Tijuana. Vila was also calling the Castillos at their apartment in Monrovia.

We set up twenty-four-hour surveillance on the Castillos' apartment, with a like watch at Vila's place. Nothing unusual happened for two days. On the third day, we followed Albert Castillo as he drove to a nearby paint store and bought ten gallons of acetone. It's a solvent, but also is used to dilute heroin. We didn't know when the heroin would arrive, but we knew where it was going. The dope was on its way.

Two days later, nothing else had happened. We had been out there 24/7 for almost a week and interest was waning among those relegated to surveillance duty. Croaking started; I heard wisecracks about bringing agents out on a case going nowhere, a "hummer."

John Bynum, one of our assistant special agents in charge, strolled into our group area. I was at my desk going over pen register information.

"Mark, what is going on with the Vila case? Does it look ready to take down?"

"We're just waiting for the load to come in." My voice was clipped. What did he want? Vila wasn't working on our timetable.

"Well, we're using a lot of manpower here, so try and make something happen."

"It should happen any day now," I said.

I thought about saying I could call Vila and tell him to hurry it up, but I kept my mouth shut.

Bynum's style was MBWA: managing by walking around. He had to do it that way; no one ever went to see him on their own. Bynum's chief business was speaking, and that ability must have got him where he was, since his rise in the agency had not been due to any accomplishments of note. Practiced at saying nothing at length, he reminded me of Nebraska's Platte River—a mile wide at the mouth and six inches deep.

Thankfully, Romero surfaced the next day at Vila's apartment. A check on his license plate showed he had crossed the border at San Ysidro earlier that morning. The chemist had arrived. Now all we needed was the heroin delivery.

Later that same day, a Chevy Impala pulled up at the Castillo apartment. A license check showed it had crossed the border at San Ysidro two hours earlier. We didn't recognize the man who entered the Castillo apartment. Was the dope in the car?

The pressure on me to take down the case increased. Everyone from the bosses down to the busboy wanted us to kick in the door and end it. The "experts" back in the office didn't have the feel for the case that Bob and I had. We felt the need to wait and watch for a while. We wanted to see some dope before we sounded the charge. We would only have one shot, so we wanted to be sure. Alas, the supervisor, Conway, superseded our caution and ordered us to make the arrests. Bynum had got to him.

As we gathered to plan our arrests, surveillance agents at Vila's place reported he was driving his Mercedes with Romero as a passenger and was headed toward Monrovia—that had to be the Castillos' place. We decided to grab Vila when he arrived. The street setup allowed us ample cover, so we could jump him as he exited his car.

Vila arrived and parked next to the Impala. As he was opening the car door, we hit them. To counter Vila's alleged toughness, we had our own tough guy: Agent Kevin Runyon. His nickname was Boom-Boom. Vila saw us coming just as his feet hit the asphalt, and he started to react. Boom-Boom was ready for Vila's move and went military on him, pancaking him face-first on the asphalt and cuffing him in about three seconds. Romero, standing rigid beside the car, held his hands up in docile surrender but still went down to greet the pavement.

We kicked in the apartment door and caught the Castillo brothers unawares. With them was Escalante—we had not recognized him when he arrived from Tijuana. Inside, the apartment was not set up for guests. No furniture adorned the living room. Instead, two large, plastic folding tables, the kind used at church picnics, were standing end to end, taking up much of the living room space. Twelve heating lamps, numerous flat cake pans, and an assortment of spoons and strainers rested at the ready on the tables. In a bedroom, we found the acetone, powdered baby milk, brown sugar, and quinine—cutting agents for heroin. We found no heroin; it had not arrived.

Two phone calls came in to the apartment while we sat hoping the heroin would drop by. We didn't answer. Pen registers showed the calls came from a pay phone at a gas station off the 605 Freeway in Whittier. That was the courier with the heroin, and he was fifteen minutes away. We had raided Vila too soon and missed the load.

Oh, well. It wasn't the dope that mattered; it was the guys selling it, and we got them.

Altogether it was a satisfying day as we ended a long and difficult investigation. We were not in the business for the money. We did it for the excitement, sense of accomplishment, and moments like this. Duty, service, and justice were fine and good, but that could all be accomplished sitting back at the office with Bynum. The reward for us was going out to confront the crooks in the street and make a physical arrest.

All five defendants decided to go to trial. With no heroin to show, their attorneys advised them they could beat the charges. Conspiracy law was still a seldom-used statute in 1978, and many attorneys on both sides of the table were unfamiliar with it.

The trial lasted three weeks, with another week devoted to jury deliberations. The trial attracted media coverage due to the presence of the first-ever Mexican source of supply captured in California. The highlight of the trial for me occurred when Luna, the one who started it and brought me the case a year before, was testifying on the stand. He was near the end of his testimony, undergoing a grilling from the defense table.

"Mr. Luna, isn't it a fact that you have not told the truth today? That you have made up a story to falsely accuse my clients?"

Luna almost rose out of his chair with indignation. "What is a fact is that if Vila and the others had not cheated me out of my share at the beginning, I would be sitting at their table with them today."

It was a beautiful comeback, and the jury loved it. One of the counts in our indictment concerned the 154 pounds of heroin we failed to grab. All the defendants went down on that charge, along with the other five counts against them, even though we did not produce one gram of heroin at trial. We spent almost a year working that case, starting with nothing solid. At the end I felt as if we had fashioned a Persian rug out of a horse blanket.

PART THREE

Holding
Our Own

14

Where America's Day Begins

DEA agent Larry Wallace was shot and killed during a drug bust at a grocery store parking lot in Agana, Guam, in December 1975. Assigned to our Tokyo office, Larry had flown to Guam to help its one-man DEA office on a heroin case.

Following Larry's death, DEA closed its office in Guam. It remained closed until the governor of Guam petitioned Congress to reopen the office, pleading that heroin traffickers were overrunning the island. The governor's appeal, corroborated by military authorities hard-pressed to keep heroin use from infecting our nuclear-armed navy on Guam, grabbed Congress's attention. DEA was ordered back to Guam in early 1978 to open a four-man office.

Having made a few decent cases in Los Angeles, I was judged competent and obtained something I had wanted since coming on with DEA: selection for overseas duty. I wanted to go foreign, to scratch that geographic itch. The timing was right too, as I had recently gone through a discouraging divorce. My ex-wife and our children moved to Seattle. I had no reason to remain in LA, and Guam was an opening to new territory.

Known as "where America's day begins," Guam is the westernmost US possession, a tiny dot in the Pacific Ocean. Guam stands at a crossroads in the western Pacific, serving a strategic role today, as it has since its discovery by Ferdinand Magellan in 1521. America appropriated Guam from the

Spanish in 1898 and gave the inhabitants US citizenship in 1952. Having no natural resources, Guam remained economically dependent on our naval outpost for most of its modern history, except during that temporary Japanese disturbance named World War II.

That dependence changed in the 1970s, when tourism began growing. With its tropical weather and proximity to Japan, Guam became a popular island retreat for the Japanese, since it offered a cheaper way to enjoy the sand and sun. They called it the "poor man's Hawaii." The Japanese tourists, isolated in tour groups at shielded resort hotels on Tumon Bay, didn't realize the truth of the setting they visited. In 1978, Guam was a thriving Japanese vacation destination surrounded by heroin.

Our new office had an enormous task ahead. I was told the population numbered about ninety thousand, not counting the assigned eighteen thousand military. I also heard the island's methadone program, a therapy plan designed to help relieve heroin addiction, numbered almost one thousand patients. That meant about one out of every one hundred Guamanians were or had been heroin addicts. I knew that heroin addicts only used methadone to try to halt the tolerance factor with heroin: the tendency to need more and more heroin to get the same high. But methadone didn't deliver a high, so many addicts used both drugs, and their lives became living hells. That explained the large amount of social ills plaguing Guam. The high rate of property crime, robberies, and murders were all linked to heroin addiction.

Obtaining heroin was not difficult. All a dealer had to do was fly to Bangkok. In the seedy, tourist part of town, anyone could approach a taxi driver near one of the hotels and get introduced to a heroin supplier. Ten thousand dollars would buy a kilogram, about thirty-five ounces of high quality "China White." On Guam, selling it by the ounce would garner about $200,000.

Guam was an insulated, small island with a small population and close family ties. The native population included only about thirty-five family names; they were all cousins. We conducted our first investigations efficiently and the word spread: the mainland had sent a team of skilled investigators with orders to clean up the island. Overnight, the grapevine draped us with an aura of invincibility. That mantle was not extended to the local police; they were not considered competent or corruption-free. Too many cousins were working both sides of the law.

Guam's society may have been in turmoil, but the rule of law held sway. Its justice system was ready and waiting—it only needed competent law enforcers. Notwithstanding our unearned heroic status, it was Guam's legal situation that gave bite to our bark. Guam had two court systems, the Superior Court of the Guam Territory, and the US District Court. The two judges were honest and hard-working. We also had two good prosecutors to help make the justice system work. The assistant United States attorney, Fred Black, was our kind of prosecutor, never reviewing a case of ours he didn't like or would not support. Unlike many federal prosecutors I had dealt with in Los Angeles, Fred liked challenges and didn't sweat the small obstacles or limit us in the number of defendants per case he would file against. The more the better. DEA would serve to supply the grist for the justice mill on Guam.

As my most productive and satisfying posting, Guam was the only place I worked where DEA made a noticeable difference. When I left Guam in 1981, heroin had virtually disappeared. We had sent all the heroin dealers to jail. It wouldn't last though; nothing ever does.

We were all new in Guam, so we started at the bottom and worked our way up. The bottom began with Song An Fairley. She was a former prostitute who upgraded to become a heroin dealer. She had landed on Guam with her navy husband, who had picked her up in a sailor's bar in Pusan, Korea, just a year before. It wasn't until he arrived for a tour on Guam that he discovered he didn't like her.

That was all right. I soon didn't like her either. Cast adrift, Fairley gravitated back to the bars, this time in Agana, and for an added touch picked up a heroin habit. To help afford the high price of heroin, she took to selling it, which allowed her to snort it for free and also make a living. When she delivered a small amount to a marine at a bar, we arrested her. The marine was our informant and had set her up.

Earlier, Naval Investigative Service (NIS) agent Ernie Maher had come to our office with the marine in tow. The marine, Private Whyte, was in trouble for drug use, an all too common problem with US military personnel on Guam. He had agreed to cooperate in order to mitigate his legal problems with the navy and said he could lead us to his heroin source. While he sat in an interview room, Ernie and I looked over his navy rap sheet and personnel record. He was twenty years old. His file disclosed he was of limited intellect, unhindered by any formal education. I read a notation from Whyte's platoon leader and mentioned it to Ernie. "Whyte's lieutenant says here he is deficient in his duties. He's slow-witted, slow moving, and can't make change for a dollar."

"What did you expect? Any proper marine wouldn't be in this mess. Let's hope he's maybe smart enough to score from Fairley."

We set Private Whyte up with a Nagra tape recorder, searched him, gave him $200 in DEA funds, and sent him to the bar to buy one capsule of heroin. Being new to Guam and unknown, I went in and watched his exchange with Fairley. It was over in five minutes, a quick and easy score.

After Private Whyte left, I stayed and observed Fairley do her work. Within thirty minutes she had sold several more capsules of heroin. All her buyers knew her well because it was just a couple of words spoken, a quick hand-to-hand transaction, and they were gone.

The next morning found us visiting Fairley at her apartment. Apparently she was still not up at eleven o'clock, and we pounded on the door until she opened up. She displayed tangled hair, caked spittle at the edges of her mouth, and crusty eyes almost closed with sleep dirt. She had slept in her clothes.

Fairley's appearance resembled that of her apartment. A torn, sagging couch and a bean bag chair failed to cover the dirt and cigarette burns on the stained, once-beige carpet. The long-standing cigarette stink blended with the odor of new mold. Personal cleanliness was not her strong point.

We found ten capsules of heroin stashed behind the toilet tank. Turning over her mattress revealed most of the DEA money she had received the previous night from our marine. We had her nailed. It took her two minutes to agree to cooperate.

Fairley came in the next day as ordered to give us her story on the heroin situation on Guam. I had just started laying down the ground rules to her when she nodded off, falling off the chair and thumping onto the floor like a sack of potatoes. Some junkies can function almost normally under the influence of heroin—Fairley wasn't one of them.

I propped her up, lightly shook her shoulders to get her attention, and seated her in the large, round trash can next to my desk. She fit in just so and didn't seem offended. Its low center of gravity kept her upright.

In between her drowsy lapses, we coaxed a story out of Fairley. She surprised us when she divulged her heroin source of supply was Rickie Sablan, the sergeant in charge of the Guam Police narcotics unit. His gang would be our next target. Fairley talked about heroin use, explaining the Guam addicts preferred smoking or snorting it. She kept a journal with a detailed account of all her heroin transactions—surprising efficiency for a junkie. Her account showed sales and proceeds revealing she grossed about $10,000 weekly.

One of Fairley's tips led us to Annie Song, another Korean hooker/junkie. We had nothing yet on Song, but upon our persuasive approach, she agreed to make a heroin buy from Kenny Shimizu. Shimizu, like Fairley, was one of Sablan's dealers and also a junkie.

Song told us Shimizu dealt out of his fortified apartment in Tamuning. The second-floor apartment reportedly featured a steel door with seven locks. With a search warrant in hand, we decided on a ruse, with Song posing as a buyer to get the door open. If we knocked and announced our intentions, Shimizu would have flushed his heroin before we could beat down his steel door.

Late that night, Song walked up the stairs to the second level, her storklike legs wobbling on six-inch heels. Five of us slinked along at a discreet distance. At Shimizu's entrance, she stood at the peephole and knocked while we glued ourselves to the apartment wall to keep out of sight. Following a sharp query from inside and an answering mutter from Song, one by one the bolts drew back. As the doorknob turned, Agent George Bannion thrust Song aside and put his shoulder and 230 pounds into the door.

Bannion was a bit early as one bolt lock had not quite cleared the jamb. We heard frantic screaming inside as Bannion gave the door another shoulder blow and the it crashed open. My role was to get to the bathroom and prevent any drug flushing, so I barely noticed the four men sitting in the living room as I dashed down the hallway. I saw Shimizu's Korean wife,

Kim, slip into the bathroom, slamming the door in my face. Hearing the toilet flushing, I gave the door a shoulder smash, tearing the flimsy door off its hinges. The falling door dropped on Kim as she was bent over the toilet, throwing heroin capsules in the bowl. She shrugged the door off her back as if it were cardboard and leaped at me—all five feet and ninety pounds of her.

I managed to holster my revolver before she reached me, kicking, scratching, and screeching. Her wild-animal attack momentarily threw me. I stretched out both arms to hold her off. While I considered how best to control the crazed sprite, Jesse Pangelinan, one of our newly minted task force officers from the Guam police, rushed up to help handle her. Pangelinan had his 9mm automatic in his hand. In the collision among Jesse, Kim, and I, the gun went off. Kim dropped to the floor at my feet. I noticed a powder burn on the right arm of my nylon DEA raid jacket. Close call.

The gun had gone off on the top of her head. Kim lay motionless, bleeding freely. Shouting for someone to call an ambulance, I grabbed a bath towel and attempted to stop the bleeding. I felt for the wound and found it, right on top of her head. She stopped breathing within fifteen or twenty seconds. As the hospital medics wheeled her body out on a gurney, they passed Shimizu, handcuffed and sitting on the couch, junkie-stoned. He called out to her. Getting no response, he said, "She was a good old lady, but I can always get another."

The investigations against Fairley and Shimizu were quick and served to set the pace for us. We had only scratched the surface of the heroin-trafficking scab that covered Guam. Unknown to us at that point but soon evident was that almost every trafficker on Guam was linked—all stuck fast on the vast spider web that represented the heroin situation. The handful of major dealers on the island had large numbers, perhaps hundreds, of lesser distributors. Almost every case we worked merged into others. We started out on the bottom feeders and worked our way up to the island's biggest traffickers.

One surprise to us was that nearly everyone we arrested soon confessed and wanted to cooperate. What caused that? Perhaps it was the island's insulated and remote existence, or the population's close association with the Catholic church. I didn't know, nor did I dwell on it, but DEA's reputation played a major role—we soon had them running for cover.

Fairley's journal gave us names, dates, and heroin amounts, to which she added more details. She was a junkie, but we were not interested in the junkies. Take away their sources of supply and they would fade away. We wanted the heroin dealers. A few dealers fled Guam, thinking that getting out of Dodge meant safety. Most of them ran away to mingle with the large Guamanian population in San Diego. Their thinking that San Diego was safe haven was a mistake, as we traveled there on several occasions to make surprise visits. Astonished to see us, all of them made instant deals at court. DEA's prominence grew with the display of its long arm.

Besides Fairley's detailed information, tips from other arrests enabled us to make a conspiracy case against Rickie Sablan. Everyone in the Guam heroin business knew him. US Attorney Fred Black convened a federal grand jury, kept busy with our parade of witnesses, and they delivered an indictment against Sablan. One of the key witnesses was Philip Garrigus. I made him an informant and planned to use him in making undercover buys for us.

Garrigus was not easy to control. He thought he knew it all, and he failed to take seriously my pointers on security awareness and the need to keep our relationship secret. Three weeks after I first talked to him and before he could do any undercover work, he and his wife were shot and killed outside their house in Maniglao one night as they were entering his car to go out. It seemed everybody knew he was cooperating with DEA.

Security on Guam was a constant concern. I never once had to show my badge and credentials when working; everyone knew who we were. At restaurants I sometimes saw other diners whom I knew to be heroin traffickers, and they knew who I was. I always checked the parking lots when leaving any commercial establishment, especially at night. Luckily, the violence on Guam attributable to heroin trafficking was exclusive to that crowd and did not apply to law enforcement.

Sablan rolled over as soon as we arrested him and offered us valuable information about his organization. He also told us about his main competition, the Lopez brothers. We would soon go in pursuit of the Lopezes, but first we wanted Sablan's source of supply—Bennie Romine.

15

The Yakuza Link

Bennie Romine looked and acted the part he played in his everyday public life. A balding, pudgy man with thick glasses, he fit in well at his small cubicle in the office of Agana Life Plan where he sold insurance. He drove a Chevy station wagon to work from the small, common home in Agana Heights he shared with his small, common wife. He seemed an ordinary man working his way through life.

But he had another side. Gambling was in his blood, and Romine's favorite bets were made at the cockfights, a popular pastime with Guam's bottom dwellers. In addition to betting on chicken fights at those gatherings, heroin traffickers set up deals and talked shop.

Romine's younger half-sister, Piilani Moore, had introduced him to the gambling nightlife and got him into his mess. She was a good-looking creature who craved the fast life and, after trying out several suitors, settled on Joaquin Nunez. Nunez was one of Guam's midlevel heroin dealers who worked in the Sablan gang; Piilani helped him sell his junk. Romine soon became friends with Nunez as well as some of the other dope dealers. That exposure began Romine's transformation from a humble insurance salesman by day into a nighttime heroin dealer.

That drama all occurred at about the time DEA set up shop on Guam in mid-1978. Nunez became one of our early victims, going down after we learned of him from Fairley and Garrigus. Following Nunez's arrest, a fearful Piilani fled to Hawaii and soon started selling heroin there to finance her gambling habit. But before leaving Guam, Piilani set up Romine, also in economic trouble, with a source obtained through Nunez. We didn't yet know about Piilani or the identity of that heroin source, since Nunez never revealed his business upon his arrest. One of the few who kept quiet and didn't perform a sentence-reducing rollover, Nunez pleaded guilty to his charges and was sent off-island to federal prison.

Our objective in narcotics cases was to find the source of supply. Stopping heroin was like stopping water, and to stop the flow of water, you must head upriver to the source. Rickie Sablan didn't know who supplied the heroin to Romine, but when Agent George Bannion and I questioned him further, he revealed another of his dealers who, like Nunez, was also friendly with Romine. His name was Tom Sallome.

Sallome had been in the navy on Guam, and was introduced to heroin dealing while hanging out at the cockfights. He became a dealer for Sablan, but also sometimes bought his heroin from Nunez when Sablan ran low on supply. I found him in Chicago at the Great Lakes Naval Base.

That was one of the appealing policies of DEA—when you had a good case going, you followed the leads wherever they led. Sallome in Chicago made my long trip from Guam worthwhile. He advised me Romine's heroin supplier was Japanese, a man who rented a room long-term on the fourth floor of the Guam Fujita Hotel. That would be easy enough to verify. We made arrangements with the Naval Investigative Service to have Sallome sent back to Guam to testify before the federal grand jury and help us put together the case against Romine.

On Guam, we wired up Sallome with a tape recorder and sent him to meet with Romine. They talked about their previous deals together, valuable evidence in court since Romine verified some of his previous sales to Sallome. Sallome wasn't able to buy heroin from Romine, so we would have to indict Romine based on testimony from his colleagues in crime: Sablan and Sallome.

Bannion and I ran around collecting supporting evidence for the charges against Romine. A check with the Fujita Hotel desk determined our Japanese quarry's name was Jungi Yamamoto. He rented room number 437. A look at his room telephone call record showed calls to Japan and Hawaii. We checked on that. With an affidavit in hand detailing our probable cause, attorney Fred Black and I dashed upstairs to see Judge Perez in his chambers. He signed an arrest warrant for Romine. We didn't have enough to arrest Yamamoto, so our plan was to arrest Romine, persuade him to cooperate, and then use his statements to obtain an arrest warrant for Yamamoto before Yamamoto sniffed the wind and fled the island. In the meantime, we obtained a search warrant for Yamamoto's hotel room.

Bannion and I arrested Romine at his office at noon in September 1979. His one-year run as a heroin dealer was over. His shock and surprise at seeing me pull out handcuffs was matched by the fascinated stares of his coworkers in the insurance office. Trembling and head bowed, Romine stiff-walked to our car for the short ride to the office. I remember thinking it would take no time to flip this mewling mouse, which was good—time was short.

Persuading an arrested doper to confess his sins and come clean could be accomplished in several ways. Knowing his motivation was crucial to turning him. What did he want? What did he need? With that, pick the right line, cast it out, and see if he went for it. If we pushed the correct button, he would consider the offer and then rationalize cooperating. Crooks often made us go through the let's-make-a-deal exercise because talking to the police ran against their criminal creed. A wasted effort, really, because once they had drawn a deep breath, righted themselves, and regained their balance after the shock of arrest, comprehension dawned swiftly. They were caught and facing prison; they knew it and we knew they knew it. Aboard a sinking ship going down fast, they had the choice of scrambling into our life raft or taking their chances on the open water. When they wavered, I would ask, "How long can you tread water?"

We placed Romine in the interview room at the DEA office to allow him a chance to compose himself, absorb the magnitude of the situation. We had shoehorned in three folding chairs and a small card table to fashion an interview space from a former broom closet. Its tight fit was perfect for those in-your-face talks. We allowed him a decent interval, then Bannion and I went in to give Romine what for and why not.

Since he was a timid man and we were in a hurry, we grabbed for the jugular, telling him what we had on him and what that meant in terms of a prison sentence. I spoke in a measured tone, pausing occasionally to let him grasp the weight of the evidence against him and the various charges he faced. I could tell he was listening as he squirmed in his chair, visibly wincing as he absorbed like body blows the several counts listed on my affidavit. Then I sat back while Bannion put on the kid gloves and took over, assuring Romine all was not lost. We could show him a path out of the woods and he could help himself, but we needed him to turn on Yamamoto.

Romine surprised us with his refusal to cooperate. He denied all our charges. Bannion started in again. "Romine, we have you cold. It's not you we want; it's Yamamoto. You can help yourself out on this, but you have to do it today, because Yamamoto will leave Guam tonight and that will be it. You'll have to carry the load by yourself."

"I'm not talking. I want a lawyer."

The man was in denial. His calling for an attorney was a stall tactic that would ruin our timetable. But we had no choice; he had not waived his rights. We let him make his calls, already knowing his attorney would not allow him to talk to us that day.

We had no choice but to press on, so we hurried over to the Fujita Hotel with our search warrant, hoping to find something incriminating in room 437. We caught Yamamoto as he was packing. He had already received word of Romine's arrest. Searching his room and bags turned up nothing solid. I tried talking to Yamamoto, but it was futile. He recognized that if we had had anything on him, we would have already cuffed him. Sphinxlike, his face remained unreadable, as lifeless as the tattoos that plastered his arms. I snapped his photo and rolled his fingerprints as a just-in-case. Yamamoto escaped Guam that Thursday night on a flight to Tokyo. I was at the airport to watch him go.

I picked up the pieces of the investigation, trying to salvage what we had. We had Romine, but his source had slipped away. Fred Black met with Romine's attorney the next day and told him what we had. Romine was on his way to the slammer. Fred advised the attorney that Romine had missed his chance at penance and would face a ten-year sentence. Meanwhile, I contacted our Tokyo office, advised them of the situation, and requested they find what they could on Yamamoto. One thing was certain: he wouldn't be returning to Guam.

Fred called me on Monday morning to say Romine had experienced a leap of understanding and was ready to talk. Four days and nights in Guam's jail had proved far more persuasive than threats from Bannion or me. The sobering news from his attorney confirming he stood to face ten years in prison convinced Romine he needed to climb into that life raft. Fred told me, "Romine is ready to give us everything on Yamamoto and—"

"That's all well and good, but he's already a fugitive and we'll only be indicting a name." I was still angry. "Yamamoto's safe in Japan and out of reach. Tell Romine we don't need him now. He wanted to be stand up, so let him. He takes the hit alone."

"I didn't finish; that's not all. Romine is willing to name one of Yamamoto's customers that he knows in Hawaii." Fred paused to get my attention. "Romine is ready to give up his sister, Piilani Moore."

Bannion and I escorted Romine from the jail to the DEA office for the interview. Trying to be more comfortable this time, we sat in our little two-man office, spacious when compared to the broom closet. Romine already knew our attitude, having been briefed by his attorney, so he didn't waste our time. He made one explanatory statement, saying he couldn't cooperate that first day because that would have meant giving up his sister, Piilani. But the first night in jail convinced him he had made a mistake. I consoled him, mentioning that ten-year prison sentences cut a lot of family ties.

Romine had known Yamamoto casually for several years from the cockfights, and knew he smuggled heroin. In August 1978, Yamamoto asked Romine if he wanted to get into the business. With money troubles, Romine agreed and soon was buying one-pound quantities of heroin for $30,000. Romine conducted several one-pound heroin deals with Yamamoto until May 1979, when Yamamoto's supply dried up. He told Romine that three of his couriers had been arrested by US Customs trying to smuggle three pounds of heroin into Hawaii. That heroin had been destined for Piilani.

Armed with everything I had on the case, as well as Yamamoto's federal indictment and fugitive warrant, I flew to Tokyo to meet with the Tokyo Metropolitan Police and enlist their help. Police Inspector Tanaka, my point of contact, was an outgoing and friendly officer. He showed me around the Tokyo police headquarters and treated me like an honored guest. I laid out our case on Yamamoto, telling him we had one witness in Guam who would testify against Yamamoto, and three pounds of heroin seized in Hawaii as evidence.

After checking names, Tanaka told me his intelligence division advised that Yamamoto was yakuza—a career criminal and a member of the Yamaguchi-Gumi clan, Japan's largest criminal organized crime group. His three arrested couriers in Honolulu were also yakuza. Tanaka said we would have a good case against Yamamoto if we could find a witness in Hawaii who had ordered the heroin. I left Japan feeling we had a good shot because I knew the witness we needed to testify against Yamamoto—Piilani Moore.

I touched base in Guam, briefed Fred Black on what I had found in Tokyo, and then headed for Hawaii and a meeting with Piilani. The Pan Am flight to Honolulu from Guam left at night and was seven boring hours over the ocean: dinner, a sleeping pill, and then wake-up for arrival at seven in the morning.

Romine had already prepped his sister for the coming storm from DEA, so I had no trouble gaining Piilani's assistance. She confirmed the three pounds of heroin seized by customs in Honolulu were for her. Yamamoto had been there for the delivery, and after his three couriers were arrested, he had run to Piilani for help.

Back on Guam, Bannion and I put the case together, gathering documentary evidence to support our two witnesses in the case against Yamamoto. His three captured couriers had already been sentenced in Hawaii to ten-year prison terms. I made a timeline and event chart to further document Yamamoto's heroin trafficking on Guam and Hawaii. I carried the whole package back to Tokyo and gave it to Tanaka. He said it was a precedent-setting case, but he was optimistic Japan would charge Yamamoto. He said he would get back to me on it.

But Tanaka never got back to me.

Receiving awards from the Guam governor, March 1980. I'm second from the left.

In late 1981 I left Guam and transferred to our office in Seoul, Korea, to work with the Korean police. A little rude, a little crude, the Koreans were my favorite Asians. They were loyal, honest, and displayed no false pretenses. What you saw was what you got. That posting would reintroduce me to the Japanese police and the yakuza.

At that time Korea was the world's best producer of crystal methamphetamine—what we called ice. It resembled clear rock salt and its purity was legend. Although living in a police state under martial law, Koreans did have rights similar to ours with two major exceptions: minimal civil rights for violations of espionage or drug-trafficking laws. For the most part, Koreans did not abuse drugs, but they were not above making money by manufacturing ice for the Japanese. All of our major investigations in Korea led to Japanese contacts. The Japanese were world-class speed freaks, consuming great quantities of ice and any other chemical charge to keep them going at speed. Most of the ice in Japan was sold by the yakuza clans.

My investigative assistant, Lim Kyong Sun, and I squeezed into our Ford LTD with four Korean narcotics agents for the ride to Pusan. The Koreans had their own cars, but no money for gas. A major shipping port located in the southeast, Pusan was a six-hour drive from Seoul. Most of Korea's meth labs were located in that area, and we had word of a big one.

Our case had started two days earlier in Itaewon, an area in Seoul for foreign shoppers by day which changed into a bar district at night. Earlier that day, Lim and I had driven to visit the Korean narcotics police at their office and make our plans. Occupying Spartan quarters, their office featured a large room with numerous desks positioned in a circular pattern around the room's center of attention—a kerosene stove. That was the sum of their heating facilities, notable because Korea's winters were about the coldest I've ever endured. As a guest, I rated the seat closest to the warm stove. For the employees, officers' ranks determined their proximity to the stove; lower-grade officers sat far from heat. Feeling toasty by the heater on that cold day, I turned and noticed three secretaries in the corner next to a window, bundled in heavy coats and typing away with gloved hands.

Out with the police later that night, we watched an informant receive a sample of ice from a street dealer in an Itaewon bar. The dealer was promptly arrested by the Koreans. Since his civil rights were negligible, information was beaten out of the dealer, and we proceeded to his source.

Korean narcotics cases all proceeded the same way. Make an arrest at the lowest level, the easy scores, and progress up the ladder to the lab. In Korea, no one accused of narcotics trafficking resisted interrogation for very long. It was simple work, not requiring all the legwork and effort needed to develop leads in America, but I wouldn't trade our system for it. There was too much chance for police to abuse their power in that system. Not that Korean police abused their power; they did not as far as I knew.

Two days later and following our fourth arrest in the case, we found the lab's location in Pusan.

On the way to Pusan, I noticed vast areas where the hillsides had been reforested, half-grown pine trees standing in neat, spaced rows like so many Christmas tree farms. I asked if the fighting during the Korean War had caused the deforestation, thinking napalm had burned off the hillsides. One of the cops enlightened me. The Japanese had clear-cut Korea's forests back when they ruled, taking the lumber to build houses in Japan while saving their own precious trees. I was interested in Korean history, but knowing the Japanese issue was a delicate subject in Korea, I dropped it.

At Pusan, we arrived at the suspected house near midnight. It was located in a neighborhood of large, similar homes, all with eight-foot-high walls and heavy gates. I scaled the wall, dropped to the other side, and opened the gate for the others. The police kicked open the front door. Then, in keeping with Korean culture, we all removed our shoes before running into the house.

We discovered the lab at the back of the house. Impressive, the gleaming, white-walled, professional set-up would have rivaled anything Eli Lilly had. The chemist was in the lab when we entered. He was dressed in a white lab coat, of course. We pulled twenty-eight kilograms, about sixty-one pounds of pure meth, out of the lab.

Our timing was fortunate. The haul represented a month's product that the chemist was preparing to send to his Japanese connection. He talked freely without persuasion and gave us all the particulars on the Japanese buyers. At the end, he asked why he needed to go to jail. "I make this chemical, which costs little to produce, and I send it to the hated Japanese, who then pay me lots of money that I spend in Korea. I'm poisoning our enemy and taking money from them to give to Korea. You should award me a medal instead of sending me to jail."

From his point of view, I couldn't fault his reasoning.

Later, I sent all the information we had developed from the lab case to the Japanese police. As usual, they were polite and thanked us for our findings. I never heard anything from them as to what they accomplished with our information.

Working with the Japanese was a study in frustration. I had heard that the yakuza had major political influence in the country at the highest levels, and that the police were often limited in their ability to suppress certain types of crime. In my experience with them, I had no reason to doubt those reports.

Patience sometimes has its benefits. Guam contacted me in May 1982, asking me to travel from Korea to Miami. Jungi Yamamoto had been arrested on our fugitive warrant as he flew into Miami from the Caymans.

His failure to pay heed to the US system of justice caught him. Lying low and waiting for the heat to cool down doesn't work on a fugitive warrant—they don't expire. Prior to removing Yamamoto to Guam, the Miami court needed someone to appear at his identity hearing, someone who could prove who he was. That would be me.

I arrived in Miami, exhausted from the long flight from Seoul, and went directly to the US Court. I was a few moments ahead of the hearing, so I asked the marshal to take me to the holding cell to see my boy. There he was, sitting like a stone statue and staring at the wall. At the cell door, I called out, "Mr. Yamamoto, it has been a long wait, but I'm very glad to see you again."

Yamamoto turned and, looking at me, did a quick double take, allowing me to catch a brief glimpse behind his mask. He remembered me, all right.

The hearing took ten minutes. I testified that he was the Yamamoto wanted on Guam, and I showed his photo and prints I had taken in that hotel room almost three years before. I next met him on Guam as we appeared before Judge Perez. In a plea bargain, Yamamoto received a seven-year sentence, a disappointing three years less than each of his couriers. Well, he had been one that got away, but not for long.

16

Bangkok Bust

Guam's drug problem was heroin, and all of it originated in Thailand. Chasing it down once heroin had spread out on the island was a difficult task. Working to stop heroin in Thailand before it arrived in Guam was more sensible.

Married at age fourteen to Jesse, a not-much-older sailor, at age nineteen Kathy Bryant had four children to show for her five years of marriage. Assigned for the past year to the Guam naval base, her husband was a submariner, and his three-month tours underwater and out of touch proved too much for Kathy. After all, an early marriage and its consequent childbearing barrage had caused her to miss out on a normal teenage social life. When Jesse returned from his last submerged voyage, she had taken up with a shore-based sailor. Intended insult or not, she relocated to naval housing directly across the street from their marital nest.

Jesse Bryant was sitting in my office, pouring out his tale. Earlier, he had been waiting for me in our office lobby when I walked in after playing water polo with Fred Black. We often swam at lunchtime with several Guam attorneys in the nearby public pool. Bryant had asked to speak with me in confidence about a serious matter, so I led him upstairs to our office for a chat.

The story about his discontent with Kathy was touching, but as I was not a marriage counselor, I expected the subject to get around to illegal drugs. First, I had to ask, "Wait a minute. She's having an affair and moved in with him across the street from your house?"

"Yeah, I know, but it's no problem. Really. I understand. She is still a kid, and I can't blame her since I'm gone so much." He seemed a good man and a saint for his patient tolerance. Teary, he continued in his beaten-down tone, "Anyway, like most of us in the military, we are short on money; I'm only a petty officer 3. But yesterday my wife came across the street and said our money troubles would soon be over because she was going on a short trip and would come back with a lot of money."

"Where is she going and what does she have to do?"

"She is going to Bangkok to carry back heroin."

"She told you that?" I was beginning to feel doubtful, but resisted the urge to glance at my watch.

"Yes, sir. She trusts me. Anyhow, I have to care for the kids while she is gone."

"Who wants her to do this? How much heroin? How is it going to work?"

Bryant admitted she had not shared that with him, telling him that it was better he not know. I assured him she was right about that, but things had changed—I was in on it now. I was still skeptical but his sincerity convinced me I had better check it out.

I telephoned Ernie Maher at the NIS and asked him to meet me at Bryant's house on the base. Ernie and I had a great working relationship, and he needed to be part of this since it involved the navy. Bryant and I drove to his house and met up with Ernie out front. I quickly gave him what I knew, and then the three of us walked across the street to see Kathy.

Kathy Bryant was not what I was expecting. Barefoot, she stood six feet tall, much of it legs, and her trim figure did not betray her frequent childbearing. Her teenager's pimply cheeks held back her looks, but with curly red hair and green eyes that fit her face, she was a semi-attractive woman. When Jesse identified us, her sudden change of posture let me know she would not be a problem. She seemed to relax; the pressure was off. At our suggestion, Bryant herded their four children across the street to his house. Ernie and I sat down with Kathy to get the story.

Peter Fisk, a sailor she knew from the gym, had met with Kathy two weeks prior and asked if she was interested in making some money, already knowing she was. He let out that he represented a smuggling group and was looking for female couriers to bring about two kilograms of heroin into Guam. When Kathy said she was afraid of being caught, he reassured her, saying they had a foolproof smuggling method. He added that another navy woman had successfully brought in a load two months earlier. Fisk told her she would make about $2,000 for a week's effort. Kathy mulled it over for a day, and then phoned Fisk and agreed to go. All her future plans involved money.

She described receiving a call a week later from an unknown man who said he was Fisk's friend. He gave her instructions to obtain a passport and a Japanese visa. He specified she would travel to several Asian countries before going to Bangkok, and he would train her for the mission. She had done as directed and was waiting for a call with further instructions from the man.

Kathy's story was plausible, so Ernie and I worked on the assumption it was true and spent the next hour schooling Kathy. We wanted her to assume the role and go to Bangkok.

Two days after our meeting, Kathy called us, saying the unknown man directed her to meet him in room 496 at the Continental Hotel for training at three o'clock on the following day. Four of us set up surveillance on the room in the morning of that day.

At two thirty, two men arrived, parked their cars nearby, and entered room 496. Both men were youthful looking, one tall and blond-haired while the other was short and dark-complexioned. Arriving by taxi, Kathy walked up to room 496 at the appointed hour and knocked. The hotel was set up bungalow-style on Tumon Beach. We watched her from the louvered windows of a bungalow located thirty feet away.

Just seconds after Kathy entered the room, the short youth left the room, got into his car, a blue Datsun, and drove away. A car license check identified a Steve Davis as its owner.

Two hours later, Kathy left the room and walked to the hotel lobby, from where she took a taxi downtown. George and I went to meet her at our office, leaving two agents behind to keep watching.

"Now then." I settled in at my desk, pen in hand. "Tell us exactly what happened. Everything."

Kathy described the man she had met. He had called himself Jim.

He was alone in the room, she observed. He was tall, wore a black wig, a paste-on phony mustache, and dark sunglasses. When she entered the room, he led her directly to the sliding glass door and onto the back patio to admire the ocean for a moment. Back inside the room, they sat at a table while he spoke about her trip. On the table lay a pistol, binoculars, and a walkie-talkie radio.

Taking notes, I said nothing but noted down that Steve Davis must have hid in the bathroom and slipped out unseen when Kathy went onto the back patio.

Kathy was to fly to Manila, Hong Kong, Singapore and then Bangkok, spending a day at each place. Purchasing some cheap tourist trinkets at the Bangkok airport and producing her passport with all the stamps would portray her as a tourist to Guam customs upon her return.

Upon arrival in Bangkok, she was to stay at the First Hotel and wait for a contact who would show her a two-dollar bill as a recognition signal.

Jim instructed her to buy a loose-fitting, dark-colored dress and an oversize bra because she would body-pack the heroin in custom-fitted plastic pouches under the dress. He would pay all her expenses and then give her another $2,000 when she returned.

Jim closed by saying he would make flight arrangements and call her in for one more training session the day before she left, which was to be in about six days. On her way out the door, he peeled off $200 from a large roll of money and gave it to her to cover the expense of obtaining her passport.

While Kathy was filling me in, the agents observing the room followed Jim when he departed fifteen minutes after Kathy left. He carried a cloth bag, probably containing the wig, mustache, and other stage props. They followed his car north toward Andersen Air Force Base. He entered the base and drove into the base housing area. Surveillance dropped off at that point.

We had agreed to be discreet in our surveillance as we didn't want to risk being seen by any of the crooks. We had an insider, Kathy, in this caper and didn't want to hazard the deal. We would let them make their plans and go to Bangkok. I was going to shadow Kathy every step of the way. We would make the arrests when the source delivered heroin to her.

Then I would come back with her, and we would take down the group in Guam when they met with Kathy to recover their heroin.

We spent considerable time on the phone coordinating with our concerned offices to cover the logistics and contingencies. In Bangkok, any heroin seized was the property of the Thai police and would remain in Thailand. However, for evidence purpose, they would give me a small sample, which we could mix with flour to fashion a load similar to what was seized. We'd bring it back and perform a controlled delivery to the suspects in Guam, thus wrapping up everybody involved. A lot could go wrong on this complex operation; remaining flexible was important.

Three days later, Kathy received a call from Jim with instructions to meet again at the bungalow hotel at six in the evening. She would leave on her trip the day after the meeting.

We started surveillance on room 496 at nine in the morning. Jim arrived at four that afternoon, parking his car nearby and walking in with a large paper shopping bag. About fifteen minutes later, a Guamanian man walked up and was let into the room. One Guam police detective on our task force recognized him. "That's Robert Borja; he's a big-time heroin dealer."

We found Borja's car parked next to Jim's. Borja stayed in the room with Jim for only half an hour and then left in his car. We had two cars follow, but they lost him in a neighborhood near his home. No problem; we knew where he lived. We now had four men involved in the crime: Jim, Peter Fisk, Steve Davis, and Robert Borja.

After meeting with me at our office for a last-minute pep talk, Kathy rode to the hotel in a taxi, arriving at six. She met Jim, who was again working his disguise. He gave her the body pack, consisting of plastic bags filled with flour. Jim had her try everything on for a dress rehearsal, taping the bags on underneath the girdle. She modeled the dress, turning and twisting as he instructed. He announced it looked perfect—no telltale bulges.

Kathy took off the bags and gave them back to Jim. He advised her that she would meet someone in Bangkok named John Moore, who would fill those same bags with two pounds of heroin and tape them shut. She was to wear that dress when returning with the heroin.

For one final order, Jim said, "Buy yourself a green dress. You will wear it in Bangkok so John Moore can recognize you."

Jim went over the instructions again and made Kathy repeat them back to him. She was to check in to the First Hotel and wait until six in the evening for John Moore to come, bringing his two-dollar bill. If he didn't show, she was to go to the Dusit Thani hotel, wearing the green dress, and sit in the coffee shop until he contacted her there. If John Moore didn't come that first day, she was to repeat the schedule until he did arrive. Jim explained that sometimes they encountered small delays in obtaining the heroin from their Thai source.

Then Jim gave her a gold chain with a small gold pendant resembling a Buddha. "This is for luck, so wear it always."

Handing over $1,500 in expense money and her air tickets, Jim reassured her everything was in place. John Moore was set to meet her in Bangkok in four days. He reminded her to come directly to the same hotel from the Guam airport upon her return and check into a room; he would find her.

I waited at the gate for Kathy. It was fifteen minutes until flight time and she had not arrived. We had not shadowed her to the airport from her house, fearing that Jim and his gang would be doing the same thing—he was paying for the trip, so it made sense for him to keep an eye on his investment. Besides, he had warned her they would be watching her throughout.

Our plan was for each of us to travel alone to Manila and hook up at the Silahis hotel. Bannion, waiting at the gate with me, ran over to a pay phone and rang Kathy's house. No one answered; she must have been on her way and running late. I asked Bannion to grab her, put her in a hotel that night if she missed the flight, and keep her incommunicado. I got on the flight just before they closed the doors. I needed to get to Manila and meet up with a DEA agent at the airport.

Bannion met Kathy as she ran up to the gate. The aircraft was already on the runway, so she had missed the flight. She apologized, saying her taxi had arrived late. He went to Plan B and placed her in an airport hotel with orders to call no one. She would have to catch the next day's flight to Manila.

Bannion made sure Kathy was onboard the next flight. I had talked with him on the phone and I was set to pick her up with Howard Shaw, the DEA agent in Manila. Thirty minutes out from Guam, however, the plane developed mechanical problems and had to turn back. Kathy wasted another day at the airport hotel as I simmered in Manila.

The third attempt worked, and Kathy arrived in Manila. Howard and I met her and we headed for the Silahis Hotel in his car. She was distraught over the problems with her flights, but I dismissed her concerns.

"Don't worry about it," I said. "Those things happen. Battle plans never turn out as scheduled."

"But what about my timetable? It's Sunday. How can I go on to Singapore and then Hong Kong and still be in Bangkok on Monday to meet with John Moore?"

Howard and I had already been working on the problem. "It doesn't matter if you miss Singapore and Hong Kong. Those trips were only to get stamps in your passport. Here's what we're going to do. We're going to wait around and relax, and then tomorrow take the morning flight into Bangkok. You'll be in your hotel on time and waiting for John Moore. How's that sound?"

She brightened. "That sounds good. And that means I'll have a chance to go shopping today," she added, giving me her innocent look. "Because I forgot to bring the green dress."

Kathy was working out well. She was a good listener, enjoying her role and the burden placed on her. She told me it was the first time in her life she felt valuable.

Howard and I drove Kathy to the Glorietta Mall in Makati. Shopping is a cultural mainstay in the Philippines, and on Sundays the mall packs them in. People go just to walk around, be seen, and spend a day out of the heat and humidity.

We were on a mission, though, since Kathy needed a green dress. An ordinary task, except finding a green dress that fit a six-foot-tall woman was problematic in a country populated with short women.

Strolling along and window-shopping for likely stores, at one point we passed a mirrored wall. We naturally looked at our images while walking by and had to laugh. There we were: a woman whose heels put her at six foot five, towering above the two men standing five foot eight and stepping their tallest on either side of her. Glancing behind, we discovered a large crowd following her. I wished I had a camera that day.

Finding a dress her size was hopeless, so I hunted for and found a reasonable alternative. One store had a large green shirt that almost fit, but hung loosely from her shoulders like a bowling shirt. Kathy, looking down her nose, spurned it. "I won't wear this in public."

I knew better than to step between a woman and her wardrobe, but time was getting short. "Kathy, you won't have to. Simply carry it in a bag. Slip it on in the restroom, and then take it off when you leave the coffee shop. No big deal."

Our arrival in Bangkok was smooth and soon busy. Agent Brent Walters from the Bangkok office was assigned to help me on the case. His opening guidance was to cancel placing Kathy at the First Hotel. "Every doper in Bangkok goes there to score heroin," he advised. "The hotel employees are wrong and they know our police on sight. Surveillance is impossible. We have already made arrangements to put her in the President. It's safe there, and management is friendly."

We booked Kathy into the President Hotel. It wasn't what Jim had instructed her to do, but she had the backup plan in place to meet John Moore that night at the Dusit Thani. At a few moments before nine, Kathy and I rode with Brent to the hotel, located across the street from Bangkok's Lumpini Park. She wore her green bowling shirt over a skirt. We entered separately and she went straight to the coffee shop on the ground floor and sat down. Brent and I sat in the corner while some Thai undercover police scattered about.

At nine thirty, Kathy ran her fingers through her hair, her prearranged signal to me that she had noticed something. Most of the customers in the restaurant were foreigners, and we didn't pick out anyone special.

A few minutes later, a waiter approached her, verified she was Kathy, and advised she had a telephone call. She took the call at the register. It was John Moore. He said he had spotted her drinking coffee. At his questioning, she explained the First Hotel was full, so she had gone to the President and was staying in room 305. He said it was no problem and told her to stay in her room until he came with the heroin, which might be tomorrow or might take two to three days.

Kathy caught a taxi back to the President and went up to her room. Brent and I came in through the adjoining door from my room to get her story. She informed us she had signaled because she saw someone familiar to her from Guam. She didn't know him, but he was young and short with a dark complexion. I thought of Steve Davis, whom we had not seen since Kathy's first training day. We had missed him at the Dusit Thani, but that was okay; he would deliver the heroin to Kathy, and us, at the President. We just had to wait for it.

Two days later, we were still waiting, but Kathy received a phone call in the morning from John Moore. We taped the call.

"We're having some trouble filling those bags with the stuff. It's taking longer than we planned, but we'll have it put together by tonight. I want you to be ready to get it. Wear the green dress again and be set to go by eleven."

"Why can't you bring it to me?" She was whining now. "Jim said you would deliver it to me."

"We could have at the First Hotel, but you are at a hotel where it is not safe. We have this all figured out, so don't worry. Just be available to go. You'll be done in thirty minutes and can catch the noon flight tomorrow."

Kathy was doing a good job—a born actress. I knew she was having fun; heck, so was I.

John Moore called her again at ten thirty that night.

"Take the hotel taxi to the Manhattan Hotel, go to the coffee shop on the ground floor, and sit in the corner in the back. A Thai man named Mr. Ron will approach you. He'll know your name and he will show you a two-dollar bill. Go with him in his car. He'll give you the package and bring you back to your hotel. Go now; he's there waiting."

By changing the deal at the last moment, John Moore was acting like a true doper. We followed Kathy's taxi to the Manhattan, another lowbrow, low-rent tourist hotel located not far away, off Sukhumvit Road. Kathy strolled into the coffee shop and sat in the back as directed. She'd been waiting not five minutes when Mr. Ron slid up to her, having come in by the back door. He voiced her name and gave her a glimpse of a two-dollar bill.

Without any lingering, they left together out the back door, which led to an alley. They got into Mr. Ron's red Toyota. He drove back and parked on a side street next to the President. Brent and I followed along with several police. Mr. Ron gave Kathy a blue shopping bag, which contained a kilogram of heroin. As she rose out of the car, Kathy ran her fingers through her hair again. The bust signal.

The Thai police moved in and arrested Mr. Ron, who identified himself as Prateep Sriwatta. Behind the backseat they found an additional blue shopping bag containing a half kilogram of heroin. Heroin trafficking was a crime punishable by death in Thailand. Prateep, knowing he had been caught with 1.5 kilograms of heroin, started talking before they had handcuffed him. Confess and cooperate, and the Thai court would spare his life.

Prateep wasted no time directing the police to John Moore, who was holed up in room 104 of another hotel located near the Manhattan. The police proceeded there straightaway and arrested him in his room. John Moore was registered as Steve Davis. My hunch was correct; he was the guy who had been with Jim on that first day in Guam.

Brent and I met up with Davis at the Thai police station. He was sitting at a table in a large room. Two Thai police officers guarded the door. I identified myself to the glowering Davis and asked for some personal identifying information. Then Major Virat, head of the police narcotics unit, strode into the room.

Davis chose that moment to say his piece. Looking at Major Virat he opened up in an angry tone. "I am an American citizen, and I have rights. I demand to talk with someone at the embassy. Right now! I know my rights."

After Davis's outburst, Virat's Teutonic half reared its head. (Thai culture strives to avoid coarseness and displays of anger. Major Virat was Eurasian, with a Thai father and a German mother). Brent, knowing Virat well, nudged me under the table with his foot, signaling me to watch. Virat sprang to his feet and slammed both fists on the table, leaning forward with his face inches from Davis.

"You are in the Kingdom of Thailand!" he shouted. "You have no stinking rights."

Davis shrank back. It was one of those Kodak moments that I would not forget. I would have the opportunity to work with Virat in the years to come when I transferred to Thailand; he was one of a kind.

It seemed to us a good moment to withdraw, and we left Davis to his fate. In the meantime, I decided that night I wanted to come back and work in Thailand. I had fallen under the spell of that strange, exotic land. It was the world's major source country for heroin—the dragon's lair. I would get my chance within a few years.

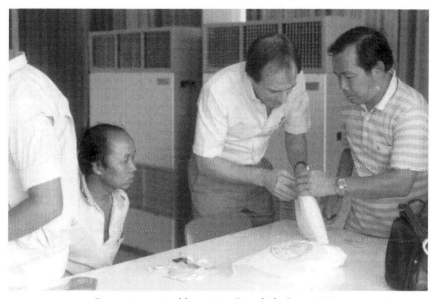

Processing seized heroin in Bangkok, June 1979.

I spent the next day, Thursday, tying up my end of the case with Brent. I contacted Guam and advised Bannion of our situation. He would set the trap for Jim and the others. Brent and I went to see Major Virat at his office. His men had taken out two ounces of heroin and added flour to make a 1.5 kilogram package. It was diluted, but still counted as heroin in US courts.

After his arrest, Prateep informed the police that it had been his second transaction with Davis, Prateep having sold him a pound of heroin in March. For this deal, Prateep bought 1.5 kilograms of heroin for $7,000 and sold it to Davis for $15,000. It could have generated a half million dollars on Guam.

One thing kept bugging me, though. Kathy had received the bag with one kilogram; who was to receive the other bag, the half kilo?

I returned to the President that afternoon about five o'clock and found a message under my door. It was from Kathy, asking me to contact her as soon as possible. I rang her next door and she came to my room, breathless.

"I think there's another courier here from Guam!"

I held up my hand to halt her while I thought a bit. Then I tumbled into it—the half-kilo package. Kathy didn't know about it, so I replied, "Take your time, and tell me what you have."

"Well, the day I left Guam, you know, on the plane that had to turn back, I saw this girl in the waiting area. We were the only two white women on the flight, so I noticed her. She was also wearing a baggy dress, just like me. I saw her again today. Here, at the President. She is staying here and we just had coffee together. Jim told me another courier was involved, and I think she's here just like me."

I thought so too. Thinking out loud, I wondered, "Do you think you could hook up with her now and find out for sure? We don't have much time, because we're leaving tomorrow."

"I've already set it up. We're having dinner together downstairs at six. Oh, and she's staying in room 1148."

Kathy called me at eight from the hotel coffee shop. "Agent Lloyd, I'm here with Carla Chun and she needs to talk with you. Can you come down now?"

She had spoken in a professional tone. The girl was growing up. Fast.

Before going to the coffee shop, I phoned Brent because we needed two agents to conduct the interview. I hurried downstairs to them and Kathy introduced me. We sat around making small talk until Brent arrived, and then I excused Kathy so we could get the story from Carla.

Carla started at the beginning, saying Robert Borja was an old flame who had contacted her about bringing heroin back to Guam from Bangkok. She decided to go since she was broke and jobless. Carla detailed her meeting the mysterious "Jim" in his masquerade get-up in room 496. Her story matched Kathy's almost word for word, including their quick stroll onto the patio so Davis could slip out the front door and the dress rehearsal with the flour-filled body pack. We missed seeing Carla since we had only watched the room on the two days Kathy was there—Carla came on alternate days.

When Carla spotted Kathy on the aborted Saturday flight from Guam, she suspected her because Borja had mentioned an extra courier would also make the trip. He said that courier was large enough to body-pack a bigger load. Short and slim, Carla had been told she would carry back a half pound of heroin. I didn't bother telling her the greedy buggers had been set to double up her load and saddle her with over a pound of the junk. Carla spotted Kathy again on the Sunday flight to Manila but didn't say anything to her, preferring to mind her own business.

After stopping a day in Singapore and Hong Kong as planned, Carla arrived in Bangkok on Tuesday and checked in to the President Hotel, as instructed by Jim. A fortuitous coincidence. She received a phone call from John Moore that afternoon and verified her safe arrival. He phoned later that night and advised her to stand in front of the Central Shopping Center at 11:00 p.m., wearing a blue dress. Someone named Mr. Ron would drive up in a red car, pick her up, give her a bag with the dope, and return her to the President.

Carla put on her blue dress and rode in a taxi to the Central Shopping Center. She stood there from eleven to midnight and no one approached her. Giving up, she walked back to the President and stayed in her room, wondering what had gone wrong.

The next afternoon, Carla stepped onto the elevator to go downstairs and have a look around. The lift stopped on the third floor and Kathy got on. They nodded to each other and rode down in nervous silence. They both headed for the coffee shop and sat separately for a few moments. Finally, gathering her courage, Carla walked over and sat down with Kathy at her table. The two women opened up with some general news about Guam and, feeding off each other's conversational tidbits, ended up sharing that they both were going through divorces and just needed to get away from Guam, alone.

Carla revealed she had made one-day stops in Singapore and Hong Kong before arriving in Bangkok, just to see something of the Orient. On hearing that, Kathy gave her a knowing look and asked in a low tone if she had already met her contact in Bangkok. Carla then noticed Kathy was wearing a Buddha necklace just like the one she wore.

Dropping the pretense at last, Carla admitted she had not met her contact. Kathy informed her she wouldn't either, given that John Moore had been arrested and the heroin seized. Kathy had quickly divulged her own cooperating role in the operation and suggested that Carla talk with me and try to sort her problems out.

To keep up with Jim's timetable, Kathy, Carla, and I left Bangkok the next afternoon and flew to Tokyo. I was carrying the 1.5 kilograms of floured heroin that represented the pure heroin we had seized from Davis and Prateep. I had sent a terse telegram to Guam from Bangkok relating the turn of events. Bannion would arrange the surprise reception.

Riding on a Japan Airlines plane full of Japanese tourists, the three of us rolled up to the Guam terminal at one thirty in the morning. The ground crew pushed the staircase to the front door. My two couriers and I were seated in first class and watched the door open. Peter Martin, the DEA agent in charge on Guam, stepped into the cabin.

"Mark, we have it all set up. After getting your bags and going through customs, the two couriers are to get into the green taxi out front. Ernie Maher is driving. He'll take you to the hotel, where you will check in to room 572. We have DEA and NIS agents all over the place covering it."

We joined our agents in the room adjoining 572. Bannion went over a game plan as we waited for Kathy to check in at the front desk. When Kathy and Carla came into their room, Bannion and I entered through the connecting door. Three agents remained behind, listening at the door. They pulled the pins from the door hinges to make it easier to open later. I placed the carry-on bag with the heroin on the table. The agents in the next room received a radio call advising that Jim and Borja had pulled in to the parking lot. Bannion gave the two women a few words of instruction, and then he and I hid in the closet, looking out through the louvered doors with guns drawn.

Kathy answered the knock at the door, and Borja walked in. She didn't know him, so he flashed a two-dollar bill at her, keeping to the script.

"How was the trip? Any problems?"

Borja was smiling. He hadn't seen Carla, not knowing she was there until she opened up on cue.

"There's your dope. You tried to set us up!"

Borja, startled, looked over and saw Carla.

"What? How did you get here? Wait! You're not supposed to be together!" He looked into the bag, noticing the heroin packaged in one plastic bag. "What did that guy do? Well, you're here, aren't you?"

He pulled an envelope out of his pocket and handed it to Kathy as Bannion and I burst out of the closet. He reared back at the sight of us with our brandished guns. He backpedaled close to the connecting door. It flew off its hinges and knocked him flat. Bannion lifted the door off Borja as the three agents from the other room rushed in. I pulled a revolver out of Borja's waistband before placing cuffs on him.

Out in the parking lot, Guam police rushed Jim's car and placed him under arrest. He had a gun in his pants too. Our big surprise for the night: Jim's real name was David Johnson, and he was the son of the colonel in charge of the US Air Force police on Guam.

Johnson came to his sentencing dressed in a white shirt and black tie, the uniform he wore when attending high school at the Father Duenas Academy. That was a touch not lost on Judge Perez as he also was a graduate of Guam's finest school. Looking at Johnson, who seemed clean-cut, respectful, and remorseful, Judge Perez must have wondered how an obviously nice young man like him could have become involved in a scheme to import heroin to Guam. The judge had already heard Johnson's guilty plea and admission to earlier distribution of one pound of heroin on Guam and Hawaii. But, wearing his benign, pensive look, Perez inquired, "The court wants to know for what reasons you embarked on these criminal acts."

Johnson looked right at the judge and related his story. "Last year, the DEA agent in charge here, Mr. Martin, came to our house for dinner. My dad is the head of air force security at Anderson Air Base, and he knows Mr. Martin. They were talking about drug dealing, and I heard Mr. Martin mention that there was a foolproof way to import drugs. It was the scheme shown in the movie *The Thomas Crown Affair*, where Steve McQueen kept himself unknown to his helpers while directing them to perform a robbery. Mr. Martin said someone could do that with a drug courier, remaining unidentified while sending the courier off to Bangkok to bring back the dope. If the courier was caught with the drugs, they couldn't turn you in, because they didn't know who you were. I used that method when I recruited the two girls to bring back my heroin."

That explained it to me. Johnson's initial mistake in his half-baked scheme was listening to Martin, an agent who had never made a case in his career and wouldn't know how to set one up if it bumped into him. His second blunder was using Fisk and Borja to do his recruiting. The dolts had enlisted couriers who did not know Johnson, true enough, but they did know their recruiters. That move canceled out all of Johnson's nonsense play-acting with his wig, fake mustache, and the other props. The couriers didn't need to know Johnson: Kathy knew Fisk, Carla knew Borja, and all four of them would have rolled over and led us to Johnson if caught.

"But why did you undertake this criminal scheme?" questioned the Judge.

"Your honor, it has always been my goal to attend medical school and become a doctor. I have a 4.0 grade point average and will graduate from the University of Guam next year. The money I would have made from this enterprise would all have been used for a good cause, to pay my medical school tuition. That was a mistake, and for my errors I apologize to my family and to the court."

Judge Perez was known as a kind-hearted idealist who believed that second chances and soft justice were the rule and not the exception.

In David Johnson he found his exception.

"How about the heroin addicts and those lives ruined by heroin? Do you apologize to them too?" Voice rising, Judge Perez started getting into it. "How can you tell me you want to be a doctor and save lives, yet you attempted to sell a poison that destroys lives in order to achieve that goal?

With a rare look of disgust, Judge Perez handed down a seven-year prison sentence for Johnson. Borja caught an eight-year sentence. He was an experienced heroin dealer, after all, a fact worth an extra year to the judge. Fisk, for his minor yet important role, received a three-year deal.

Davis spent a long four months in a Bangkok jail before his attorney arranged bail. Bail was not normally allowed in Thailand for foreigners because, once out of jail, they immediately fled the country. However, paying off the attorney, who in turn paid off a judge, who then granted bail, gave one a chance to flee.

For Davis, his father emptied a retirement account at the Guam Naval Shipyard, where he had worked for thirty years as a welder. He sent $65,000 to Davis' attorney in Bangkok. Upon making bail and without a passport, Davis went south, sneaked across the Thai border into Malaysia, and made his way to the US consulate in Penang. They gave him a replacement passport and put him on a plane to Guam, but not before notifying us. I was waiting for Davis at the airport when he arrived. He seemed almost glad to see me as I arrested him.

Davis made a quick guilty plea, as everyone else had already cut a deal. At sentencing, Judge Perez, having vented his spleen on Johnson, reverted to his standard leniency and gave Davis a one-year prison sentence. The judge announced that the spell Davis had served in a Bangkok jail was equal to several years served in a federal penitentiary. He had it about right on that score, but I thought Davis should have received more. Without remorse, he had squandered his father's retirement fund.

Prateep Sriwatta confessed, so the young man avoided the death penalty and earned a life prison sentence instead. I imagine he's still in there.

17

The Three Amigos

I checked in with the head of personnel upon returning to Los Angeles to begin my second tour in the City of Angels. "SAC Brown left a note for you to see him as soon as you arrived."

After my tours in Guam and Korea, I had been assigned to Thailand for four years. It was June 1987, and I was returning to America after spending nine years abroad. I hadn't even checked in yet. What could the special agent in charge possibly want with me? I didn't know him, but he had a good reputation, the kind not easily earned.

I entered his office and he wasted no time at laying it on me. "I've got an OPR case here that I have been holding for you for the past three months," he said. OPR, or the Office of Professional Responsibility, was the DEA division concerned with agent behavior; they were the headhunters. "Do you remember Agent John Jefferson?"

Surprised, I told him, "Yes, I knew him well. We were in Group Four together for two years. Back when I first came on in '74."

"Well, he's been named on a cocaine trafficking allegation. I want you to take a look at the case; work on it for thirty days and either develop the case or close it."

I sat down and read the case file on Jefferson. A thin folder, the file showed nothing new written in several months. The case had started with a traffic stop in Los Angeles by the county sheriff's department in June 1985.

They had pulled over Roger Goodwin for running a red light. Goodwin was an aspiring rapper who held a day job as a cocaine trafficker. The deputies arrested him after finding two ounces of cocaine and $7,000 in his car. To avoid jail, Goodwin agreed to cooperate and work off his beef.

Goodwin set up a couple of small street dealers for easy arrests and then dried up. The sheriffs saw through his foot-dragging, suspecting he had more to offer. Under pressure, Goodwin gave the deputies a final bone he hoped would make them go away. He told them his coke came from "an FBI man." He didn't know the man, having obtained the cocaine through a middleman (Goodwin's brother-in-law, Sherman Poole), but he knew the man's house in Alta Loma. He took them on a drive-by to view the house. It was the home of DEA agent John Jefferson.

At first, the sheriff's narcotics squad tried to develop the case on their own, but Goodwin told them he was on the outs with brother-in-law Poole, who had the only connection with Jefferson. Sergeant Baker and his squad then contacted DEA in Los Angeles and related what they had—an allegation from a doper with nothing to back it. DEA agreed to let the sheriffs carry on and try to make a case. Goodwin continued to protect Poole by keeping him out of the loop, so by January 1986, the sheriff's narcs had grown tired of it and yielded the case, along with Goodwin, to DEA.

Goodwin had made an allegation against a DEA agent, so DEA's OPR got the case. OPR was centralized then, with all of its investigators working out of DEA headquarters in Washington, DC. They often delegated their responsibility to conduct an internal investigation to an affected field office and did so here.

Two supervisors in the LA office were tapped to conduct the Jefferson investigation. It wasn't a popular assignment because now they had to undertake an internal investigation while already having full plates supervising field agents. That was possibly a vindicating factor in their not devoting all their efforts to working the accusation. Regardless, the case was not an easy one to pursue. After sitting down with Goodwin and getting his story, which included brother-in-law Poole's role, they made a few stabs at Jefferson: two were reasonable and one was a huge mistake.

First, Goodwin made a controlled call to Poole, recorded by DEA, and asked to buy some more cocaine from his "FBI man." Poole was testy, telling Goodwin, "Man, that's over with; he's made his million and quit."

It was a nice try, but Poole's dialogue was vague evidence. And Poole's telephone statement was truthful, as it turned out in the end.

Next the supervisors placed Goodwin in front of a federal grand jury. He testified as to his actions in the case, which included him purchasing about twenty kilograms of cocaine from Poole, who said he had received it from Jefferson.

The supervisors then screwed up by pulling in Poole for questioning. The investigation drove into a ditch at that point. Poole denied the allegations completely, and sounded the alarm to Jefferson. Jefferson was in Hawaii on vacation when Poole called him. A month later, during a trip to conduct undercover work for our New York office, Jefferson reported his badge and credentials lost. That was not an unknown occurrence in DEA, but it happened only a month before Jefferson managed to attain stress leave. He left the job in March 1986 and never came back to work with DEA. His "lost" credentials would later become significant.

At that point, Goodwin decided it was an appropriate moment to disappear. He dropped out of sight. The case remained open, but no one was working on it. The two supervisors had enforcement groups to manage and didn't have time to look for the evasive Goodwin.

The case had been on life support for months by the time I showed up in June 1987. It was time to revive it or, resuscitation failing, pull the plug.

Now I understood why Brown told me to just give it a month—he must have figured it was gasping for breath too. However, it was not over. Instead, it was the beginning of a consuming, grueling, and ultimately frustrating investigation that absorbed the next year of my life.

When looking at somebody as a criminal suspect, you find out what they're doing and who they know. I needed to update the records on Jefferson, so ordering telephone toll records on his home phone was first on the list. While waiting for the toll records, I went through his personnel record. He had changed much since he and I were young agents together in 1974. The only black agent in our group, his easy-going, quick-to-laugh manner fit in with the group. Ours was an arena in which friendly insults and deprecating jibes were served up with regularity. Thin-skinned personalities would have been offended.

He was strange, though, because he couldn't speak the street jive. He couldn't even swear properly. His father was a minister, and Jefferson had been raised as a devout Christian. He was known to sometimes read from the Bible while sitting at his desk. As a black man, he was not suspicious-looking to crooks. He had an Afro hairstyle, dressed well, and looked the part. The other groups in the office often utilized Jefferson in undercover roles, acting either as a buyer or as a bodyguard/money man to another undercover agent acting as buyer. He was known around the office as an undercover specialist, flash and dash.

I had covered him on numerous occasions when he worked undercover, but I never felt he was a star in the role of dope dealer. I remembered listening to a few taped recordings of his negotiations with dealers. He came across as less than effective: not particularly threatening nor somebody to be taken seriously. He talked too much and should have let his money close the deals, not his mouth. Many of his undercover negotiations did not prove fruitful.

I recalled one important characteristic about Jefferson from our early days. He was greedy; the lure of money had a terrific hold on him and often flavored his everyday conversations. He sold Amway products on the side and tried to recruit his coworkers to join him in selling, or at least to buy the stuff. With a trunk full of soap, he drove around in his government-issued car to deliver to his customers and spent an unreasonable amount of time tying up one of only two phone lines in our group while he pushed his goods. It was on that topic that I first heard of Sherman Poole, his neighbor, close friend, and Amway partner.

Right away, I met at the US courthouse with the assistant United States attorney handling the case, Matilda Kennedy. She had a solid reputation at DEA as an aggressive prosecutor—someone who didn't avoid a challenging investigation. Her work ethic and exuberance had a continual positive effect on all of us. Also on board were two other DEA agents: Brian

Nelson, recently added to the case, and Allen Pavlik, one of the supervisors who had conducted the preliminary work on the case.

We discussed what we had going and what we could do to find a solution. Goodwin had mentioned that Poole told him the "FBI guy" (Jefferson) had two other partners in his cocaine dealings—one large black man, and a Hispanic man who acted black. Pavlik theorized they had to be two other agents in the office, Donnell Reyes and James Cannon. The three agents had hung out together, running around like the three amigos.

What caught my attention was Matilda's early certainty as to Jefferson's guilt. I made mention that we would find out the truth, whether Jefferson had gone wrong or not. She gave me a determined look and made it clear in a few words that he was guilty. Her strong-minded will was infectious. It wasn't long before I was at the task wholeheartedly, bolstered by the added resentment of an old acquaintance gone wrong.

We had to bring Goodwin to the surface. Bothering his family was the tactic that worked. We paid visit after visit to known family addresses, disturbing them with our presence. Finally caving to family pressure to get us off their backs, Goodwin found an attorney and sent us a recant of his grand jury statements in a videotaped segment. He renounced all he had previously said. That tactic wouldn't save him. We obtained a material-witness arrest warrant and brought him in so he could repeat his original story to the grand jury.

Soon I had Jefferson's toll records in hand. I realized we were dealing with a doper—who else would go to every public phone booth within a mile of his house to make his toll calls? Paranoia about law enforcement tapping his home phone must have driven him to the public phone booths. The knucklehead should have taken a bag of quarters with him to make those calls, though. By using his telephone calling card, every call he made from anywhere was listed on his monthly phone bill.

His carelessness revealed much. From those public phones, not from home, he had phoned his two amigos Reyes and Cannon, travel agencies, Swiss banks, and numerous closely situated phone booths in New York City. Phone calls to numbers associated with other active cocaine cases also turned up.

Jefferson had been investigating dope dealers from one side of the law for well over ten years. He was too smart; he had seen too much to leave a clear trail like that. Or so one would think. We obtained phone tolls for Reyes and Cannon and, no surprise there, found several suspicious phone numbers all three of them were calling. Clearly, the three amigos worked together.

Donnell Reyes had always been in trouble while at DEA. He was fired in late 1985 for insubordination after he refused a disciplinary transfer to another office. But he sued DEA for discrimination and won. When Reyes came back to work in June 1987, I met him in the office. Bad first impressions are usually accurate. You know the type: after shaking his hand, you wanted to go wash yours. Reyes was patronizing, with an oily delivery. I put him down as a crook at first glance, if only because he looked like one. American justice presumes innocence; I do not.

My friend and academy roommate, Bob Patrick, took me aside and told me to watch out for Reyes. Bob didn't know I was already watching out for Reyes, but I appreciated the warning.

Reinstated, Reyes was placed in the same group where Brian and I were sitting. After obtaining the phone tolls and Goodwin's reemergence, we had something to go on. But we needed privacy, since no one at the office knew our assignment. We solved the problem by obtaining spare office space at the federal courthouse. It gave us plenty of room and required just a hop upstairs for our frequent strategy meetings with Matilda.

We had dozens of leads to follow on the phone calls. The IRS was brought in because of the Swiss banking connections, and they started a financial investigation of the three. The IRS was slow but thorough, and they were good at looking at the financial part of dope dealing—something most DEA agents loathed.

We also wanted to follow the amigos around to see how they spent their days. Like Jefferson, Cannon had quit the job in 1986, going out on a partial disability. We didn't yet realize it, but the amigos had all left the job at nearly the same time for a particular reason. We needed help. Brian and I couldn't do it all, and we certainly couldn't conduct surveillance on the three amigos because they knew us.

Management's support was half-hearted. Half a dozen agents were plucked from offices around the country and flown in on temporary duty to conduct surveillance. That didn't work at all, since they didn't know LA and were lost more than not. Almost useless to us, they left within a week.

Next, they gave us several spanking-new agents just out of the training academy. They didn't know LA either, and their surveillance skills were only budding.

It's been said that police don't notice when they are being followed: the predator only looks ahead, never behind. Looking behind is for the prey. Reyes was different. His countersurveillance moves on the street indicated to us he was the prey, and he well knew it. He burned any surveillance on him within five minutes of its start.

We dropped the surveillance program; it didn't work. As it turned out, we really didn't need it. But the newbies had their uses. We put them to work organizing the phone toll information, which was steadily growing.

Everybody analyzed the phone records, hour after drawn-out hour, linking calls to people, places, and events. We wrote the information down on three by five cards, separating the phone numbers from the license plates from the addresses and so forth. Personal computers were not available to us yet in 1987, and the information we received quickly became unwieldy. To keep current with all our data, I put together a timeline and link charts. These visual reports served to answer questions we always had during an investigation. We call them the five *W*s: who, what, why, when, and where. That was the value of visual reports. A picture quickly gets to the point, cutting out a lot of verbal or written explanations.

Major cocaine cases in Chicago, Detroit, and Minneapolis showed linkage to our three suspects based on phone records. We worked long and hard with the FBI on a major money laundering and cocaine case they had going in Detroit. Their chief suspects, the Wilson brothers, were federal fugitives, having disappeared before the net dropped. The list of suspects, witnesses, and persons of interest to us grew. Our daily to-do lists were always at least two pages long. Matilda began a grand jury investigation, and we started serving subpoenas, requiring people to come in and testify.

Following leads was often unproductive, but we had to keep at it and be thorough, going after every clue. It was not a case of casting a few lines in the water here or there; it was dragging a net instead. We collected as much information as we could because we didn't yet know what was significant or what would turn into only a sidetrack down a dead end.

The long hours we spent on cases that related to the Wilson brothers were due to numerous telephone calls made from Reyes's phone at his apartment. Reyes lived near our DEA office in downtown Los Angeles. The doorman had told us several different people would come down to the lobby from Reyes's apartment just to use the pay phones. He found it odd, since Reyes had a phone in his apartment. We didn't find it odd at all.

Our tech man placed a hidden camera outside Reyes's apartment door. We got it going just in time to see the Wilson brothers moving out; the FBI's fugitives had been hiding there. We found out later Reyes and the Wilson brothers had been juvenile friends in south Los Angeles. He was just helping out his fugitive pals.

But the hours spent on the Wilson case and other leads, which drew us to travel to Minneapolis and Detroit, were not relevant to our case. They turned out to be false leads, but every case—that is, every case lasting past sundown—has false leads. It comes with the territory. We had to back up and take a different tack.

I liked the complex cases. They were a challenge. Our progress, measured by the information we collected, came slowly, like trying to walk through a bamboo thicket. Sometimes the thicket became impenetrable and we had to retrace our steps, change direction, and go off on a new angle to keep moving toward the goal.

Early on, I found that narcotics work was not a job; it was a mission. Many of us lived that purpose-driven life. For some, what zeal they had at the beginning faded under the withering realization they were laboring at the impossible task of quashing drug trafficking. Their DEA lives altered, providing only a job and a paycheck. And there were those who shamelessly worked other jobs on the side, such as selling real estate or going to law school. They were the part-time investigators.

DEA agents received pay for ten hours a day. Some worked only eight hours and then knocked off, but many worked twelve to fourteen hours daily much of the time. The types of cases we worked were a determining factor. The lengthy, involved investigations brought big challenges, big difficulties, and long hours. It all depended on one's dedication to the mission.

The first several months on the three amigos case were the dark days. We had collected a mountain of telephone call records and grand jury testimony; getting a handle on the information became a grind. Complicating the issue was my own equilibrium. I had recently returned to the United States after living abroad for nine years, the last four in an area of southern Thailand devoid of any western influence. I was suffering from culture shock. I had spent too long a time away from America. Six months passed before I felt comfortable again, felt that I was at home.

My work schedule soon became a routine. I usually left the courthouse about eight or nine at night, the last man out, and headed for my condo in Whittier. Built on a hill, it overlooked the Rose Hills cemetery. At night or on a foggy morning, my view from the balcony was of a beautiful park—no one had to know it was a graveyard.

Coming home to my deserted house after a long day spent analyzing telephone records was emptiness. I popped a frozen dinner in the microwave—one of Marie Callender's—and seven minutes later I was sitting in front of the TV and eating. I tossed the empty plastic plate into the trash can and it was bedtime. Thinking back, my single-mindedness about finishing the case was helpful in sidestepping my less-than-happy personal life. It kept me from dwelling on my failures as a husband and father. Self-inflicted wounds are the slowest to heal. I read in bed until my eyes started burning, and then it was lights out. Tomorrow always dawned early.

Despite many dead ends, we made progress. Most helpful were the phone tolls, which laid out most of the story. After months spent running down numbers and linking them with dates, events, and places, I felt we were close. We didn't have all the details, but we knew the story. We knew what direction to take and who to go after.

What did we know? We knew the amigos had been selling drugs for at least three years and that they had sold a great quantity of cocaine—at least twenty kilograms to Goodwin on just one occasion. And they reaped enough profit to make it worth stashing the money in Swiss banks. Their phoning to Federal Express and the phone booths in New York told us how and most likely to where they shipped the coke. We found calls to an apartment in Baldwin Hills, rented by Reyes, and that showed us from where they had likely operated and stashed their coke. We knew much, but not everything. We didn't know where they found that much dope to sell.

Anyone who has worked in major narcotics enforcement knows the job comes with hefty rations of temptation due to the frequent opportunities to steal. Large amounts of narcotics, worth more than their weight in gold, and sacks of cash, often found in small denominations, are regularly seized during investigations. Sometimes, though not often, not all that is seized finds its way into the evidence vault. But when motivation meets opportunity, crime occurs. With those three agents in mind, we took a close look at documented drug and money discrepancies at the Los Angeles office for the previous years. The record was not pretty.

The list of irregularities started in 1982 with the disappearance of $14,000 in cash at the office. No one was disciplined for that loss. The worst year for losses was 1984. In July, the office cashier left her booth to use the restroom, leaving the door ajar. She returned in five minutes to find a sealed evidence bag containing $100,000 in seized funds missing. That security lapse cost the cashier her job. In October, Jefferson and Reyes went into the evidence vault. Jefferson told the evidence custodian he wanted to check out a piece of nondrug evidence. As Jefferson signed the receipt, he distracted the custodian while Reyes nosed around the room. At that time, drug and nondrug evidence were stored in the same room. Shortly afterward, one kilogram of heroin worth $100,000 turned up missing out of the evidence room.

In January 1985, two Thai heroin couriers arrived from Bangkok with fifteen pounds of pure heroin. They were arrested in a hotel room near the LA airport after delivering the heroin to a DEA undercover agent. Jefferson was assisting on the case that day and volunteered to transport the heroin to the office for processing. Only twelve pounds made it into the evidence vault. Later, in court, the Thais pleaded guilty to smuggling in twelve pounds, but told their attorney they had actually brought in fifteen pounds of heroin. They wanted to set the record straight. Besides, they had not gotten away with it; why should anyone else?

Altogether, more than a dozen incidents involving money or dope losses occurred between late 1982 and early 1986, dates that coincided with some of the amigos's trips to Switzerland.

Those were only the chance targets of opportunity. Jefferson also systematically stole drugs. We looked at the evidence reports he prepared. It seemed he often volunteered to process the evidence after a drug buy or seizure. No one liked the chore, so he was welcome to it. It involved weighing and sealing the drugs in an evidence envelope, writing the report, and then mailing the evidence off to the DEA laboratory in San Diego for analysis. DEA regulations dictated that two agents together handle all money and drug processing, but Jefferson often managed to do it alone.

In those days the average purity of the cocaine seized in Los Angeles was around 50 percent. Almost all of Jefferson's submissions came back from the lab at 10 percent pure. We concluded he was cutting every bit of cocaine he touched. On a pound seizure, he could take out 75 percent of it, add a diluent to restore weight to the evidence, and walk away with twelve ounces of cocaine.

We began to believe the three thieves were stealing all or part of anything they touched. By no coincidence, the drug and money thefts stopped after the three amigos left the job by mid-1986. Why not? They had made their million dollars and quit, just like Poole had told Goodwin at the beginning of the investigation.

We had no positive proof of the three amigos stealing dope and money, not yet. But we had our suspicions. We spent considerable time forming hypotheses based on incomplete information. Our time was not wasted; supposing is one of the steps to proving. Their tactics showed bold and careless actions. Those actions proved they had no respect for or fear of DEA's ability or investigative expertise. They were sure we could not catch them. Such arrogance only served to stiffen our resolve. Go ahead, call us plodding, call us disorganized; just don't call us stupid. We would stay on the case and see it through.

Who were these guys? We backed up a step and took a close look at our three suspects. Maybe something in their backgrounds could shed light on who they really were. I had known Jefferson well, inasmuch as we worked in the same group for two years. He was not on a mission like many of us; he was a part-time agent and full-time soap salesman. He was greedy, but I had never figured him for a brazen thief. Cannon was not someone I had known well, and I saw him as a follower. In the office, he had never shown any drive or enthusiasm, but rather looked around for someone's coattail to grab on to and pull him along.

Reyes? Well, he was a different story. We conducted a thorough background study on Reyes—something not properly done by DEA prior to his hiring as an agent in 1978. If the background check had been done, he would never have known us. Born in New York to a Puerto Rican father and a black mother, he was brought to LA as an infant and raised in South Central Los Angeles. He grew up and thrived amid the crime and gang activity of that part of town. He had a few arrests as a juvenile and finished high school with a GED. We found he failed to list three earlier employment terminations on his DEA job application.

Since he had been friends with the Wilson brothers as a youth, we assumed he, like the Wilsons, had been a gang member. But why would a gangbanger apply to the Los Angeles County Sheriff and the Los Angeles Police Department as well as DEA? I felt I knew the answer: he wanted the gun and the badge and all the power and authority he imagined that entailed. The other agencies found him not suitable, but DEA did not. One DEA supervisor in Detroit told me that he had been a member of Reyes's agent selection board and remembered discussing Reyes's application. The head of the board, John Landers, had recommended hiring Reyes, despite his spotty background and poor oral interview, remarking, "Let's hire Reyes; we need Spanish-speaking agents."

Reyes was hired. Only later did it come out that he couldn't speak a word of Spanish. Ironically, John Landers was appointed special agent in charge (SAC) of the Los Angeles office in July 1987, replacing SAC Brown. SAC Landers was overseeing our case.

From the outset, Reyes did not fit in with DEA. He experienced frequent disciplinary trouble with his supervisors, suffering four different suspensions for various violations. None of his peers cared for him either— except for Jefferson and Cannon. Besides their race, they also had other similarities. All three had jobs on the side even though agents were not allowed to have outside work. Jefferson had his soap, Cannon did private investigation, and Reyes had his gold gig.

While working with the Los Angeles airport group, Reyes evidently began his criminal behavior by helping an LA gold dealer avoid paying taxes on imported Italian gold. Reyes would meet the Italian gold courier at the gate upon arrival from Rome and, using his airport identification, carry the gold himself to avoid customs inspection and the import tax due. His behavior at the airport got him transferred to Detroit in 1985. He refused to go and was fired. He won his discrimination suit, coming back to DEA in June 1987.

But why would he ever want to come back to DEA? We found out soon enough.

Four days after arriving at our office, Reyes went to the LAPD and checked their records for information on the Wilson brothers, telling the LAPD he was working on a related investigation. That was at the same time the Wilsons were hiding out in his apartment. Showing his brass, Reyes came to work just long enough to take a look around at what we had going. Reyes had just moved into his new home, paying cash for a nice location to park his new Porsche. It was a $580,000 place in Rancho Palos Verdes. With an ocean view. There was nothing subtle about him.

After doing research on his background, it was clear to us that Reyes had crossed over and embraced corruption at an early age. We all agreed on the amigos hierarchy: Reyes was the instigator. He had shown his verve and boldness while at the airport. He probably seduced Cannon first, spotting that plodding, financially overdrawn, and agreeable agent as an easy recruit. He then had no trouble hooking Jefferson and reeling him in with talk of easy money, since Jefferson was ever ready to discuss anything related to his own financial gain. He'd had his own disciplinary troubles with DEA management over his soap peddling and was recruitment-ready.

Since the three amigos appeared to have stopped their stealing and dealing, our lone option was to draw together an historical conspiracy case against them. That required documenting the overt acts (who did what, when, and where). To gather the necessary details and connect the dots, we couldn't look forward. We had to look back to past deeds. We had only circumstantial pieces of the whole. It was rather like looking at a large jigsaw puzzle, only the pieces were not interlocking. We needed a catalyst that would organize and hold those fragments together to make a clear picture.

Circumstantial evidence is critical but doesn't send anyone to jail on its own. The glue we required was a live witness, one who could appear in court, verbally cement the pieces together, and tell the jury what took place. We knew who he was and where to find him.

His name was Stuart Mosley. The New York office had successfully used him as an informant for several years. At one point in 1982 he had gained entry among some Mafia drug dealers. Jefferson was tapped to travel to New York, pose undercover as Mosley's nephew, and arrange heroin and cocaine buys. Reportedly, the two hit it off quite well and became close and chummy—despite DEA regulations against such fraternization with informants. Mosley "retired" from the informant trade in late 1986.

Brian and I traveled to New York in late 1987 to talk with Mosley. Since his apartment was positioned within a block or two of those same public phones called by Jefferson and Reyes, we suspected he had not retired from the drug trade at all. We believed Mosley distributed cocaine and heroin for the three amigos.

Mosley met us at the New York DEA office. He denied our every probe pertaining to his activities with the suspected agents. He remarked he knew only Jefferson, not the others, remained good friends with Jefferson, and that was that.

At one point, he pulled out his little black book to find a phone number. Brian asked to see it, and reluctantly Mosley handed it over. Imagine his surprise when Brian spotted Reyes's pager number.

We had heard enough lies for one session, so we served a subpoena on Mosley to appear before the grand jury at Los Angeles.

Mosley arrived in Los Angeles as ordered and came to the courthouse. Matilda joined us for the meeting. Mosley stonewalled, playing dumb. But he was a career criminal, had spent time in prison, and soon realized that we knew the story. Averse to prison, he recognized it was time to make a deal.

Wavering, on the edge of rolling over and giving up, he begged Matilda for a favor. "Look. I need to see Jefferson first. I will see him tonight. I think I can bring him in and we'll both talk."

That night he stayed with Jefferson, who had recently moved into his new $750,000 home in Claremont. Whatever was said between them must have been intense, because Mosley had a heart attack while sitting on Jefferson's couch. We didn't hear about it until two days later.

We drove out to see Mosley at the Pomona Valley Hospital. The cardiologist who had performed the open heart surgery warned us Mosley's condition was grave and cautioned us not to talk to him for at least six weeks.

We didn't bother Mosley for two months, giving him time to heal. But his recovery was slow and he remained weak. Meanwhile, we fought off attacks from another direction. The New York US attorney handling Mosley's earlier case involving the Mafia did not want us to prosecute Mosley. He advised that charging Mosley would discount his past testimony and create appeal issues if Mosley was found to have been a dope dealer while working for the New York prosecution.

It didn't matter much at the time, since Mosley was in no condition to travel or testify in court. In any case, Matilda would take on the New York prosecutor concerning Mosley's status. We had Mosley in hand, if he survived, but we had yet to get his statement.

18

Judgment

While Mosley had his troubles, I had mine. Early one Friday morning in April, I rode the elevator up to the DEA office on the eighth floor. Riding with me was Dempsey Washington, one of the young, up-and-coming agents in the LA office. He greeted me and added, "Congratulations on your promotion, Mark."

He had received a call from his close friend, the secretary of the DEA career board, and I was to be named supervisor for Group Four on Monday. Within minutes the word spread around the office, as it always does when someone is promoted. The congratulations and back-slapping were short-lived, though.

The promotion cable from the career board came out on Monday, but my name was not on it. I called the career board secretary and he hesitated, since he wasn't supposed to give out inside information. I told him he already had, but promised not to disclose him as my source. The career board had selected me, but the head of the board, the DEA assistant administrator, had to sign off on all the board's choices. He had redlined my name. The board named another agent to the position.

I knew the assistant administrator, having run into him in Thailand two years before. He was then new in the position, having come over from the FBI, and the Bangkok visit was his first trip abroad. Like most FBI agents, he knew very little of our work overseas.

I traveled up from my office in Songkhla to attend a meeting with him and all the other Thailand supervisors at the Bangkok Hilton. He questioned me about post differential and why we agents living in Songkhla deserved to receive 15 percent more pay than those living in Bangkok. I explained that the State Department set the pay differential rates. It authorized extra pay for those working and residing in difficult environments. In Songkhla, we had unhealthy living conditions, physical hardships, and a total lack of western culture. I told him we deserved the extra pay.

I could see he was having difficulty summoning up an image of a wretched Songkhla while staying at the beautiful Hilton Hotel in Bangkok. After all, Songkhla was still in Thailand; how bad could it be?

I should have left it at that, but I didn't. "Why don't you check out of your five-star hotel and come down to see for yourself how we live?"

What had perturbed me was that no one from Washington ever came to visit us in Songkhla—the carpetbaggers rarely ventured far from Bangkok when visiting Thailand. I had not realized it at the time, but he remembered my wisecrack. In fact, he had made more out of it than I had and taken it as a personal chide. Maybe it was the way I had said it. See, in Vietnam we sometimes had commanders circling safely above in Hueys, telling us below, unseen under the triple canopy and under fire, how to get out of a fix. I was sensitive to someone who didn't have a clue to the situation telling me what it was. At any rate, he had scratched my promotion.

It was an embarrassing and humbling snub. I may have let it go except I was telephoned not two weeks later by an Australian police friend stationed at the Australian embassy in Washington, DC. We had once worked together in Thailand. He was coming out to the Australian consulate in Los Angeles and wanted me to join him for dinner. At dinner he related that he had been to a diplomatic reception in Washington a month before and met the DEA assistant administrator. During their chat, he mentioned he had worked with me in Thailand. The assistant administrator chuckled and told him, "Mark Lloyd? Now there is an agent whose career is over."

A truck loaded with disappointment had run over me. I had always had hopes, but not towering expectations. That way, if hopes were dashed, it was less painful. I had learned to be conservative in my dreams and keep them curbed and unvoiced.

Fortunately, a good friend and confidante helped me get through my brooding self-analysis. Telling me to stop whining, she consoled me by saying, "Don't worry. Cream always rises to the top."

But it doesn't always, not if there is agitation. I sulked, had self-doubts, and briefly pondered why I kept trying—especially at the thankless, unpopular case I was working.

For a short while I felt sorry for myself, but I didn't collapse in a corner and allow my discontent to fester. I stayed on the rails and kept moving, working the case. I did it because I loved the job. I had been rejected, but I was still in love.

That incident clarified for me that advancement in DEA was not my driving force. I wasn't there for the rank or salary. Not that I would work for free, mind you, but if I believed in the mission, just give me a little rent money and I was your man.

In the army it was sometimes said that you go to war and fight for the men who sent you. I imagine there may be leaders who could instill that type of loyalty in their men, but I failed to meet any. I never felt that way, not in the least; I was there for my country, yes, but not for those who sent me. I was fighting for myself, to do my job and return home alive.

I carried that same mind-set with me into DEA. It was an attitude easy to retain, what with much of the leadership I had to work under. I sometimes held the view that I was not working for those at the top but despite them.

Our investigation was not wholly supported at the DEA office. OPR, or internal affairs, was not popular at any police agency, and ours was no exception. The problems I had stemmed from the attitude of upper management—they wanted the case to go away.

After I had been working on the case for six months, the negative comments and questions I received from management mounted. The case was dragging; they wanted Brian and me back in the office. I didn't get it. We had before us three former agents, corrupt to the bone, who had committed more crimes than we could count. And management was trying to hide the case under the mattress.

Management had motives for burying the case. They were embarrassed.

Weak supervision had played a major part in the mess we uncovered. Corruption of that duration and magnitude flourished only in the absence of good supervision. Most of the group supervisors in the office did not go out on the street with their groups, and without that oversight, any agents inclined to cheat or steal could get away with it.

I felt the leadership in Los Angeles was poor from the top down. Likewise, management would not come out looking well in any post-investigation inquiry—how could they have let this happen?

Race may have been another factor to the front office. Our suspects were black, and I realized that the extensive drug-dealing charges we were pursuing could possibly precipitate a media circus, especially in Los Angeles. While our office environment was without racial complications, racial unrest always bubbled just below the surface in the City of Angels. But management was kidding itself if it thought the media would not jump on our case in any event—the number of agents involved and the amount and breadth of their corruption was big news, regardless of race.

SAC Landers, well aware of the case's implications, voiced nothing. Instead, he let his deputies take the shots at me. Between George Conway, the number two in the office, and Conway's favorite toady, Jim Hancock, I was taking sniper fire on a weekly basis.

Conway, a black agent himself, was the black agents' champion in the Los Angeles office. I had known him for all my years on the job. He had been my group supervisor for two years in the 1970s, and I had always got on well with him. During that time I observed he took care of his own when possible. Most of his actions had been equitable as far as I was concerned because I realized every supervisor had his favorites.

Management's rationale for attacking the case was twofold: we would never make any arrests, and they needed Brian and me back in the office. As one of the office's few senior agents, I was needed to mentor the young agents.

A typical jab was one I absorbed from Jim Hancock when, in all seriousness, he challenged me one day, "When are you going to quit milking that dead case and come back here and start earning your paycheck?"

However, if they supposed taking me off the case would see it wither and blow away, they didn't know Matilda.

By then, everyone in the LA office knew of our investigation. Several of the employees had been friends with, or at least felt kindly toward Jefferson and Cannon. As for Reyes, I didn't think he had one supporter in the office. Nevertheless, it seemed there was some sympathy for the three suspects. That was understandable. No one knew what I knew. But I could sense their feelings when I went to the office, sometimes feeling like I was the bogeyman. They had me figured wrong.

Law enforcement is not about retribution, and I was not an avenger. My motivation was the need to see punishment for evil acts. Schooled at an early age, I bought in to the necessity of regulations. I believed order was a precondition for progress. It validated my law-abiding philosophy. Besides, no one likes to see others get away with it.

DEA management chose to set up a showdown meeting in Matilda's office. We knew they were coming to kill the case and take Brian and me back to the office, and we knew their strategy. The case against the three amigos had started almost three years previously, having been dormant a good portion of that time. All three agents under investigation had since resigned. They were off the job now; why not let them go? At any rate, what we had was circumstantial evidence and conjecture. Where were our live witnesses?

We had our arguments ready, points crucial to our continuing the case. For twenty minutes or more, I spoke in a matter-of-fact voice, unrolling our chain of knowledge and circumstantial evidence, the likes of which left our audience listening with interest. When I concluded, SAC Landers, true to form, passed on voicing an opinion and turned to his deputy for comment. Conway had been nodding his head as if he liked the story, but then played devil's advocate and inquired if and when we would have a witness who could testify to what we had surfaced. I replied we were working on it and it was close. Conway's pessimistic response was expected. "You're wasting your time on a case that you will never make."

I had kept Conway in the know during all our progress in the case. Then he made a statement like that. So much for a vote of confidence from the top.

Matilda sensed where Conway's remarks were heading and made a well-timed preemptive strike. Eyes flashing, she was impressive. "If you take Mark off this case and let those crooks off, I'm going public with it.

Those three are totally corrupt, and this office will see them answer for it in court."

The reasons for the boss's negative attitude remained unspoken; it was best not to look in there. I thought Matilda wasn't serious about her threat to go public, but Matilda's intensity and projected will were compelling. Landers and Conway wilted before her. The meeting was soon over, and they stole out, apparently beaten. We had won the skirmish, but the war continued.

Susan Bates had ten years on the job with the IRS. She led the small IRS team that moved in with us at our courthouse office to facilitate close cooperation in the case. It was my first time working alongside the IRS. Fitting in with my vision of a typical IRS agent, she was not a tall woman and carried a few extra pounds. She wore no makeup and had her hair cut short, a look that declared, "I'm too busy to fritter away time on myself."

She was on a mission too. She told me early on in our teamwork that since illegal drugs and money were joined at the hip, our agencies should also work that way. It made sense to me. A straightforward sense of duty stemming from her armor-covered spirit was tempered by her always-on sense of humor. That was a personality bonus for someone relegated to the mundane accounting and document-scrutinizing life in the IRS.

While our investigation moved along in intermittent ebbs and heaves, the IRS kept going forward at their methodical pace. We were the hare, they were the tortoise. Bates and her team were looking at money laundering and income tax charges for the three amigos. They had uncovered a massive amount of structuring by the suspects. Structuring involved making many small financial transactions to disguise a large movement of money. This was done to avoid examination, since financial laws called for banks to document any cash transactions exceeding $10,000. The IRS documented several dozen money orders and checks made out to the amigos' Swiss banks and totaling over $750,000. That, along with the unknown amounts of cash they carried, accounted for their trips to Switzerland.

Several witnesses had revealed to us that the amigos had sent and received packages through FedEx and also confirmed their travels to Switzerland, but no one yet had described what was in those FedEx boxes or why the amigos had gone to Switzerland. We knew, but we needed someone else to tell us. We needed Mosley to tell us. We had stashed him at a hotel for two months, ostensibly to heal some, but we couldn't wait anymore.

We brought Mosley to the courthouse in a wheelchair. He looked terminal, displaying worrisomely feeble movements and shortness of breath. He was a black man, but you wouldn't have known it to look at his whey-faced paleness. Nonetheless, it was time for him to stand up and choose sides.

Thinking he may expire before he was able to testify at any trial, Matilda made arrangements to videotape his statements for the grand jury to consider. However, we first needed to get his mind right because, as we suspected he would, he started out with falsehoods, spinning out a story that fooled no one and served only to waste time.

Mosley whined about the closeness he had with Jefferson, how he considered Jefferson like a son, and all they had done together to fight drug trafficking in New York. Mosley's story was touching, but we knew he was lying. He had the guilty body language and downcast eyes of a thief caught in church. He became angry and frustrated, but that was acceptable, as we needed to get him going. I could see the muscles of his jaw working, his furrowed eyebrows and darkening face. His realization was coming to life. We could read his face like an AAA road map: no town names, rivers, or roads—instead fault, admission, cooperation.

Words poured out like an exorcism as Mosley confessed to the drugs Jefferson and Reyes had sent to him in FedEx boxes. He sold the cocaine, over one hundred kilograms, and sent them $20,000 per kilogram in payment. He received about two kilograms of heroin, pure China White, and he paid them $8,000 for each ounce—about a half million dollars. He maintained he did not know where they obtained the drugs; they had only disclosed it came from "work." The drug amounts Mosley admitted receiving from the amigos were far more than we had suspected.

The IRS had their case together by early November 1988. Matilda needed more time to get the numerous drug charges together, so we elected to go ahead and indict our three suspects on the financial crimes first, charging them with thirty-four counts of money laundering and income tax evasion. We intended to arrest them at their homes simultaneously in the early morning and conduct search warrants after they were in custody. I chose to arrest Jefferson, my old buddy.

We assembled at five in the morning at the parking lot of a Vons market in Claremont. Bates had requested I lead the raid since I knew Jefferson and had more door-kicking experience than her IRS would-be commandos. I went over the action plan and assigned roles. Looking almost comical, the assembled IRS agents had arrived overdressed in new, all-black SWAT gear and carrying AR-15 rifles. Bates saw me looking at them sideways. "It's company policy; we have to go in well-armed."

I didn't say anything as I didn't want to spoil their adventure. I could see from their body language they were nervous and not experienced in entering homes and making arrests. One man was shifting his weight in a nervous dance from foot to foot. Another rearranged his unfamiliar equipment. A third kept yawning; the adrenaline had kicked in.

When I finished the briefing, we leaned against our cars, waiting for darkness to end so we could deliver Jefferson his dawn surprise.

Approaching from all angles, we surrounded Jefferson's spacious house. Jefferson's wife, Alicia, opened the door to our pounding and announcements. She gave a short scream and fled upstairs at the sight of the IRS ninjas. We swarmed into the house. I noticed one IRS agent tracking heavy mud over the white carpet in the living room as we spread out to clear the downstairs.

We heard Alicia sobbing upstairs and Jefferson calling out, frightened. I was a little nervous too, because the ninjas were crouched, pointing their rifles at the stairway. Who wouldn't be scared at the sight of them? I called up to the unseen Jefferson, trying to calm him, and advised him to come down as we were there to search the house.

After a few tense moments, he came down. Without any formalities, I searched and cuffed him; he was just another dope dealer under arrest. We began our search of the house.

While searching, an IRS agent called me into Jefferson's bedroom closet. On the insole of one of his shoes, Jefferson had a piece of paper. It listed the names of several of us working on the case against him. The paper was worn and it appeared he had been walking on it. He explained that his father had told him about a verse in the Bible instructing one to write the names of one's enemies on the bottom of one's feet and walk on them.

Years later, I was in Egypt and visited the Cairo Museum. The tour guide showed me a pair of sandals found on the feet of one of the mummified pharaohs. One sandal had the names of the pharaoh's enemies inscribed in hieroglyphics on the insole: Nubians and Hittites. Despite the deployment of podiatric hexes, Egypt fell. And so did John Jefferson.

I drove to the DEA office with Jefferson cuffed in the back seat. An IRS agent sat next to him. He was subdued—heavy in thought, I supposed. Perhaps during that one-hour drive he was reliving his life until then—thinking about the past was the easiest way to handle it. The present was depressing, seeing as he sat handcuffed in my car, and the future looked bleak. He realized the good times were over.

My mind was working too. I was disgusted, thinking what a fool he was and how his life choices had gone wrong. Crossing over the frozen pond of criminality is always dangerous. For some, the ice is thick at the beginning and the passage easy, for a bit. The crook is thinking, *I can make this!* But somewhere on the way across there is always that patch of thin ice. Jefferson had found it. Now flailing, he had broken through and was fast sinking.

Although I wasn't smug, I did feel some satisfaction that the untold hours we had put into the investigation had at last paid off. Jefferson may have got away with it for a while, but now he would have to pay it back.

In any event, we didn't speak to each other on his ride to jail.

At the office, most of the agents were already at work. When we came off the elevator on the seventh floor and walked down to the booking area, the crowd began forming. News of Jefferson's arrest spread through the office like a fire alarm. I ended up kicking the gawkers out of the booking area so I could process Jefferson—mug shots and prints. Cannon soon came in under arrest, and we afforded him the same service.

That Reyes was not found did not surprise me. All through the investigation he had operated with one ear to the ground. He must have spotted the arresting team parked around his house and made his getaway. He would be on the run for the next seven months.

An international manhunt was on for Reyes; his money was in Europe, so we believed he wouldn't stray too far from it. We found out he obtained a false Mexican passport. We made sightings in Mexico, Brazil, and Spain. Good detective work by some of our overseas agents found he was heading to his money, stashed in a bank in Switzerland. He was arrested by Swiss police outside his bank with an empty suitcase and a phony Mexican passport. Reyes' wife *and* his girlfriend were arrested three months later walking together out of Reyes' bank with two suitcases containing $1.8 million in cash. While Reyes did a six-month jail term in Switzerland for the phony passport, Matilda worked through the extradition bureaucracy. Reyes was not brought back to judgment for several more months.

Jefferson and Cannon had shown me from the beginning they were not master criminals. Their lack of telephone security had early on demonstrated their greenness. Yet they both possessed enough smarts to know the early criminal gets the deal. Persuading one or the other to plead guilty and make a deal would make the case against the remaining defendants easier. We knew Cannon was the trail dog on the team, so we supposed he would prove the easiest to flip over. Get one to roll over and the others had no chance to beat the charges.

It came as no real surprise that both of them determined it was time and both made deals. Jefferson, after finding out what we had for evidence and hearing about Mosley's capitulation, said, "The *Titanic*'s going down, and it's time to get off." Pleading guilty and cooperating would cut considerable time from their prison sentences.

Attaining Jefferson's story was not a problem, as he had always been a talker. When we worked together, our group sometimes had to tell him to just shut up. Realistic, if nothing else, he knew how the procedure went. Since he had agreed to full cooperation, he sat down with us and laid bare the whole sordid tale.

Beginning in late 1982, when he first worked undercover with Mosley in New York, they had planted the seeds of the plot in a discussion of the pointlessness of enforcing drug laws. Stopping drugs was impossible, so why shouldn't they be like everyone else and make some money off those who demanded drugs?

Later, back in Los Angeles, Reyes and his devotee, Cannon, related to Jefferson how they had stolen $14,000 in seized money at the office. The three talked over how they could steal seized dope and money from DEA. The seeds were sprouting.

Once Jefferson mentioned he had someone to sell the stuff on the street—Mosley—they began their unbridled thievery, laying bare DEA's supervisory and security weaknesses.

With Jefferson presenting a meticulous story, we documented that the three amigos were responsible for every case of missing dope and money in the LA DEA office. From Reyes's rented stash house in Baldwin Hills, they mailed out the dope in FedEx packages to Mosley, who then used the same boxes to send the money back. It was satisfying to hear Jefferson verify that the places and procedures they used were the same as those we had gleaned from his telephone tolls back at the beginning; we had followed the right scent from the outset.

Jefferson related how he had often volunteered to stay behind "to finish up" after late drug buys or seizures, allowing the other agents to go home. Once alone in the office, he cut cocaine at his desk before sending diluted drug to the lab and taking the pure. He kept a convenient box of Sugar Twin in his desk for that purpose. Sugar Twin was an artificial sweetener resembling cocaine in appearance, and was often used to dilute cocaine.

When he decided it was time to leave DEA, he falsely reported losing his badge and credentials. He continued to use them to avoid official scrutiny on his money trips to Switzerland.

As we watched him speak, his smug, prideful tale flowed over us like a cold wind. Voicing no I-have-sinned admissions and displaying not a trace of remorse, he calmly related the manner in which he had broken his oath and cheated his society. Perhaps he was relieved that the wait for us to arrive, warrants in hand, was over, and he lacked the energy to continue the deceit about his real nature. In any event, as his words settled, it was hard to believe how he had changed from the person I thought I had known before. He'd been snakebit by the lure of quick money.

We listened in astonishment when Jefferson revealed how they made their biggest score. Another group in the office was shadowing a Colombian cocaine group in late 1985, and planned to get a search warrant and hit the suspected stash house in Pasadena. Jefferson heard they would move on it on a Saturday, so the three amigos opted to check it out themselves two days before that. They watched the house and noticed two people leave; it was dinnertime and the traffickers were off to eat. The three broke into the house and found $120,000 stuffed above the ceiling in a hallway. In the garage, they found the big one: a cardboard box containing 180 one-kilogram bricks of cocaine.

They sent almost all of it in parcels to Mosley to sell. Jefferson yielded to Sherman Poole's plea for a cut of the action and sold the last twenty kilograms to him. Poole delivered them to his brother-in-law, Goodwin. The last few ounces of that consignment were grabbed by the sheriff's officers when they pulled over Goodwin. That had started the investigation—three and a half years before. The three amigos made well over one million dollars each on just that one score and concluded it was time to get out while they could.

We had Mosley on ice and Jefferson had spilled his guts. Cannon was the first to flip and, having a lesser role in the thefts, verified Jefferson's account. Matilda marched in over eighty people to testify to the grand jury. Some of them were helpful to our case; many were not.

We needed to get Reyes extradited to Los Angeles to wrap up the case and get it to court. Matilda hacked her way through the red-tape extradition process and Reyes arrived. The government was ready to prove the thirty-four tax and thirty-two drug counts in the indictments on our defendants.

During the three-month-long trial in mid-1989, Matilda mounted a massive frontal attack on Reyes. The key witnesses were Jefferson, Cannon, and Mosley. They related every detail of their drug and money thefts and the drug sales they consummated. A large supporting cast of other witnesses corroborated those stories, all fortified by the physical evidence obtained during our investigation.

The tidal wave of testimony and evidence against Reyes forced him to invoke a defense strategy different from mere denials—the evidence against him was too condemning. Throughout, Reyes claimed that his accusers alone were the thieves and dope dealers. He was crooked, yes, but his criminality stemmed only from smuggling untaxed gold through customs at the airport—crimes for which he had not been charged.

When deliberations started, the jury had a heap of data to review. After three weeks, it returned guilty verdicts on all charges against Reyes. The jury didn't buy any part of his ridiculous story.

Besides garnering substantial prison terms for the three, we took their money and their houses, which they had bought with illegal funds. We seized cash in the amount of $1.8 million from Reyes, $1.1 million from Jefferson, and $800,000 from Cannon.

At the end, the three amigos stood as DEA's worst-ever case of corruption. At Reyes's sentencing, federal judge Terry Downs showed his disgust when he remarked from the bench that perhaps the DEA, too, should have been indicted for allowing the corruption to go on so long. "We have been served poorly by that agency. How could the DEA have looked away for the length of time they did?"

The meaning of Judge Downs's words were lost to most that day but not to me. He had not reprimanded DEA for having problems, but for how it had handled them. Still, he sentenced Reyes to eighty years in prison— twenty years more than recommended by Matilda in her arguments.

The press was kinder to the Los Angeles DEA management than Judge Downs had been. SAC Landers made several damage-control statements to the press about the corruption, mentioning that the crooked agents' actions had a detrimental effect on office morale. He also tried to soften the situation by saying the amount of money involved in the nation's drug trade escalated the issues and intensified management's concern (whatever that meant). He noted that sometimes there were more resources seized in a single case than what an agent and his coworkers combined would make in their entire careers.

His words sounded almost as if he had expected agents to turn dirty and then tried to justify their behavior. Anyone in law enforcement, and especially anyone involved in fighting drug trafficking, understood and embraced the fact they were held to higher standards. Landers should have underlined that point to the press and trumpeted the convictions instead of saying, in effect, that the temptations proved too strong for any agent to resist. Maybe this kind of problem was inevitable because of the huge financial temptations; it just should not have been.

On the positive side, those three crooked agents served to strengthen DEA in the long run. Their criminal capers caused DEA to tighten up the oversight of some of its practices and change some of the mandatory responsibilities of its supervisors.

May we always learn from our mistakes.

PART FOUR

The Amazon Basin

19

Operation Snowcap

Illegal cocaine use in the United States was getting out of hand. By the mid-1980s, the use of cocaine and its even nastier spawn, crack, was skyrocketing. It was everywhere in great quantities, an oversupply that made prices drop. When I joined DEA as an agent in 1974, a one-kilogram coke seizure, then selling for $100,000, was a big case. Ten years later, an agent had to make a seizure of at least ten kilograms, valued at only $50,000 per kilo, before he could walk around the office with the same flair as before.

Cocaine suppression grew into DEA's main priority, displacing heroin. Coke became the drug of choice for many, especially young professionals with money to spend. Hollywood glamorized it and the media often called its use benign. DEA agents' efforts to stop, or even slow, the growth of cocaine trafficking did not show any progress. Sure, we arrested and jailed many dealers, but new dealers waited in a never-ending queue to take a chance to make the easy money.

We had to try to stop cocaine from crossing our borders. Was this task possible? Not likely. Most of the cocaine came into the United States overland along the Mexican border and by air or ship into Florida. The United States–Mexico land border, along with the length of our coastlines, make up almost seven thousand miles to watch. Fighting against cocaine *after* its arrival in our cities was coming to the battle too late. That was a lesson I learned while posted to Guam in the late 1970s. We went to Thailand to stop heroin *before* it came into Guam, and that strategy worked.

Finding cocaine source countries was easy. Cocaine was produced by processing the leaves of the coca plant. Those plants grew only on the eastern slopes of the Andes Mountains—in the countries of Bolivia, Peru, Ecuador, and Colombia—with about 90 percent of the plants grown in Peru and Bolivia.

In 1986, DEA experimented with a new type of enforcement operation in Bolivia. US Army helicopters airlifted DEA agents and Bolivian police into several huge cocaine laboratory sites. Cocaine production in Bolivia temporarily came to a standstill with the destruction of the labs. The success of that operation planted the seed of Operation Snowcap—DEA's extraordinary effort to stop cocaine production.

Operation Snowcap began in 1987 with goals to find and stop cocaine production and traffickers in the source countries—Peru and Bolivia for the most part. DEA sent teams of agents out to the growing areas with specially trained local police and conducted paramilitary enforcement operations—destroying cocaine-processing labs and jungle airstrips and seizing cocaine. To staff these teams, Operation Snowcap depended on agents volunteering for temporary assignments in those countries.

In late 1987, I was working in Los Angeles, and DEA headquarters sent out a couple of recruiters to sign up volunteers for Snowcap duty. In front of an all-hands meeting, they explained the Snowcap plan. They took the high road on the program, describing how effective Snowcap tactics were and promising extra money for the hazardous duty, as well as other benefits to encourage volunteers. They also said that all volunteers for the two-year assignment would have to undergo military jungle training before going.

The concept seemed good and the work sounded exciting, but I did not want to undergo any more military training. I felt my year in Vietnam combat had established my bona fides. At any rate, the timing was not right as I was in the middle of a sensitive internal investigation against three corrupt DEA agents. I was making headway after having put in several months on it, so I passed on Snowcap. Things change, however.

A few years later, in early 1993, I was the agent in charge of the Spokane, Washington, DEA office. I had been there three years and was coming due to serve a three-year stint at DEA headquarters as a staff coordinator (a glorified paper shuffler), as was required of almost all supervisors.

A vacancy announcement came out seeking supervisors to serve two-year assignments as team leaders in Snowcap. I called a couple of friends in Snowcap and, after hearing their opinions of the program, decided I would rather serve in South America than ride a desk in Washington. Headquarters selected me for the job.

The downside was the requirement to undergo military training and Spanish language school before I was eligible. Despite my military experience, DEA insisted everyone undergo the training for liability reasons. I decided to face the situation and do it.

Having just celebrated my forty-fifth birthday, I set out in June 1993 for Ft. Benning, Georgia, to start the Snowcap training. DEA had contracted with the US Army Rangers to conduct the training. It consisted of a seven-day assessment and selection process—seven days of physical hardship and misery to weed out the weak and uncommitted volunteers—followed by a ten-week Ranger course. After that, providing I survived and could still muster, it was on to five months of Spanish language training. Looking back, that summer I spent at Ranger training was "middle age having a go at youth."

Sixty-six volunteers arrived at Ft. Benning on a Saturday evening. Besides me and one other supervisor, the rest of the volunteers were junior agents. Most were in their midtwenties, and their average time with DEA was only two years.

After drawing supplies and gear, we found bunks in the barracks and went to eat dinner. Eating in an army mess hall again was strange after so many years. At least the food had improved; there was a soda dispenser, ice cream machine, salad bar, and plenty of decent food. I chatted a little with the head cook, and he told me their policy was to give out enough food to supply us with four thousand calories daily. We were going to need it, starting the next day.

The Rangers started up in earnest on the following day. They rousted us from our beds at four o'clock in the morning and ran us in formation at high speed for the two miles to the pool. These predawn runs were a

Ranger favorite, and the ruthless pace served to point out what kind of a course this was. Our tightly spaced running formation broke down within a quarter mile. With Rangers yelling at the winded laggards to keep up, our strung-out column arrived gasping, wheezing, and coughing.

At the pool, we had several events to test our water survival skills. Four agents who did not make the grade were immediately sent home. At six o'clock, we ran in our wet clothes back to the company barracks, again at high speed, had breakfast, and then reassembled with our empty rucksacks.

The Rangers marched us over to a sandpile and ordered each of us to fill an empty sandbag. They had a scale conveniently placed and made sure our sandbags each weighed thirty pounds. We placed them in our rucksacks and carried them on a six-mile forced march to Victory Pond, a small lake. We ran through a series of confidence tests over the water to test our balance and fear of heights. We lost three more agents on that segment; vertigo got to them. Wet and tired, we put on our sandbagged rucksacks and marched back to camp. I fell into bed that night.

The next day was another four o'clock wake-up and more physical tests, such as the notorious "Darby Queen" obstacle course. The course was one mile in length and contained twenty obstacles that we had to negotiate, testing our running, jumping, climbing, crawling, and balancing skills, as well as our strength and stamina, to reach the finish. Through it all, the Rangers were constantly screaming at us to speed it up. Darby Queen was grueling, and four more agents dropped out.

The weeding-out process continued over the next two days as our numbers thinned. We started each day with strength training done to excess and a road run, and then attended a few classes. One night we had to make a timed twelve-mile walk with our sandbagged rucksacks.

By the end of the fourth day, we were down to forty-two agents. We had a couple of more days of physical testing and underwent personality evaluations to determine how much fun we were having.

After seven days, we were finished. Our sixty-six volunteers from the first day had been winnowed to only thirty-eight left standing. That number would later be reduced to a final figure of thirty-two agents completing the training course, or less than half the original number of candidates.

As the group's old man, I felt good about enduring that test—especially running with those young ponies in their twenties. With a significant feeling of pride and accomplishment for making the cut, everybody went home to get ready for our return in three weeks to start the real course.

The Army Ranger School training staff put together a ten-week course for DEA that covered the basics of the Ranger training course, with (fortunately for me) a few modifications. For one, we usually got the weekends off. That really saved me, as I would spend Saturday and Sunday recuperating from the previous week's physical strain.

The course was physically punishing from start to finish. In addition, the Ranger cadre harassed us throughout—up to our final day. The Ranger cadre made it difficult for us, but we were not in the army and in the end that made all the difference. The training consisted of typical light infantry techniques, but always practiced at high speed and always conveyed to us in a stress-producing manner.

Our training instructors were eight Rangers, all sergeants, with a master sergeant as the lead instructor. They were all young and knowledgeable enough, but most of them were too full of themselves, as elite military men often are. Master Sergeant Meadows, the lead instructor, was the biggest prima donna of the lot. He wasted no time in telling us about his combat feats; he had made combat jumps into Grenada and Panama during those brief operations and strutted around as if he were the real deal.

I have always found that actual combat veterans do not feel the need to impress others with their exploits. Maybe Meadows impressed the young agents, but I did not buy in to his bravado act, and I showed it. He and I were destined to have a long, unpleasant ten weeks together based on my refusal to pay homage to him. Since I was the agent's group leader, he took extra pains to single me out for special "attention" throughout the course.

The army designed Ranger training to develop small-unit leaders. To accomplish this, the cadre appointed candidates to leadership positions on the many training patrols we conducted. Ideally, almost everyone would have had a chance to plan and lead a patrol. That entailed writing up an operation order, which contained all the details of the plans. A lot of extra work went into preparing those orders, and it usually took away from the little sleep time we received.

Since most of the agents had no military background, Meadows assigned only a few of us to plan and lead. He stuck me with over half the patrols, including all the major ones. That was all right; I would be doing it anyway once I arrived in Peru. I like to think I made good plans, but I did not enjoy all the extra work. Although I am sure Meadows thought he was punishing me for my attitude toward him, I took it as a challenge—I knew how to play the game, and he never got to me.

We suffered the first few days until we got into the rhythm of the training. Up at 5:30 a.m., form up, and run to the "pit," a large, sawdust-covered ring where we did an hour's worth of calisthenics. Then we formed into our running groups and took off for a forty-minute, high-speed run.

After breakfast, we had classes on various subjects mixed in with plenty of fieldwork: land navigation, communications, weapons training, and a lot of patrolling. We trained long hours, usually not finishing up until eight or nine at night. At least we spent most of our nights in the barracks and not sleeping out in the woods like the real Army Ranger candidates.

Near the end of the course, we went for the mountain phase of the training at Dahlonega, Georgia, located in the Blue Ridge Mountains. The mountains are not very high, compared to the Rockies or Cascades, but are very steep, a steepness that reminded me of Vietnam's central highlands. We spent several days patrolling up and down the slopes and going without sleep while practicing battle drills.

The course ended with a raid on a mock cocaine laboratory. Of course, I got the nod to make up the plan. The entire class was involved. We conducted the raid and did rather well, finishing up just before dark.

After consolidating, we piled into trucks for the ride back to camp—or so we thought. After a mile ride, the trucks stopped. The cadre told us to get off and make our way back to camp while avoiding all roads, as the "enemy" was patrolling roads looking for us. We reached camp, and our beds, at four. At six, they rousted us out for our final exam and fitness test. We were done.

As I mentioned, most of the agents were young and averaged about two years with DEA. About ten were military veterans. During the training, I had occasion to speak with and get to know everyone. I was to be a team leader and one benefit of that assignment was I could choose my team members to go to Peru with me. Consequently, I spent a lot of time vetting and watching everyone perform. I knew the slackers and shirkers. Likewise, I quickly spotted the stand-up agents, the ones I would recruit to go south with me.

I asked each agent why he was there, and to a man they replied it was for the extra money and the quick promotions—a mercenary answer. I suspected some of them, especially those with no former military time, also wanted to experience putting on a camouflage uniform, painting up their faces, and running around in the jungle carrying an M-16 rifle—maybe even get a little trigger time. I have always been a bit naive, but I was still disappointed in their motivations to volunteer for Snowcap. I expected something more than that out of them.

As I was to find out later, there was an inverse relationship between an agent's Snowcap experience and his DEA investigative skills. Many of the Snowcap-qualified agents scattered about the country attempted to deploy with Snowcap whenever they could—for the money. Snowcap commonly kept four teams deployed for three months each, posting teams continuously in Colombia, Guatemala, Bolivia, and Peru. Enterprising agents could fit in two deployments a year.

Being away from the home office half the time did not allow much opportunity to learn proper narcotics investigative skills or develop good investigations. Three-month periods away from the office did not endear agents to management either. Consequently, I knew more than a dozen agents with several years of DEA experience who, while able to perform acceptably in South America, were minimally satisfactory in their home offices.

Working in Peru was a different environment than, say, Los Angeles, New York, or Miami. The work was paramilitary in nature, although some of the same narcotics investigative principles applied, especially in recruiting and developing informants. Signing up young agents to work in Snowcap after only a year on the job, and then allowing them to stay in for four or five years, was a mistake that needed correcting, as they were not developing into effective investigators. Events would soon settle that issue.

A six-month Spanish-language training course was next on the program. DEA has sent me to three language training courses, but Spanish was the only language I studied in the United States. I trained at a government contractor company in Rosslyn, Virginia.

Like all my previous language work, this course entailed immersion training—five hours of one-on-one conversation daily followed by several hours of homework. I had two teachers: Jose, a likable Ecuadorian, and Lydia, a seventy-year-old, testy Argentinean.

I learned much from Jose, as his teaching method was comfortable for me. Our discussions often centered on history—a favorite topic for both of us. He enjoyed excoriating the Spanish explorers and brought new meaning to the word "conquistador."

Lydia was a piece of work. Really, she was something to watch. Sharp-witted, she snootily practiced perfect enunciation and hopelessly expected the same from me. She once told me that besides the Spaniards, only people from Argentina spoke proper Spanish, unlike "those Mexicans" or, even worse, the Cubans. I remember she liked to eat apples in class. That was all right, except she would often talk with her mouth full and spit pieces of apple at me. She never seemed to notice.

I am no whiz with languages but I can get by. I took two years of high school Spanish, which meant I had learned some words but could not converse with anyone. While serving in Korea, I studied Korean, but only spent eighteen months there before I transferred to Thailand, so I never became proficient at it. As soon as I started learning Thai, I completely forgot what little Korean I knew.

My Thai was decent and I had retained it for ten years. When I started Spanish, it became a problem because it kept colliding with my Thai. While not too difficult to read and write, Spanish was complicated to speak. Conjugating verbs was my biggest problem. Although I managed to score well enough to pass the oral examination, I never felt comfortable with Spanish. I always had to think carefully before speaking. Peru would afford me ample opportunities to practice.

20

Peru

After finishing Spanish language training in March, I had to prepare for leading a team to Peru. I called around the country to the agents on the Snowcap eligibility list and picked out the best nine agents I could get. I wanted Spanish speakers who had previous experience in Peru. I picked only one agent from my Ranger training course.

What I ended up with was a team that typified the work ethic and expertise of a regular DEA enforcement group anywhere. A group of ten will have two or maybe three agents putting together investigations (the workers). Add to that four or five sporadic case makers who are always available for support on surveillance or arrests (the helpers). Then, count on having one or maybe two chunks of deadwood who sit around the office avoiding work while collecting pay (the slackers). As it always works out, the workers, with valued assistance from the helpers, carry the load, while the slackers pretend to be part of it. In the end, we all receive the same credit and pay. Life is never fair.

Ten days before leaving for Peru, the team assembled at the DEA Academy in Quantico, Virginia. We met there for a week so I could get acquainted with the team members, conduct training, make assignments, and obtain all the equipment, weapons, and supplies we needed. Most of us were meeting each other for the first time, and there was some time spent getting to know one another. We went to the range to fire our assigned weapons, and went over the list of necessary explosives—we used the explosives to destroy illegal airstrips.

Aboard an Air Force C-141 Starlifter, we took off from Andrews Air Force Base outside Washington, DC one midnight in April 1994. Four Snowcap teams were aboard, with all the supplies, equipment, and weapons each team would need for the next three months.

Our first stop was in Guatemala City. Next stop was Bogota, Colombia. The C-141 dropped my team in the early afternoon at Lima, Peru, and then took off to deliver the final team to La Paz, Bolivia. The plane would turn around the next day and fly by to pick up the four teams we had replaced. The team we relieved happily met us at the airport while we prepared ourselves to spend the next three months in Peru.

Snowcap leased a house in Lima that we used for an administrative base. There was a seven-foot wall around it. The house featured six bedrooms, a swimming pool, and a full-time gardener and housekeeper. We didn't stay there much, as we all spent most of our time out in the jungle. But I rotated agents two at a time into Lima for three-day stays every two weeks or so. They tended to their administrative duties at the embassy and just got a break from the jungle.

While settling in our Lima house and sorting out our equipment, I attended various briefings at the embassy on the current drug trafficking situation in our operational area and started framing our plan of action.

Descriptions of Peru come in threes. Geographically, the west coastal plains are arid, very much like the southern California coast—without the natural beauty. Most of the population lives there.

East of the plains, the central corridor holds the Andes Mountains. They are not wide, about fifty to seventy-five miles, but rise to heights above twenty thousand feet. Flying over, one sees only rock and snow as the peaks stand high above the tree line.

Once over the peaks, the mountains drop away swiftly into the Amazon basin—jungle. All of the numerous rivers on the eastern slopes of the Andes drain into the Amazon River.

The Peru climate also comes in threes. Arid Lima and the coast are temperate, cooled by the ocean. The ancient Incans developed irrigation techniques to bring water to the coastal regions. The towering Andes are cold and windy much of the year. The Amazon basin is hot and humid, as a jungle should be.

Three races live in Peru. The Indians, the majority of the population, look like their ancestors—images preserved on Inca pottery still found around the country. The Spanish, European-looking and representing the social elite, are concentrated in the larger cities near the Pacific coast. The third group, the mestizos, comprises those of racially mixed blood, and they live all over the country.

Cocaine originates only from certain species of the coca plant, a rather plain-looking shrub native to South America. Since time immemorial the leaves of that bush have been chewed by the Indians to stem fatigue and hunger and to stimulate their mood. Only the leaves contain any drug; the remainder of the plant serves no purpose.

At that time, nearly two-thirds of the world's coca crop grew in Peru. The most widely grown variety of coca, that with the highest concentration of cocaine alkaloid, was cultivated only on the eastern slopes of the Andes Mountains. This area's tropical climate, high amounts of rainfall, and sloping hillsides to keep the plants from drowning in the acidic soil offered perfect growing conditions. The primary growing area was in the Upper Huallaga Valley (UHV), which encompassed an area about the size of New Jersey.

The conversion of coca leaves to US-preferred cocaine (cocaine hydrochloride) involves numerous steps requiring several chemicals and solvents. Workers in Peru grew and harvested coca leaves, processed the leaves into cocaine base and sent it on to Colombia for final processing into cocaine hydrochloride. Only the Colombians had the expertise and chemicals necessary for hydrochloride processing and, most importantly, had the established customer bases in the United States and Europe.

Cocaine production is a drawn-out process. It begins by converting coca leaves into paste, always done very close to the coca field to cut down on the hassle of transporting large amounts of leaves. The conversion starts in a *pozo*, a crude, roughly square pit measuring a foot or two deep, lined with heavy plastic. It is usually located near a stream that provides a constant water supply.

Workers throw dried coca leaves in the pozo and mix them with water and soda ash. Kerosene is added, and the mixture is stirred to help extract the cocaine alkaloids. The stirring is accomplished by several workers stepping into the pit and stomping the leaves. If lucky, they do this wearing rubber boots. One giveaway in spotting pozo workers was their feet. If they stomped shoeless, long exposure to kerosene and other caustic chemicals absolutely ruined their feet.

After draining off the leaves and fluids, adding soda ash crystallizes the solution, which when dried produces coca paste, a light-brown, puttylike substance. Usually, processing 250 pounds of dried coca leaves could provide about one kilogram (2.2 pounds) of coca paste.

Converting coca paste into cocaine base is more complicated, requiring more sophisticated equipment, additional chemicals, and educated skills. Cocaine base labs were sometimes near the coca fields, but usually were located near rivers or close to a clandestine airstrip to simplify the movement of cocaine base from Peru to cocaine hydrochloride labs in Colombia—the final processing stage.

Offhand, working in the cocaine industry appears dismal. Harvesting the leaves, carrying and dragging one-hundred-pound sacks to a pozo pit, endlessly stomping the leaves, and breathing caustic chemical fumes add up to hard and unhealthy employment.

Nevertheless, there were no labor shortages in the UHV. By 1994, the area's population had quintupled in size from ten years earlier. Why? A farmer growing bananas or citrus could expect to earn five hundred dollars a year. Working in a pozo would bring a worker about five thousand a year—decent money in Peru.

Operation Snowcap was DEA's most extensive and unprecedented enforcement effort. The program was also DEA's most controversial drug war strategy. Originally working out of a fortified, Vietnam-style firebase at Santa Lucia, located in the middle of the UHV, Snowcap teams accompanied Peruvian police on US-supplied Huey helicopters to raid cocaine labs and destroy hidden jungle airstrips.

The rationale for building a base like Santa Lucia was to protect US personnel when conducting antidrug activities. DEA agents flying into the heart of the UHV drug-trafficking area were increasingly at risk because the Sendero Luminoso (Spanish for "Shining Path"), a Maoist organization attempting to violently overthrow the Peruvian government, had taken control of much of the area in the late 1980s. The Senderos protected cocaine traffickers in return for monetary support.

Built in 1989, the base at Santa Lucia housed and protected a force of Peruvian police, DEA agents, ten Huey helicopters, and two fixed-wing aircraft and their crews. Because the base was in a tropical area with no safe, accessible roads, fixed-wing aircraft transported personnel, equipment, and supplies to the base from Lima several times each week. For safety's sake, we used only twin-engine aircraft to fly over the Andes—if one engine failed, the other could keep the plane flying.

To find the coke labs and hidden airstrips, we had the assistance of several assets. The *pajaritos*, Peruvian police who listened to trafficker radio talk, analyzed the conversations and gave us key information on the movement of coke by boat and by air. In addition, we had the frequent help of US Air Force surveillance planes that could find and track everything in the air. When the air force detected a small plane flying out of the area toward Colombia and determined it was not legally identified, the Americans notified Peruvian air force fighters, who could respond and investigate.

This program caused the traffickers to exercise more caution when planning their flights, but it abruptly stopped in mid-1994 after a Peruvian fighter, alerted by a US surveillance plane, shot down a small plane that refused to identify itself and land. Unfortunately, the plane was carrying Christian missionaries, not traffickers with cocaine, and the outcry was great. In damage-control mode, the US government abruptly stopped using the air force surveillance planes. Cocaine flights between Colombia and Peru resumed in full force.

Nevertheless, our best asset was human sources. Informants gave us timely information on the movements and locations of traffickers and their coke labs, caches, and airstrips. We paid well for their information and they remained anonymous. Most of our informants were walk-ins, coming to us seven days a week at all hours to give information.

To help us pinpoint that information, we had the use of twin-engine planes to conduct surveillance. After receiving an informant's tip, we flew to the target area (usually with the informant on board to point the way) to verify the information. If the target proved promising from the air, we returned to our base, planned a raid, and then conducted the operation in our helicopters with the Peruvian police.

Geography determined how we operated, and it contributed to our successes. Transporting cocaine base from the UHV in Peru to the labs in Colombia was a major problem for the traffickers. The Colombia border is located about five hundred air miles from the center of the UHV. Only one road existed, and it called for a roundabout, almost thousand-mile journey on a twisting, rutted, generally dirt route that passed through most of the little towns along the way. Transport by river was possible, but only along a serpentine, sometimes dangerous route requiring ten to fifteen days to complete. Naturally, the road and river routes both required a trafficker to finagle his way past police and army security blocks. Flying the coke out to Colombia was the quickest and only sensible way.

The traffickers used small, single-engine aircraft (Cessnas were a favorite) to ferry the coke to Colombia. A Cessna could carry up to one thousand pounds on each trip. The coke merchants built illegal airstrips in the jungle to enable that plan, since the area's few commercial airstrips were under military control. Coke merchants built their strips near a river or road to allow for easy delivery of the cocaine to the plane. They used bulldozers or road graders to clear a patch of ground for the landing strip. In some locations, a straight stretch of existing road could be used to land on. The traffickers having blocked off both ends with guards, planes quickly landed, loaded up with cocaine, and then took off.

Upon the team's arrival in Peru, I had a new operational plan in mind based on a historical review of previous enforcement work accomplished in the UHV. The situation had changed since the first Snowcap teams started operating in 1989. Due to our successful efforts, the traffickers had learned from our methods and changed their own ways of doing business.

The base at Santa Lucia was centrally located in the Upper Huallaga Valley, and from there our helicopters flew teams out to conduct raids. That worked very well—for a while. The operating range of a Huey helicopter was only 150 miles out. The traffickers knew that and started constructing airstrips and labs beyond Huey range from Santa Lucia base. As a result, good targets became hard to find.

Our plan was not to concentrate our resources at Santa Lucia, but to spread out in the UHV—break up the team into small sections and establish base camps with the local police. The Hueys could come pick us up, refuel, and then ferry us farther to conduct our raids. This tactic extended our range and allowed us to operate in new areas.

We set up bases in the towns of Tingo Maria, Tarapoto, and Pucallpa, and kept our base at Santa Lucia. These towns gave us geographical coverage of the UHV. Although I did not want to, I was required to keep two agents at Santa Lucia. There was not much action, but our CASA continued to be based there. The CASA was a twin-engine aircraft resembling a flying bus and we used it almost every day, whether for tactical missions or reconnaissance operations.

Our team's arrival coincided with a base change by our Hueys. They moved from Santa Lucia to a new base in Pucallpa. Pucallpa was the region's largest city, located on the Ucayali River. The vast numbers of vultures that inhabited the city was Pucallpa's chief feature and served to represent the place. The ugly black birds seemed to perch on every rooftop and electricity pole, or just circled overhead looking for food. It was spooky. A large town, Pucallpa was regional headquarters of the police, army, air force, and navy. Its commercial airport was better suited to support our Hueys.

All US personnel in Pucallpa operated out of the Inambu Hotel, a run-down, three-story structure. Fortunately for the owner, who made out financially on the deal, it was strategically located. The US embassy leased the entire hotel and fortified it with a perimeter fence, concertina wire, and sandbags, and built two guard towers on the roof. It was an uncomfortable, crowded dump and the food was terrible—everything fried, every day.

We divided the team into four two-man groups, leaving the assistant team leader, the team medic, the communications specialist, and myself as the headquarters group. The medic was a former US Army Special Forces medic and the communications expert was a former Navy Seal. Both were contractors working for DEA and both were very good at their jobs. I kept two agents each at Santa Lucia, Pucallpa, Tingo Maria and Tarapoto.

My headquarters group usually worked out of Tingo Maria. I had already identified a couple of slackers on my team, so I put them at Santa Lucia, imagining they wouldn't have much action to avoid. Two seemingly aggressive agents went to Tarapoto to get something going. Pucallpa was likewise new territory. Pucallpa had roads and the Ucayali River, both avenues for potential interdiction efforts.

Each team hooked up with the Peru National Police (the PNP) based in their respective towns. For any planned operation at any location, I would bring together four to six agents to go out with the PNP and conduct the raid.

We conducted all our enforcement operations in the Upper Huallaga Valley. At the time of our arrival, the Peruvian army was conducting military operations at various locations in the UHV against Shining Path insurgents. Due to that activity, the US embassy in Lima insisted on reviewing and approving all our planned enforcement events prior to us going out.

As usual, political considerations mattered. The embassy would not allow us in an area if there was even a remote chance the army would also be operating in that vicinity. The embassy's concern was human rights violations by the Peruvian army; it wanted reassurance that we had not witnessed anything like that. It wanted no chance of anyone in the media linking the United States to Peruvian army killings.

Consequently, for our first three weeks in the UHV, we planned several raids that the embassy nixed. All were canceled to avoid any possible contact with army units supposedly in the area. We had heard stories, mainly from informants, of the army going into a village and wiping it out, but I never saw any evidence of army misconduct. After all, they were fighting against a violent organization the United States had labeled as terrorist, and much fighting and bloodshed occurred on both sides.

The embassy in Lima ordered us to keep a low profile in Peru. We were armed agents running around the countryside—worrisome to the diplomats. The State Department's diplomatic mission in Peru had its priorities, but it seemed the cocaine situation did not head the list. It may not have been in the top five. Dealing with the State Department became bothersome during my time in Peru. I felt the embassy would have preferred Snowcap not to be in Peru. Diplomacy and drug enforcement operations often clashed.

Our PNP comrades were special paramilitary police; that is, they were police officers but walked, talked, and operated as soldiers. They dressed like soldiers in camouflage uniforms and carried military arms—the AK-47 rifle. The cocaine traffickers were equally armed.

On their own, the PNP were not very active and did not recruit informants. They preferred to stay in their camps waiting around for us to initiate something. Their hearts were not in it. I had several PNP tell me cocaine was an American problem, not Peru's. All we had to do was stop the American craving to use cocaine, and we would soon all be out of business. A ridiculous thought.

Though they were reluctant warriors, we never had to goad the PNP into action. When it came time to get on a chopper and fly out to destroy a lab site, they were ready to go and were the first to jump off the chopper and mix it up with the traffickers. It was the Latin machismo at work. Although unenthusiastic about the mission, they always showed up and took care of business.

Our first two operations were airstrip demolitions. The PNP and we loaded up all available Hueys and went out to the target. There were never more than six Hueys available to use. The Vietnam War–vintage machines constantly broke down for one reason or another.

Upon landing at an airstrip, we secured it and then set up a defensive perimeter while we searched the area for suspects, any coke hidden in *caletas*, and equipment. Caletas were drug caches: simply large holes dug in the ground and filled with waterproofed bags of cocaine base, then covered with a tarp and dirt to hide them.

Traffickers literally carved airstrips out of the jungle. The strips were nothing but narrow tracks of compacted dirt. Blowing the airstrips was a straightforward process that involved creating big craters in the runway so planes could not land. Military explosives accomplished that task. Setting off a twenty-five-pound shaped charge drilled a borehole straight down into the ground for six to ten feet, depending on the type of soil. Then we lowered cratering charges into the holes and set them off. To deny a plane space to land, we strategically spaced the holes, blowing two, three, or more craters. Hidden in the trees we often found the road graders or bulldozers used to construct the airstrips. Though it was wasteful, we set explosive charges on the engines and blew them since we could not drive them off.

Those explosives made impressive holes and appeared effective. Unfortunately, they did not work. When I would fly back over a few days later to check on them, the airstrips were almost always repaired and ready to go. The traffickers must have brought in every person with a shovel within twenty miles to get them going again so soon.

I soon caught on; blowing craters, although offering a sense of accomplishment, was a waste of time and resources. We were just making noise out there.

In May, our agents in Pucallpa interviewed a walk-in informant who offered information about a trafficking group that used boats to ferry cocaine to an airstrip located beside the Ucayali River. We made plans to intercept them. Two small rubber Zodiac boats with outboard engines had come with us to Peru, and this was our chance to use them.

A flyover in our CASA enabled us to spot the airstrip, sited next to the river. We also found a good place to set up a river ambush about two miles upstream from the airstrip, one that featured a narrow choke point in the river.

Two days later, we lifted off with six agents, twenty-two PNP, and a Zodiac loaded on all the Hueys we could get flying; only five were available. Landing two miles inland allowed us to arrive at the river without alerting anyone in the area. Our Huey pilots were PNP and they always flew "nap of the earth" (low, just above the tree line). Their feeling was that no one on the ground who wanted to shoot would have much of a chance because a trafficker would not hear or see the Hueys except briefly, just as they flew over. After dropping us, the Hueys flew back to Pucallpa to await our call for pickup.

Carrying the inflated Zodiac and its small outboard motor, we made good time walking through the flat, woody savannah and arrived at the ambush site in the early morning. At the river choke point, we set up with all the DEA agents and half of our PNP, along with the fiscal—a Peruvian government prosecutor. Fiscals came out on every arrest situation, ostensibly to give arrest approval and to ensure the police upheld the rule of law.

In my area, the fiscal's name was Vargas. He was not like any attorney I had ever met. Vargas may have looked the part, being a bespectacled, scrawny little man weighing in at about 125 pounds, but he always carried a small .38-caliber snub-nosed revolver and acted as if he knew how to use it. He reminded me of a bantam rooster, displaying a hard-charging attitude. I was to find out it was no act.

About 150 yards downstream from the choke point and hidden just around a bend, we placed the Zodiac with five PNP, and another five PNP were concealed directly across the river from them. After three hours of watching and waiting, right on time with the informant's report, we saw two boats coming downriver.

Looking through my binoculars, I saw they were typical riverboats, about four feet wide and twenty feet long, with outboard motors chugging away—glorified canoes. Each boat carried six men and several bundles, packaged as what could only be cocaine base. Traffickers in Peru transported their cocaine in bundles of one-kilogram blocks, totaling twenty-five kilograms (fifty-five pounds) per bundle, all wrapped in taped, heavy black plastic. As a confirmation, I spotted two men in the leading boat holding AK-47 rifles. These people were not out fishing.

When the boats were about fifty yards from us, Captain Llosa, the PNP leader, and three other PNP stood up from our concealment with raised rifles and called out to the boats. He ordered them to cut their motors and come in to him. At the sudden sight of uniformed men with raised guns, the boats complied and started drifting in toward us. By then we had all stood up, watching as the boats came closer.

When the boats were still about twenty yards away, the lead pilot gave a quick pull of the cord and the engine sprang to life. He opened it up and the boat surged forward. The trailing boat did the same. Instantly, both boats were racing downstream.

With not a second's hesitation or a word of warning, the PNP opened up and began shooting at the boats. Both boats overturned as some of the traffickers rolled over the sides to get away from the firing. Surprised, we Americans just ducked and kept out of it. As I was to learn, the PNP were inclined to shoot first and ask questions later. To my amazement, I also caught a glimpse of Fiscal Vargas banging away at the boats with his little gun—I took his actions as a positive sanction. The man was quick to slap leather.

The shooting was soon over. As the mess of boats, men, and cocaine bundles flowed downstream in the swift current, our Zodiac came into sight and tried to help. The traffickers stroked hard toward shore, the quick thinkers aiming for the far side, away from us. Our five hidden PNP on that side were waiting for them and scooped them up as they pulled themselves out of the river. The PNP also grabbed the men crawling ashore on our side.

The officers in the Zodiac fished cocaine bundles out of the river. We saw several bundles floating away, but due to the fast current they drifted out of sight before they could be retrieved. The final tally was six bundles, weighing out to 150 kilograms of cocaine, and nine traffickers arrested—two of them wounded but ambulatory. Three more were lost in the river—whether shot, drowned, or escaped, we never found out. The PNP likely shot them, as we managed to recover one bullet-riddled boat from the river.

For good reason, we tried to keep our informants' identities secret from the PNP whenever possible. The informants' personal safety was always an issue with us. Word had spread that DEA not only paid well for information, but also took steps to protect our informants. When we took our informants out on operations with us, and we usually did, they were clothed in PNP uniforms and wore masks to hide their faces and identities. Some of the PNP even wore masks for the same reason. In the UHV, being on the side of law and order was not safe.

21

Tingo Maria

Nestled in a scenic river valley where the Monzon River enters the Huallaga River is the town of Tingo Maria. Surrounded on all sides by mountain vistas, Tingo Maria calls itself the entryway to the "Peruvian Amazon." One could follow the river downstream, eventually link up with the Amazon River, and reach the Atlantic Ocean—about two thousand miles away.

Tingo was well situated for us in the middle of cocaine-growing country. It was also untouched territory. Notwithstanding the presence of a sizable PNP unit and an army contingent, law enforcement had not been an influence in the area.

We rented a house for our base camp. It backed up to the airport and was located only a mile from the PNP camp. The modest, two-story, concrete-block house had a ten-foot high block wall around it with a metal gate, and provided us with reasonable security. Two PNP stood guard at the gate twenty-four hours a day, but I never counted on them to actually risk their lives for us. I told our men to be ready for an attack if the guards ever failed to show up or suddenly disappeared.

Since we were vulnerable we had security procedures to deal with attack threats. For starters, we never went anywhere unarmed or alone. A high hill was located just a rifle shot away from the house. To help cope with that possibility, we filled sandbags with dirt from our backyard, placing them against the house's inner front walls. We also kept the front curtains closed at all times—no sense in giving anyone a clear shot at us.

In the event of a sustained ground attack, our strategy was simple. We would call the PNP and then hold out until the cavalry arrived. If the attackers got into our compound, our plan was to retreat out the back door to a couple of ladders placed at the wall, get over those, and run across the airstrip to the airport security office, which was manned by Peruvian air force.

Still, we were not defenseless. Each of us always carried a Glock pistol and an M-16 rifle when out on field operations. We also had one Colt squad automatic weapon, equipped with a one-hundred-round drum magazine and a 40mm grenade launcher, so we were fairly well armed.

I was amazed how the word about our location got out. Soon we had informants coming right to our house with information to sell. That meant, of course, that the traffickers also must have known where we lived. The informants usually came around under cover of darkness to keep their identities safe from curious onlookers.

We paid out reward money for information leading to arrests and seizures—usually ten dollars per kilogram of cocaine and one to two hundred dollars per arrest. For tips on hidden airstrips, we paid out a hundred dollars or so, depending on the situation. Not much money, really, but it was decent wages in the poor Upper Huallaga Valley economy.

Many of our informants were "one hit wonders," able to give a tip for only one target and that was it. However, we had some professional informants, people who were able to penetrate trafficker organizations and obtain information valuable to us. During my limited time in Peru, one intrepid informant managed to earn over $10,000 from Uncle Sam.

My first function at Tingo entailed a visit to the PNP camp to introduce myself. The PNP base held about one hundred police and an unknown number of camp followers with unknown duties, but all eating from the government trough. Located at the foot of a jungle-clad hill, the base consisted of several buildings laid out military style, containing offices, barracks, and supply, all surrounding a central parade ground. A brick wall topped by barbed wire encircled the base.

In the back was the motor pool, which served as the parking spot for disabled police vehicles. Haphazardly parked around the mechanics' shed were at least twenty trucks, jeeps, and cars. Most of them were not serviceable, as verified by the tall weeds and bushes growing undisturbed around them. On my first day's tour of the base, a mechanic killed a six-foot-long bushmaster snake while showing me the motor pool. The PNP cut it up and grilled it for that evening's dinner, and it was delicious.

Commandante Diaz, a police lieutenant colonel, commanded the PNP in Tingo Maria. Overblown and overfed, his English was limited to "hello" and "good-bye." My Spanish was stumble-ready, but my assistant team leader, Donny Garza, was a native speaker. I usually kept him with me when we needed to plan an operation with the PNP.

Diaz was from Lima, and after a few moments of conversation, I knew how he came to an appointment in backwater Tingo Maria. He had nothing going for him. Nevertheless, although I could see he was neither very bright nor experienced, he was ambitious—when he was not drinking. The man shamelessly made it clear to me that if we made some significant arrests and seizures, he could move back to Lima with a promotion. I told him I wanted nothing more than to see him get his wish.

Soon after our arrival in Tingo, we had our first chance to try out Diaz and his PNP on an operation. An informant approached us with a story concerning a trafficking group that backpacked bundles of cocaine overland from a coke lab to the Monzon River. At the river they placed the bundles on boats for transport to an airstrip. The informant had observed the couriers, usually in groups of ten or more and typically on Sundays, walk by carrying heavy backpacks of cocaine. They used a well-beaten trail on their way to the river that ran close by a location in the jungle where his family had a small farm.

We flew out with our informant on our CASA transport plane. We spotted his farm and the visible trail. After looking at the surrounding terrain and the river situation, we decided a trail ambush was our best approach. I met with Colonel Diaz to plan, and he wanted to set up the ambush at the informant's farm. Tactics were not his strong suit. I patiently explained to him that any police seen at the farm would implicate the informant, and the whole family would likely pay for that with their lives.

We decided on a location well away from the farm and closer to the river to set up the trail ambush.

On the following Sunday, we flew out at dawn with five DEA agents, Fiscal Vargas, and twenty-one PNP, including Diaz. That surprised me as I had thought he was strictly a stay-in-the-office type. We landed in a grassy area about five miles from our intended ambush site, waved good-bye to the Hueys, and conducted a brisk trek through the woods toward our ambush site. After a robust two-hour walk, we arrived at the trail. Diaz was exhausted.

We found an abandoned shed alongside the trail and chose that location. Two deadfall trees near the shed lay almost parallel to the trail and could offer us good cover. Commandante Diaz lounged about, still tired from the walk and obviously not comfortable in the jungle. I asked him how he wanted the men deployed for the ambush. I pointed out the fallen trees as being good concealment, and Diaz agreed, saying, "Put half our men behind the trees on this side and half across the trail from the trees, so we have them in crossfire and none can escape."

I knew then we were in trouble. I tactfully explained to him that if shooting started (knowing it would with the PNP), we would have our two groups shooting at each other. I could see that some of Diaz's men listening to our conversation were hanging on our every word. Their safety was at stake and they well knew it, but they were not about to question their commander's orders.

I subtly persuaded Diaz to deploy everyone in an L-shaped ambush, with most of the men behind the fallen trees and a small group on each end of the trail, effectively covering all avenues. Fiscal Vargas insisted on a concealed site in the middle ground, ostensibly so he could shoot in any direction. I was starting to like his style.

In the end, it did not matter as no one came down the trail. We waited all day and then had to hustle to get back to our Huey pickup site before dark. During the walk there, we radioed the Hueys. They informed us two of the aircraft had mechanical problems and would not be available until the following day.

We would have to spend the night in the jungle. Once again, I had to explain tactics to Diaz, showing him how to put everyone in a circular perimeter for security and the necessity for having someone on watch all night. The man had no noticeable common sense. I made sure we DEA agents kept watch all night too, everyone pulling a turn. Except for the mosquito harassment, we survived well enough sleeping on the ground in a grassy meadow.

The next day, we received word that the Hueys were still down and we would have to stay out another night. We spent the day bonding with the PNP and conducted some improvised training, so the day was not a total waste. Diaz's aide had the foresight to bring a bottle along, so the lush was no bother to anyone.

The Hueys arrived the following day at noon to take us back to Tingo. I never again saw Commandante Diaz outside his base. That was fine with me.

With the Peru police at a jungle ambush site, April, 1994. I'm kneeling on the left.

Burning cocaine labs near Tingo Maria, May 1994. I'm on the left.

Jungle cocaine labs were crude but effective, Tingo Maria, May 1994.

Just after my team departed for Peru in April, DEA gained a new administrator. In May 1994, as part of his fact-finding duties and to become familiar with DEA operations, especially overseas operations (with which he had no experience), he sent a team to Peru to evaluate Snowcap. The team included the administrator's new chief of staff, Steve Llewellyn; Bob Brandon, his new head of operations; and Dick Wharton, the new head of foreign operations.

I met them in Lima and took them around the embassy for the obligatory briefings. Then we flew over the Andes so I could show them what we were doing in the UHV. I had plans to show them our bases, introduce them to the PNP, and take them out on an airstrip destruction operation—basically, a dog and pony show. Our first stop was Santa Lucia, the base that had not been productive of late.

Our two Santa Lucia team members had recently returned to camp after being out with a platoon of PNP to check a tip concerning a lab in the vicinity, with no results. On the walk back to Santa Lucia, the unit had to cross a fast-flowing mountain stream. The PNP on point stepped into the water and started across. He lost his footing on the slippery rocks and went under. The water was only hip deep but the current was fast, too fast for him to regain his feet. The water likewise swept down the young PNP lieutenant in charge of the patrol when he jumped in to help. The strong current carried both of them out of sight. A frantic search finally found both men almost a half mile downstream, caught in tree branches and drowned.

The patrol had just arrived at camp when we flew in from Lima. I asked Brandon if he wanted to go over with me to the PNP and offer our condolences. He looked at me as if I was kidding and stayed where he was.

The next day, we were in Pucallpa and flew from there in our Hueys to raid a newfound airstrip. It was located near a river about forty-five minutes from Pucallpa. The pilots flew their usual nap of the earth flight pattern, traveling only a few feet above the trees at about ninety miles an hour. On landing, the raiding unit jumped out, conducted a search, and began setting explosives to crater the airstrip.

Brandon complained to me about the helicopter ride, accusing me of showing off by flying too low. I told him the PNP was flying, not me, and that was their standard flying procedure in the UHV. The team was efficient in laying the explosives and blew three craters in the airstrip. We found a Caterpillar tractor off to one side and blew the engine on that too. Going back to Pucallpa, we flew nap of the earth. Brandon said nothing, but I knew what he was thinking.

The evaluation team stayed three days in Peru. We had conversations on every aspect of Snowcap, and I could gather from their line of questioning that they had come with one mind-set: find justification to end Snowcap. Our extraordinary program in South America did not fit in with the new administrator's plan for DEA.

Snowcap was a huge and expensive undertaking involving not only DEA, but also the State Department, the military, the CIA, and other federal law enforcement agencies such as customs and the border patrol. As such, the decision to end Snowcap could not be made unilaterally by the administrator. He would have to show justification to the other players in Washington.

Many of our efforts involved flying around the UHV to search for targets. We had a list of known illegal airstrips in our area, and we flew over them often to check for activity. We also flew out to newly reported airstrip sites to verify their existence and locations. After spending six weeks in Peru, I had a list of over twenty-five illegal airstrips, and those were just the ones I knew about. How many more out there was unknown and frustrating. I could not hope to subdue cocaine smuggling out of all those airstrips with the measly few, aged Hueys I had.

Flying over the area, I became amazed at the number of coca bushes under cultivation. Coca was everywhere, the only major moneymaking industry in the Upper Huallaga Valley. The numbers and sizes of farms growing products such as bananas or vegetables were miniscule compared to those growing coca plants.

A few years earlier, someone at the US embassy in Lima had floated a brilliant plan for the United States to subsidize potato farms in the UHV to counter cocaine cultivation. A forlorn hope. Farmers could sell potatoes for five cents a pound and coca leaves for ten times that amount. Besides, no decent roads existed to send the produce to market across the Andes, so food could not be delivered before it rotted. On the other hand, Colombian coca buyers flew in with money in their pockets to pick up the finished product; no need for roads.

I soon concluded that our enforcement methods, as they stood, were hopeless. There was just too much cocaine produced in an area that was too large to watch. To cover an area the size of New Jersey, we had ten DEA agents, a CASA airplane, and ten old helicopters, half of which were down for repairs at any one time. The PNP gave us personnel and authority, but they were not investigators and had little initiative. They were hired guns just waiting around for us to form a posse.

The traffickers repaired the airstrips as soon as we destroyed them, so blowing holes in the ground was a waste of time. Likewise, finding and destroying the cocaine labs and pozo pits was not fruitful, as they were soon producing again. Equally, making arrests did nothing to deter anyone from working in the cocaine trade. It was the only way in the area to make decent money, despite the risks. We simply did not have enough men and aircraft to lessen the cocaine amounts being processed and sent on to America.

Statistically, we were golden. Our teams made many arrests and seized lots of cocaine during our three-month tours in Peru. But the numbers game meant nothing to me; I knew our mission was hopeless unless we changed our methods. After thinking hard on it and talking to some key people, I felt I had a solution to our problem.

The traffickers' weakness, or bottleneck, was their transportation system. Carrying cocaine by road or riverboat to Colombia was out of the question. They could not easily run the gauntlet through police and military checks, and the distance was too far, anyway. They had to use airplanes. However, airplanes needed airstrips to land, and that was their small but serious vulnerability.

We had the ability to exploit that exposure. Between the PNP pajaritos intercepting trafficker radio talk and our successful informant pipeline, we received substantial information about airplanes coming in to load up with cocaine. Knowing that, we could hide out and watch the airstrip, witness the loading of cocaine, and then report the aircraft's tail number and its take off direction to the Peruvian air force. The Peruvians could intercept the plane and either force it down or shoot it down; it was up to them.

The supply of cocaine was limitless, as were the numbers of growers and traffickers. What were limited, however, were the number of airplanes available and the number of pilots willing to land on a primitive airstrip and then take off, overloaded with coke, for a long trip back to Colombia.

Forming a plan of action on the way, I flew to Lima to pitch my proposal. It was the middle of May and our tour was half over; I wanted to make some operational changes. At the embassy, I sat down with all the parties that had a stake in cocaine suppression. Everyone reluctantly acknowledged my analysis of our ineffectiveness in the UHV.

I got a rise out of one self-important embassy official when I mentioned sneaking out, lying up to watch a plane load coke at an airstrip, and then alerting the Peruvian air force. He informed me we could no longer share target information with the Peruvians if they were shooting down aircraft. I knew better than to argue, so I went to plan B (always have a plan B).

Since we could not stop the drug planes in the air, I proposed that we send out a team of PNP and DEA agents, lay up in ambush, and then arrest the traffickers and seize the aircraft on the ground. That idea did not go over well either. I heard a chorus of disagreement due to the dangers inherent in such a scheme. I allowed that it would take careful planning and require extra logistical support, but in the end, after some lengthy arguments, I got my way—with some conditions.

What swayed them was this question: Putting aside the natural danger of flying a small airplane onto an improvised airstrip, would the added prospect of armed PNP waiting in ambush affect a Colombian pilot's desire to take the job? My belief was that capturing pilots and planes would cause the Colombians to make immediate changes in their trafficking methods.

To obtain embassy consent, I had to agree to some reasonable restrictive ground rules for our airstrip ambushes—careful planning, close support from our Hueys and other aircraft, and full PNP support. Flying back to the UHV, I felt the trip was a success. Although I was restricted in some respects, the PNP was not—they were officially in charge. We were "advisors" going along to assist. I had no doubts about the PNP's performance. If we were lying in wait as a Colombian plane landed on an airstrip, the PNP would do whatever necessary to bag the plane.

I could not wait to break the news to Fiscal Vargas. We had authorization to ambush airstrips, and I already knew the location of our first target.

22

Longer Is Faster, Shorter Is Slower

Cachicoto was a small town of about five hundred souls located twelve miles upstream from Tingo Maria on the Monzon River. It was a dusty, nondescript village with several tin-roofed houses, a few small shops, and other buildings. The buildings surrounded a dirt and gravel-strewn town square that doubled as a soccer field. The town supported the Sendero Luminoso to a man. Visible from the air, the village square still showed the faded red remnants of a large hammer and sickle painted on the gravel. That had been done before the Peruvian army established a small outpost about five miles away, in 1992. Since then, the Senderos had toned down their public insurrectionist displays. The town's population and that of the surrounding Monzon valley depended almost entirely on coca cultivation for its income.

Commandante Diaz disclosed to me that the army had an arrangement with the Sendero-sponsored traffickers in the area to live and let live. If the Senderos refrained from attacking, the army would overlook Sendero cocaine production. I reckoned the army was also making money from the arrangement.

I met on occasion with the local army commander, Flores, an older captain, and at each meeting he made mention of their latest arrests or antidrug operations. Fiscal Vargas, whom I trusted, told me it was all nonsense, as he would have had knowledge about every arrest in the region. That confirmed it for me: Captain Flores was on the take.

Cachicoto sat in the middle of prime coca-growing land in the Monzon Valley. We flew over it often looking for targets. Seeing that it was Sendero territory, the traffickers did little to hide their coke labs and pozo pits. I spotted numerous lab operations from the air. But I was looking for airstrips and not finding any; with that many labs in the area, an airstrip had to be near the river.

A gravel road, not much wider than a jeep trail, led east from Cachicoto, staying close to the Monzon River and heading toward Pueblo Nuevo. About four miles outside Cachicoto, it ran on a straight stretch for well over half a mile. From the air it appeared suitable for use as an airstrip. We took many photos, and a close-up photo study found visible tire tracks and a wide spot in the road resembling a turnaround point. The road had to be the airstrip.

Puzzling though, was the presence of a crater dug in the road one hundred yards from the turnaround. That spot would have been the approximate midpoint for a landing. The crater was two to three feet deep and about six feet in diameter, reaching out from the edge of the road to the middle. It seemed capable of prohibiting any aircraft from landing.

We kept looking at the area for a couple of weeks, taking more photos. Comparing photos taken weeks apart showed new tracks on the road and at the turnaround point. Airplanes were definitely landing there, but how did they avoid the road crater?

I went to Commandante Diaz at the PNP base and talked it over with him. I asked him to send out two or three men undercover, posing as workers, to survey the road and the crater and verify aircraft had been using the road. He said the army had blown the crater the year before to keep away airplanes, and it was working. I showed him my photographic evidence to the contrary. He still refused to give me any men, citing the dangers of crossing the Monzon River and going to Cachicoto. That was Sendero country, and he would not go in without a large posse.

I could not fault him much there, as his men would be killed if found out. We talked some more on the ambush idea. To his knowledge, a successful airstrip ambush had never occurred. However, I could see him warming to the concept—bagging an airplane would send his stock up with his superiors in Lima.

As we continued to plan the Cachicoto operation, my foremost problem was inserting an ambush team into the area without alerting any residents. The area around Cachicoto featured scores of coca farms with their attendant small houses. Traffickers would notice any Hueys approaching the area. Even dropping off miles away and walking in would not work, since the sound of helicopters in the UHV was a sound of warning: police or military were coming. If the alarm went out, the traffickers would radio to Colombia and cancel any planned flight to Cachicoto. I thought back to my earlier experience with Hueys and came up with a possible solution to the problem.

While I was in Vietnam, we had a similar stealth challenge when trying to insert long-range reconnaissance teams into enemy territory. Sometimes we made dummy insertions over a wide area to confuse the enemy—having several helicopters simultaneously swoop down into widely separated areas, with only one Huey actually unloading a recon team. Consequently, the enemy did not know which sector we were in, and it forced them to try to cover all the possible landing spots to find us. That trick would not work in the Monzon, as any Huey presence in the area was a showstopper, but maybe tweaking the ruse would.

Our plan would exploit the traffickers' conditioned responses to our tactics. When raiding labs and pozo pit sites, we routinely swooped down in Hueys, jumped out, carried off the cocaine and any suspects we could grab, and blew up the labs and pozos before leaving. After we left in a whirl of dust, life returned to normal. The lab workers came out of hiding and rebuilt.

For this operation, we would change that cycle. I called for two insertions into the general area, set about three or four days apart, to raid and destroy some of the labs we had identified—get them used to seeing us come. Then we would do it a third time—only, on that raid, half of the assault team would stay and hide while the remainder of the force flew off. In the noise and confusion of our running around and setting off explosives, no local person was liable to notice that fewer police left than had arrived. If the stay-behind team could remain unnoticed, we were in business. We would lie up in bushes until late at night, then walk to the preselected site and set an ambush before morning's light.

We conducted our first diversionary raid on June 17, 1994. The area we hit was located about three miles away from the airstrip road. Our six Hueys landed in a coca field, loaded with four DEA agents and twenty-four PNP. Spreading out and following the many trails, we found six pozo pits full of coca leaves and one lab busily processing base cocaine. Also present were several gallons of chemicals such as kerosene, sulfuric acid, and ammonia. All the workers had fled upon hearing our arrival so we made no arrests. We set off explosives in the pozo pits and the lab, set fire to the workers' huts, and flew off while everything burned.

I wanted to pull off a similar raid in two or three days, but once again, the lack of helicopter support derailed our plans. No Hueys were flying on the days we needed them. Our Peru tour was ending in just two more weeks, so I decided to scrap the second raid and get to our main objective—ambushing that road.

Conducting a landing too close to our ambush site was risky, so we chose an area about five miles away for our second ruse-raid. A small mountain separated our diversion area from the road airstrip. The mountain was only 1,500 feet high, but it was steep-sided. The target area seemed ideal since it contained a few labs for us to destroy while we made our presence known, and it seemed close enough to the road airstrip to reach during a night march over the mountain.

Hoping to avoid having to force our way through the heavy jungle covering the mountain slope, I had noticed from the air a boulder-strewn streambed that climbed nearly to the mountaintop. I thought that would work as a rapid route up the mountainside. The airstrip road actually curved around the mountain and drew close to our Huey landing site. One member of my team suggested we just walk the long way around on the road. I pointed out the several farmhouses scattered along the road and cautioned him on our need to reach the ambush site undetected. Besides, I said, "Shorter is faster."

We set out in the late afternoon on June 21 with plans and enough provisions to stay out for up to five days if necessary, waiting for a traffickers' plane to land on our road. Traveling in five Hueys this time, we landed on an overgrown vegetable field and jumped off. Again, we were four DEA and twenty-four PNP, plus Fiscal Vargas with his trusty .38 revolver.

We found four pozo pits nearby and one cocaine base lab, idle at the time but well-stocked with chemicals. We blew up the pozos and the lab, burned a few huts, and finished up within an hour. We saw no one while we did our work and, hoping no one was hiding and watching, eleven PNP and one DEA agent boarded the five Hueys and lifted off. Three DEA agents and eleven PNP were left behind to hustle uphill into the jungle before the sound of the departing Hueys had faded.

We silently paced up the mountain slope for fifteen minutes and then sat down to wait for the night, when we could safely move out. We had good maps and some photos, and I was confident we could find our way, even in darkness. We outlined our route of movement, with Rich Babich, my radioman, a former Navy Seal, and a good man in the field, walking on point. I followed second, then Major Quesada and his men trailed. Agent Donnie Garza brought up the rear. I wanted one of our own men back there so we would not suffer any straggler problems without knowing.

At nine o'clock, the moon rose—what there was of it—and we set out. Rich soon found the boulder streambed, which was dry, and we started working our way up the mountain.

Two hours later and exhausted to a man, we halted for a rest. We had covered much less than half a mile. Fiscal Vargas seemed ready to expire as he lay on the ground, gasping and retching. I had been ready for the mountain's steepness all right, but the boulders in the streambed ruined us. Some of them stood up to ten feet in height, requiring us to help each other up and over or, groping in the dark, simply to find a way by climbing around. At that pace, we had no chance of making it to our ambush site in one night. The streambed had not looked so demanding when I viewed it from the air—boulders appeared smaller from two thousand feet above.

Major Quesada was good about it, but I could see he and his men were knackered, and time was not on our side. We quickly determined our exact location, plotted a direction to the road at its closest point to us, and declared the mountain the winner.

I could not see his grin clearly in the dark, but Rich gave off a triumphant air as he whispered, "Longer is faster, shorter is slower."

I sighed and mumbled, "Okay, okay. So much for the shortcut. Take us to the road."

We angled off the mountain toward the road. In the dark with the thick jungle, it was no easy maneuver, but we stumbled upon a decent path that led down in the right direction, and we met the road at about one in the morning. Once on the road, we spread out and strode as quickly and quietly as we could. We passed several farmhouses, and a few dogs barked at us, but no lights came on and no one came out. It was cellar-dark, so anyone peeking out would not have seen who or what we were. We stopped once for a short break and stepped off the road. Everyone seemed to be handling the march well, and we soon pressed on.

After rounding a sharp bend in the road, we came upon the turnaround point of the airstrip first, it being farthest away from Cachicoto. There we split up as planned, with the PNP and Fiscal Vargas moving off the road into the bushes to find a hide site from which to observe the turnaround point. If a plane landed, it would taxi to that point to turn around and load up. The PNP would make the arrests. We three DEA agents kept walking down the road toward the touchdown point. At our position, we would serve as rear security in case a threat came from the direction of Cachicoto.

About a hundred yards farther down, we came upon the road crater. It was a real crater, over two feet deep, and it would prevent an airplane from landing. However, snooping around in the bushes off to the side, we discovered several planks hidden in the underbrush. Custom cut to varying lengths and six inches in width, they could easily handle an airplane's weight. We had found the answer to the puzzle. The traffickers simply planked over the crater for a landing and then dismantled the planks to leave the crater intact.

We continued on to a spot we guessed to be the touchdown point, crept about fifty yards into the thick brush, and lay down to wait. It was four o'clock in the morning; we had walked all night.

We kept watch by turns for an hour while the others dozed, waiting for the coming day. I had the third watch, and right at seven o'clock I heard people walking down the road from the direction of Cachicoto. I poked Rich and Donnie alert, and we low-crawled through bushes closer to the road. It was an army patrol, about ten men. They were armed and walking in a tactical formation, but talking and joking as they passed. They continued walking the road past the turnaround point, past the bend, and out of sight. Was that a regular occurrence, or were they clearing the road for a purpose? Since I did not trust Captain Flores, I had not queried him about the army's local patrolling patterns or revealed any of our plans.

I did not wonder for long. At eight o'clock, more people came down the road from Cachicoto. There were four of them, young men, and they paced in a line abreast. We saw one of the men bend over, pick up a stone, and toss it into the brush as they walked along. Were they grooming the road for an airplane?

A few moments later, although out of our sight, we could hear them talking, obviously stopped on the road. Were they at the crater? I had to find out, so Rich and I low-crawled through the bushes parallel to the road. Donnie stayed behind to watch our backs. We crawled into a position close enough to observe the four men carefully fitting the shaped planks into the crater to cover it. Clever buggers—it was an ingenious deception.

We crawled back to Donnie, and Rich used our small radio to contact Major Quesada and tell him to get ready for action. After the road-clearing crew had finished the crater repair and returned past us toward Cachicoto, I asked Rich to assemble the satellite radio. I called our Tingo base and advised the team what was developing, but asked them not to alert Commandante Diaz. I knew Major Quesada did not have a radio strong enough to reach the PNP base, and I wanted to keep a lid on the news, just in case.

I could not believe our luck—we may have arrived just in time to catch a plane on our first day. We lay down again, having no trouble staying awake.

When the airplane suddenly landed at eleven thirty, our first warning was the noise of the reverse-thrust propeller as it put down just in front of us. We had not heard it coming. I had imagined a plane landing on that road would have at least made one pass before landing, just to check out the situation. Obviously, the pilot was in radio contact with someone on the ground, had been there before, and knew the road.

The plane taxied toward the turnaround point as we crept out to the road. There, Rich and I lay down on the edge facing the aircraft just as it was turning around. Donnie lay down facing toward Cachicoto—we did not want any surprises from behind.

The plane throttled down but did not shut down. A pickup truck and several motorcycles drove to it from around the bend in the road. Each motorcycle carried two people, while a lone driver sat in the truck. The truck was loaded with black plastic-covered cocaine bundles. The men on the motorcycles parked close to the plane and started unloading the truck and placing the bundles in the airplane.

A man was pushing the second bundle through the aircraft doorway when the shooting started. Rich earlier had trained the Colt automatic rifle with the one-hundred-round drum magazine at the airplane. I carried the 40mm grenade launcher. At the sound of PNP gunfire, Rich fired off a short burst at the plane. I could see the pilot inside, and he started to accelerate the engine.

I had noticed from a tracer round that Rich's burst had been a couple of feet high (every fifth round in the drum magazine was tracer). I told him to drop it down two feet. He did so and fired again. A tracer round must have hit the wing tank because the plane suddenly flared and then went up like a Roman candle. The PNP continued their shooting as the fuel tank exploded with a loud whoosh. Suddenly, behind me Donnie opened up and began firing. He yelled out he had seen two men coming toward us. I turned and saw no one; they had gone to ground.

Casting a look back to the burning aircraft, I caught a glimpse of one of the loaders running for his life away from the plane and around the bend in the road. I was worried there may be more traffickers around the bend since they had come from that direction, so I loosed off two grenades from the launcher, aimed to land on the road around the bend about three hundred yards away. The loud explosions of the grenades seemed to heighten the PNP rate of firing.

For all I knew, the army was involved in this too. I kept a close watch on the road and bushes behind the burning plane, but no one appeared. High explosives are quite persuasive, having the ability to take the fight out of anyone. The PNP firing slowed, then stopped. Nothing happened for a moment; we stayed down on the edge of the road and watched the airplane burn.

Then some of the PNP come out on the road. One of them saw us and waved. We got up and went down to join them, walking through the brush and staying off the road.

We arrived at the blazing wreck as the PNP were beginning to take account. I saw Fiscal Vargas reloading his revolver and wearing a grim face. My hero: he saw plenty of action that day. Two PNP pulled a terrified trafficker out of the bushes. He was unhurt, and someone handcuffed him to one of the motorcycles parked off the road. Three traffickers were lying down, wounded. Two of them had multiple wounds that appeared fatal, while the third had a stomach wound that could turn mortal.

The PNP carried the wounded from the roadside to the motorcycles, where one of the PNP, acting as a medic, attended to their wounds. He started IVs on them and applied dressings.

I had not seen the pilot get out. I found his skeletal remains in the wreckage after the fire receded. In addition, one loader had been in the act of placing a cocaine bundle aboard when the plane's gas tank exploded. I found his body, burned beyond recognition, lying beside the wreckage. We found one other dead loader in the bushes. Shot in the opening volley, he had tried to crawl away.

As we sorted out the mess and took stock, Rich got the satellite radio going. I called Tingo and notified our team what had happened, asking them to advise Commandante Diaz and to get our Hueys out to us as soon as possible, as we had wounded crooks.

I then called DEA headquarters in the United States to advise them what had transpired. The reception was clear. I found it remarkable that I could talk to someone sitting at a desk in Washington while standing next to a smoldering airplane in the Peruvian jungle.

Adding the two mostly-burned cocaine bundles that we fished out of the burning plane, we had seized five hundred kilograms of cocaine base. Seven traffickers had driven up to meet the pilot, and one got away. Although the PNP seized four AK-47 rifles, it appeared none of the traffickers got a shot off.

While we were waiting for our Hueys to show up, a Peruvian army helicopter flew in. The word was out on our ambush, and we were the center of attention in the region. I reported to the colonel on board about the army patrol we had watched that morning. He said he knew nothing about it but would check it out. I would have liked to have been a Spanish-speaking fly on the wall when the colonel talked with Captain Flores. I knew he was in for some direct questioning. No surprise to me, I never heard any more on the subject.

Our Hueys did not arrive for over three hours. Thankfully, none of the good guys were in need of medical attention. In the interim, the PNP interrogated the one conscious and unhurt trafficker. He and all the others were local Cachicoto men and had spent the night at a cocaine lab getting the bundles ready for the plane. The pilot was someone they knew well, who made the trip from Colombia to Cachicoto a few times monthly. His brother was also a pilot for the Cachicoto runs.

The PNP took the time to salvage the valuable propeller blades off the burned plane, a Cessna 206. The Hueys had brought us some thermite grenades, and I put two on the engine block. Only the burned engine and tail section remained of the aircraft. The thermite burned hot enough to disable the engine, turning it into scrap iron. With the Hueys' arrival, we loaded up, flew off, and left the burned wreck lying on the road.

I saw Commandante Diaz that evening and he was positively jubilant, greeting me with a bear hug. I could see he was mentally packing his bags for a posting in Lima, because capturing a plane was a huge accomplishment. His only question to me, sadly, was why we had to burn it up—delivering an airplane intact to the PNP would have made him a star. I was quite sure Major Quesada got a chewing out for not saving the plane. How could we explain what happened to someone that ignorant?

The following day we had a celebratory dinner at the PNP base. We had a good time and everyone seemed happy—there's nothing like a victory. Yet, during a serious moment, Major Quesada and two other PNP of the ambush team got me in a corner and revealed how they really felt. They had been out there in a gunfight—they had been scared and afraid to die. They had families to support and lives to live, and they had put those lives on the line for what they felt was an American problem: cocaine. It was not their job to die for America's predicament.

What could I say to make them feel better? I knew they were feeling the effects of post-traumatic stress, heartened by alcohol, so I did not get into it much with them. I muttered something about how our respective countries must call police officers to duty, however miserable or dangerous it may be. I thanked them for being there and doing their duty. It was weak, I know, but I did acknowledge their sense of duty and effort, and in the end that is all any of us should expect to receive.

As I hoped, our success at Cachicoto had an immediate impact on flights from Colombia. The PNP pajaritos did not pick up any radio traffic from Colombian airplanes coming in to the UHV for several days; that indicated the Colombian traffickers were trying to address our new tactics.

Unfortunately, we did not have the resources to conduct airstrip ambushes on a continuing basis. Our operations could only be sporadic at best. As a further hindrance, some of the illegal airstrips were located too close to villages for us to easily sneak into position and remain hidden until an airplane arrived. The traffickers would soon figure things out and resume flying—but I doubted anyone would be flying into Cachicoto anytime soon.

We only had a few days left in Peru. Although we had faced many support problems not under our direct control—specifically with our Huey and CASA support—we left on a high note. Despite our limitations and the embassy restrictions placed on us, it had been an interesting three months. Although I was homesick, I looked forward to my next deployment in September.

Colombian coke plane burning on the road, June 1994.

Aftermath of airplane ambush, Cachicoto, Peru, June 1994.

Our team in Peru, October 1994. I'm fifth from the left.

23

Death Knell

As soon as we returned to DEA headquarters, I met with the Snowcap people and gave an operational report on our activities. I also prepared for my introductory meeting with the administrator, since he wanted to get a report from me in person.

I arrived at his office at the appointed time. After a thirty-minute wait, his assistant showed me in. He did not get up to shake my hand, and he did not ask me to sit down. Over in the corner sat Llewellyn, whom I had met in Peru in May. He never said a word. The administrator's crisp voice and clipped delivery had all the warmth of a Vermont granite wall. In keeping with his standards, I withheld any warmth from my replies, realizing it was not required.

I told the administrator the story of the airplane ambush and all that happened there. He listened to me without comment, and at the end quietly said, "I did not know we were doing that kind of stuff in Peru." He went on, "The Peruvian police should be doing that, not us; we should be seizing cocaine here in the States. Let Peru handle its cocaine situation and we will handle ours."

I should have kept my mouth shut, but I did not. I gave him a quick rundown of why I believed Snowcap was valuable. I knew if DEA were not there, the PNP would not venture outside their bases. I added that in three months in Peru, ten of us DEA agents had seized almost one and a half tons of cocaine, arrested thirty-two traffickers, and seized an airplane (burned though it was).

I thought, but did not say, "Try matching those numbers in the States."

While awaiting my next deployment to Peru, I spent three months in DEA headquarters assisting in the attempt to restructure Snowcap. The special agents in charge of the domestic field divisions had complained continually and with good reason. Snowcap drained agents from their offices, leaving them shorthanded. Furthermore, the administrator had made it clear that he wanted to concentrate on fighting drug trafficking in the United States.

Smelling blood in the water, the DEA special agents in charge mounted an all-out assault on Snowcap. They were just trying to protect their empires. Inside Snowcap, we formulated a proposal to create another division dedicated to Snowcap. The strategy called for permanently assigning Snowcap volunteers for two years at the DEA Academy in Quantico. We informally contacted some special agents about the plan, and they seemed agreeable since they would not lose any agents in the deal.

Sadly, it was not to be. A tragedy in Peru spelled the end of Snowcap.

Frank Fernandez and his team had replaced my team. On August 27, Fernandez, along with two of his agents and two DEA agent pilots, were flying the CASA in the UHV, looking for lab sites. They flew up a box canyon and crashed while trying to get out. The accident killed all five DEA agents.

DEA has suffered agent losses dating back to 1921, almost sixty lives, but never had so many died on a single day. Such a large toll was a major blow to our agency. The air crash would soon usher out Snowcap—it was the justification the administrator needed.

I returned to Lima on September 25 with a new volunteer team and a new set of orders. None of the members of my first team were available, the list of candidates was limited, and so I took what I could get. It turned out I was the best Spanish speaker on the team, and that limitation served to set the tone of the deployment.

Prior to our departure from Andrews Air Force Base in Washington, the DEA deputy administrator took me aside and told me to go to Peru, relax, and keep a low profile—the political situation was touchy, and mine was to be the last Snowcap deployment.

I arrived determined to do something constructive while in Peru, but first I had some sobering meetings at the embassy. I felt shackled after hearing my list of limitations. The PNP pilots were on strike (police on strike?) and I would have no Hueys for the next five weeks. The replacement CASA was strictly for taxi duty and unavailable for any surveillance flights, a reaction to the August crash. That was problematic since the PNP did not want to assault a target if we could not conduct preraid overflights. They did not want to fly into a target blindly, and I didn't either.

The next bit of good news was that Commandante Diaz was still languishing in Tingo Maria despite his airplane trophy. He had appeased that disappointment by taking up with a woman cocaine trafficker in Tingo and was now driving her shiny red BMW around town.

I jokingly asked the chief embassy official why we had bothered to come. He told me, and was serious about it, that they only really needed us to go out and dismantle the base at Santa Lucia. I understood then that we were not welcome in Peru.

Tingo Maria was out for us, since Commandante Diaz was obviously trafficker-persuaded, so I sat in Tarapoto for a few days to take stock. Someone mentioned the Peruvian army, so I met with the colonel, whom I had previously encountered at Cachicoto during our airplane ambush. We discussed working together. Surprisingly, when I had brought that possibility up at the embassy, I had received approval to cooperate with the army. Since the Sendero Luminoso was the colonel's primary target, and they were heavily involved in cocaine trafficking, I thought he might be interested.

He seemed enthusiastic and offered to make soldiers and helicopters accessible to us. We could go along as observers on cocaine raids that were based on our information. He asked to use our old Hueys, saying his equally aged Russian-made Hind helicopters were even worse, but he insisted the PNP could not join us. I told him we needed the PNP to go with us, but he adamantly refused to work with the PNP, so that was a deal breaker.

Meanwhile, informants continued to come in with information. As we waited for the PNP pilots to get back to work, I gave the army information on three locations, which they raided without our company. All three raids were successful, and they seized over one ton of cocaine and arrested seventeen traffickers. I knew the army's main objective was to crush the Sendero Luminoso, but if they were willing to seize cocaine in accomplishing that goal, I was all for it. Since cocaine trafficking accounted for most Sendero revenue, our efforts with the army seemed beneficial for both of us.

But the time passed and our tour drew to a close. It had been trying. I was weary from my continuing problems with the embassy over the Hueys and our many restrictions. My physical condition didn't help matters. I had contracted hookworms early in the deployment and was ailing for a month before I could get it diagnosed and treated.

I also had some problems with the team. Our unhappy situation under embassy restrictions and the specter of Snowcap's end added to the team's restlessness. My assistant team leader turned out to be immature and lazy. Only two members had deployed with Snowcap before, and none seemed ready to stand up and be a leader. We based ourselves in Tarapoto and Pucallpa, having closed down Santa Lucia, and I spent an inordinate amount of time away in Lima—fighting with the embassy—so the new agents did not have the daily guidance they needed.

Early in the deployment, one agent in Pucallpa broke the rule against leaving the hotel alone. The guards caught him trying to sneak back in over the wall at three in the morning. I had zero tolerance for safety violations, and I sent him home for that infraction. Better to kick him home than having to make a phone call to his wife explaining his death or kidnaping by the Senderos.

Without question, Operation Snowcap appeared successful. Nonetheless, it was not significant. During Snowcap's operational period from 1987 to 1994, DEA and host-nation police seized and destroyed hundreds of tons of cocaine—cocaine that never entered the United States. Yet the supply of cocaine to the United States remained constant during that time. Even so, I felt our efforts were valuable, despite the dangers we faced.

Bureaucratic fetters were responsible for most of Snowcap's problems, especially regarding the Hueys. As if the constant Huey breakdowns were not enough, the embassy sometimes held back our worn-out, insufficient Hueys and used them in administrative or training functions while we sat.

Since Snowcap only performed in foreign countries, the State Department was in charge of operations. It controlled the funds and the helicopters. An embassy representative in Lima administered our operational support, and as often as not, he and I differed as to our main objectives and priorities. The embassy held it was keeping diplomatic equilibrium and viewing the "big picture," while DEA agents in Snowcap had a narrow view and only thought about our next big raid on a laboratory.

Well, the embassy had it almost right. I thought the purpose of Snowcap was to help the local police make arrests and seize cocaine, not worry about politics. Nevertheless, as someone in the embassy once told me, "If you want to play in my country, you will play by my rules."

After I had returned to headquarters from my first deployment, and before I knew Snowcap was doomed, I wrote a detailed memorandum analyzing the Peru situation from my point of view. I put down my ideas about how Snowcap could succeed in its mission—suppressing the cocaine flow into the United States.

The main thrust of that message was the need for more teams in Peru and more and better helicopters. I recommended inserting two teams simultaneously into the UHV, along with fourteen Blackhawk helicopters and two CASAs. They would concentrate on setting ambushes on the airstrips. I maintained that a significant reduction in cocaine delivered to Colombia, and eventually the United States, could occur within six months.

The memorandum went nowhere. I think the idea was sound; the timing was not. The administrator would have nothing to do with Snowcap.

Having served two deployments in Peru, my experience evoked some parallels between the managements of Operation Snowcap and the Vietnam War. When I was in Vietnam, I spent little time moralizing the war, usually not looking beyond the protective wire of our camp. Twenty-five years later in Peru I sensed déjà vu: I had been down those trails before, already experienced those restrictions. I thought perhaps half-hearted, part-time efforts were becoming an American tradition.

Both endeavors started with the objective to assist the host country and train it to fight its particular problems on its own. However, in both those theaters, the United States started small and then escalated its involvement until it became the major force fighting the problem. The host country was never able to stand on its own.

Likewise, both undertakings presented lack of direction, determination, strategy, and, most of all, will. Our ability to win was there, but our half-measured, arbitrary efforts could not execute. That was the crux of the failures.

It was not as if the United States was forcing itself on these countries—they invited the Americans in to help. Both times, we decided we had had enough. In South America, we reached our goals, so we declared victory for Snowcap and went home.

The parallels between Vietnam and Peru diverged at one major point. In Vietnam, our limited, unsuccessful efforts did not have a direct impact on the United States' safety. Our similarly limited, unsuccessful efforts in Peru allowed the flow of cocaine to continue undiminished—a direct impact on our safety.

Mindful of that, I would offer a message for any future operations such as Snowcap: be prepared to do whatever it takes. Do it right or do not do it.

PART FIVE

Inside the Beltway

24

Bosnia

The DEA administrator walked up to the podium, voiced a few terse words of greeting, and then got right to it. "Congress dictates that DEA keep a presence in foreign countries. But if I had my way, all of you would be back working in the United States, in places such as Des Moines, Iowa, or Omaha, Nebraska."

It was our annual country attaché conference, held at DEA headquarters. The heads of all our foreign offices were present, many of them to meet the administrator for the first time. We didn't bother listening much to anything else he may have expressed. His opening statement had said it all.

I noticed a few in the audience looking to the people beside them, giving each other a look that asked, *Who is this guy? Is he serious?* In two short sentences he had effectively invalidated the efforts of all those agents working in foreign countries—about 10 percent of DEA's force. It was unsettling, since foreign operations were a major element of DEA's mission statement.

It sounded as if the administrator wanted to toss DEA's foreign operations plan into a roadside ditch on his way to Des Moines and Omaha. No use taking the fight to the enemy at the source countries; instead, we should hunker behind our barriers and restrict the hunt to our cities. Except that we didn't have any meaningful barriers. The United States had no chance of keeping illegal drugs out.

So much for the pep talk.

Housed in twin, black, tower buildings, DEA headquarters is located in Arlington, Virginia. Directly north, and separated from headquarters by I-395, the Pentagon sprawls alongside the Potomac River. After Operation Snowcap was thrown on the compost pile, I remained in the foreign operations department and served as the chief of the Europe, Middle East, and Africa section. In that calling I managed the operations of twenty-six offices scattered around a geographic area ranging from Canada east to India and from Russia south to South Africa. Our offices in Pakistan and Turkey were operational case makers. Some of the European offices were situated in drug transit countries. Agents in other offices danced on the diplomatic cocktail circuit and served generally as liaisons.

Most supervisory special agents were required to complete an assignment at headquarters. They came in hoping to get one of the few interesting jobs available, punch their tickets, and get back out to the field as soon as possible. Doing well and completing a successful headquarters tour helped them garner an office of their choosing later on. Those who failed to impress their superiors could find themselves sent to an obscure office in some slag heap city. Or, worse yet, they sometimes received a sentence to perpetual duty at headquarters, working in a coal-pit unit dedicated to administrative duties both mundane and pointless.

Though there were exceptions, from an agent's perspective one's geographic location dictated the prestige and desirability of the position. Working in foreign operations, I was among the high fliers on the eleventh floor, topped only by the bosses riding the thermals on twelve. Located in the lower pastures on the first floor was the Office of Security Programs, grazing area for the walking dead.

But not everyone looked to avoid duty at headquarters. Some agents arrived unbidden, hoping to climb that ladder for quick advancement. Climbers are found in all walks of life, and they're attracted to office politics like moths to flame. I had seen much of it before, starting in the army and continuing since then. But coming to headquarters introduced me to office power politics at a new level. Working inside the Beltway exposed everyone to a different atmosphere, heightened and potent. I observed changes in people I thought I knew—changes for the worse. I found that sucking up, backstabbing, and stealing other's ideas were talents taken too lightly, considering how well they worked.

While headquarters had its fair share of lurkers, shirkers, strivers, and those whose careers were on death watch, it also housed some of DEA's finest. Headquarters served as the stable for those being groomed for the bright lights on the top floor. But, while many were called, few were chosen. It was there that I met many of the best agents DEA had to offer. In headquarters, I served under the most able leaders I was to meet in DEA, starting with my first supervisor in foreign operations. In retrospect, I can say that I never had a truly good supervisor while serving in the field, one whom I respected above half, whereas at headquarters I never had a bad one.

Almost all of the federal law enforcement agencies were headquartered inside the Beltway. That proximity to the flagpoles of Capitol Hill, the White House, and the Department of Justice artificially elevated every agency's daily problems and concerns. Ordinary assignments and requests somehow became self-inflicted emergencies. Since we all received our operating money from Congress, all agencies were quick to please it. Constant requests for a study on this, a reply to that, and, by the way, have it done by close of business today, became our daily gruel. I often had to contact an overseas office, usually during their nighttime, and lay on an immediate task on behalf of some congressional inquiry.

These crises came with regularity, like waves washing ashore. At least our predicaments were evenly spaced—Mondays, Wednesdays and Fridays on a consistent basis. Naturally, the rare days that gave us calm, flat seas were disquieting and always drew our attention. When and from what direction would the next one crash ashore?

As one might guess, headquarters work was stressful and demanded long hours. I often came in on Sundays to catch up because Monday always dawned with new, urgent issues.

It was on such a Monday morning in late 1996 when the deputy administrator called me to his office. I took the stairs up one floor and was ushered into his office. We both stood, looking out his floor-to-ceiling windows over the highway to the Pentagon, with Washington spread out just across the Potomac.

We had known each other for fifteen years, so it was a relaxed meeting. The deputy was an astute seeker, and his ascension up the DEA ladder had been based on experience and expertise. As far as I knew, he had never climbed on someone's back to reach the next rung.

He wasted no time on meaningless chatter. "Mark, tell me what you know about Bosnia."

"Just what I have read," I responded slowly, trying to recall what I did know and to figure out where his question was going. "Bosnia was part of Yugoslavia and went through a civil war after the breakup. That ended about a year ago, and the country is divided into three ethnic regions. Of course, they're still not getting along, so NATO and the United States have troops there to keep the peace. Our Vienna office has responsibility for reporting on Bosnia, but since a war has been raging, we don't hear any news on narcotics activity."

He nodded, not showing whether he knew more about it than I did.

"Well, read up on it today because tomorrow you're representing DEA at a meeting over at the Department of Justice. The meeting is at Janine Gorsham's office at ten o'clock. I don't have all the details, but it concerns war criminals in Bosnia. I want you to go because your military and Snowcap experience fit this requirement. Besides, Bosnia is in your area."

The next morning I took the Metro's yellow line from Pentagon City to the archives station and walked a block to the main Justice building on Pennsylvania Avenue. I found the office of Deputy Attorney General Janine Gorsham on the first floor a few minutes before ten.

Joining me for the meeting were two FBI agents, Jay Mueller and Harry Wayans, along with Frank Kearney, a US Marshal. Gorsham's aide chaired the short meeting and tasked us with traveling to Stuttgart, Germany, to meet with the US Army and look into the practicality of arresting Serbian war criminals in Bosnia. After the army briefings in Germany, we would travel to Bosnia to get a firsthand look at the situation. Our reports were due back to Justice a week later.

An overnight flight from Washington landed the four of us at Stuttgart. Army representatives met us at the airport and drove us directly to the army base, home of the European command. After a hurried lunch, they ushered us to a conference room. They seated us on the front row; after all, the briefing was for us. About fifteen others joined us—horse holders, note takers, and the idle curious. We introduced ourselves around, shook hands, and promptly forgot everyone.

Colonel Mathers was our briefer. He was a practiced speaker and delivered a concise, informative story.

The Balkans are tucked into an area of southeastern Europe, situated at a major crossroads between mainland Europe and Asia. The region's mountains and violent history have produced the diverse character and fragmentation found there today. For many years after World War II, this patchwork of countries was held together under the umbrella of a single state, Yugoslavia. Following the death of its postwar leader, Marshal Tito, in 1980, Yugoslavia started falling apart.

By 1990, after ten years of internal decay, Yugoslavia's six mainly ethnic republics declared their independence one by one. All well and good, except that Bosnia was the only Yugoslav republic with a mixed-ethnic population. Bosniak Muslims constituted 45 percent of the population, Orthodox Serbs constituted 35 percent, and Catholic Croats the remainder—and they did not agree on anything.

A civil war erupted, a vicious war that would last almost four years. Pogroms occurred throughout Bosnia, and all interethnic trust dissolved. The three ethnic groups banded in separate enclaves for protection, and the killing began. I remembered it well, since my new wife and I had hosted a high school exchange student in 1991, a girl from Sarajevo. A Serb, her father had some position in the government. She had to return home abruptly just before the shooting started in early 1992.

The Serbs were depicted as the perpetrators of all atrocities, but Croats and Muslim Bosniaks got in a few licks too. However, the Serbs managed to obtain most of the weaponry, with which they soon controlled the battlefields and much of the territory. They indiscriminately shelled towns and cities, killing thousands of Muslim Bosniaks. The siege of Sarajevo would come to represent the conflict.

Sarajevo, a beautiful, ancient city surrounded by mountains, dates back to the thirteenth century. It had always existed at a religious crossroad—Muslims to the south (Bosniaks), Orthodox to the north (Serbs), and Catholics to the west (Croatians). Sarajevo's first claim to fame occurred in 1914 when a Serbian anarchist assassinated an Austrian archduke, which led to World War I. Sarajevo was showcased in 1984 as the site of the Winter Olympic Games.

The siege began when Serb forces encircled Sarajevo with a force of fifteen thousand men stationed in the surrounding hills. They rained heavy fire down, bringing ash and ruin on the city. The Bosniaks inside were poorly armed and unable to break the siege. It became the longest siege of a capital city in modern warfare, lasting almost four years. Virtually all the buildings in Sarajevo suffered some degree of damage, and thirty-five thousand were completely destroyed. Uncounted thousands of people were killed and wounded. I would get a chance to view much of that damage.

NATO forces became involved in the conflict, establishing checkpoints and refugee safe havens in several areas. Their presence didn't stop the killing. NATO troops came under fire from Serb forces repeatedly, and only intervention by NATO air strikes helped hold the Serbs at bay. One US F-16 was shot down by a Serb missile in June 1995. The pilot, a nephew of an agent in our office at DEA headquarters, was rescued a few days later by a US Marine contingent launched from a supporting aircraft carrier in the Adriatic Sea. NATO air support was instrumental in working out a peace accord in December 1995.

As part of the deal, Bosnia was divided into a Bosniak-Croat region surrounded in a horseshoe-shape by a Serbian region. The entire country was subjected to the presence of a peacekeeping force. The NATO military force, representing several countries, was divided into three spheres of responsibility administered by Great Britain, France, and the United States.

Reportedly, the number of people killed countrywide amounted to around one hundred thousand, with another two million people displaced, making the Bosnian conflict the most devastating European warfare since the end of World War II. Uncountable atrocities occurred, with Serbs responsible for about 90 percent of them. Volumes of evidence and testimony were obtained from survivors and witnesses. The International

Criminal Tribunal for the former Yugoslavia, working from The Hague, indicted seventy-four people suspected of committing war crimes in Bosnia. Sixty-six of them were still at large as of 1996, several living openly in the Serb region of Bosnia.

Colonel Mathers arrived at the purpose of the history lesson. It seemed no organization or agency was actively pursuing those sixty-six indicted for war crimes. Although the UN naively expected the warring factions to make arrests, that was not going to happen. If Bosniak police tried to arrest a Serb suspect, the war would restart in a flash. NATO military forces were precluded from active involvement in civil issues, in order not to jeopardize their appearance of neutrality. They patrolled in their armored vehicles only as a show of force to keep the combatants separated.

The tribunal at The Hague wanted something done about bringing in those charged. The US military was hoping for Department of Justice agents such as us to make the arrests, with the military's help as needed. Reportedly, at least six of those charged were known to reside in the US sector. The British and French sectors of Bosnia were evidently also holding meetings like ours, all at the tribunal's behest. The war had been officially over for a year, and the smoke had cleared; it was time to arrest the war criminals.

A military Lear jet flew us to Sarajevo the next morning. With us was Brigadier General Hampton, our guide and liaison for the trip. It was a short flight over the Alps. Looking out the window, I noticed Sarajevo was situated in a natural bowl with high ground ringing the city. As we descended, I was able to observe the devastation. I couldn't believe it. Sarajevo was a modern city shattered by warfare. The runway was operational, showing many signs of patchwork, but the terminal was a framework of destruction—windows blown out, shell-holed walls, and two jetways turned to twisted metal wreckage. We parked out on the runway, not a problem since the airport was closed for commercial business, and an embassy car drove out to meet us.

We began our assessment with a tour of the area. They wanted us to get a feel for the conflict and an understanding of what had occurred countrywide, particularly in Sarajevo, the eye of the storm. At first look, the conflict seemed complex, a clash of ancient Balkan ethnic and religious hatreds colliding at political fault lines. But after viewing the destroyed buildings at street level and looking down upon them from former Serbian gun positions high above the city, it seemed simpler. Bosniaks had been trapped inside the city; Serbians above with guns had shot at them.

The Holiday Inn had housed all the foreign press corps covering the war, and we stayed there as well. It still bore bullet scars and shell holes. A nearby park had a wrought-iron fence around it. I noticed several bullet holes in the fence's bars, demonstrating the amount of fire that had come down. Some of the trees bore bullet holes too, their trunks trying, but as yet unable, to grow bark over the scars. We drove and walked around several parts of the city, just looking, and I didn't see a single structure that had escaped war damage.

I was a war veteran and had seen combat, but never in a city, especially a city that had suffered through a lengthy siege. The experience was unforgettable.

Destroyed apartment building in Sarajevo, March 1996.

Assessing the situation in Sarajevo, March 1996. I'm standing third from the right.

After that sobering look at Sarajevo, General Hampton took us upcountry to view the proposed operational area. An army helicopter flew us north about eighty miles to Tuzla, home of the US Army garrison in Bosnia. Arriving in time for lunch, we joined the soldiers in their huge mess hall. Having been away from the army for over twenty-five years, I was surprised by the large number of women soldiers. General Hampton mentioned that women made up almost 20 percent of the army. The army had changed, but the lousy chow had not.

We rode in official UN vehicles thirty miles north to Brcko, located in Serbian territory. Brcko was a small Bosnia town situated on the Sava River. Just across the river was Croatia. Brcko was placed at the top of the arch, the toe of the horseshoe-shaped Serb sphere of influence. It served as the Serbs' main transportation and communication hub between the two sides of its horseshoe. It wasn't safe for Serbs to travel cross-country directly; they navigated by staying within their own ethnic territory.

Brcko could have been any rural town in America except for the unique Balkan-European style of the houses. Small, two-story homes with yards and vegetable gardens were the order of the day. We drove down several streets, actually passing the home of one suspect. We took notice of the roads, intersections, and cleared areas that could be used as improvised helicopter landing zones, as well as the likely avenues to get in and get away from the houses—a military-style reconnaissance.

A US special forces team was staying in a house near the edge of town. They were not in uniform, supposedly operating incognito, but everyone in town knew what they were. They kept a low profile while they tried to get close to the populace. A few of them spoke Serbo-Croatian and that helped some, but the locals were Serbs, and they felt Americans supported the Bosniaks.

Our military boys knew that the two suspects living in town were looked upon with respect by the townspeople, and they knew that both suspects, who had been Serb leaders during the war, had some subordinates living near their homes. The special forces sergeant who briefed us said that getting into a house to make an arrest could be done, but getting away without a fight would be hard to accomplish.

We had seen enough. On returning to Tuzla, the chopper flew us back to Sarajevo and the Holiday Inn.

The next morning it was back to Stuttgart for another briefing session. This was a review of what we had observed and deduced, including the military's take on the problem. They proposed that a team of federal agents drive up to each house in the dark of night to make a forced entry and grab the suspect. After dragging him to a waiting vehicle, it would be off to the nearest landing zone for pickup by chopper. Following a short flight to Tuzla and a rendezvous with a waiting C-130 cargo plane, morning would find them in jail at The Hague.

What they proposed was a direct military-style mission, except that federal agents, not soldiers, would form the sharp end of the stick. Besides lots of luck, the operation would require a complex command and control arrangement throughout, and mixing civilian and military cells would likely weaken the plan.

We in the assessment team had earlier discussed the situation among ourselves. It was obvious that the military did not want to be on point in this operation. They were averse to getting the army bogged down in a skirmish in Bosnia. The military was willing to handle the logistics and support, but the Department of Justice would be out front.

We could see the military's point. There was no future in America getting too involved in a European conflict, especially one in the Balkans, Europe's political version of the La Brea tar pits. As a Vietnam veteran, I didn't want to see America again take on a mission with no clear limits. While each of us on the team would each write an assessment report to our own agency, we were in complete accord: let the military do it all. And that was what we did.

A few months later, the British military took a run at making an arrest in their sector. Naturally, they got into a firefight while entering the house and had to shoot their way out. Who needed that?

It took several years for the UN to round up their suspects, and not all were found, but the United States managed to stay out of the limelight of actively arresting war criminals in Bosnia. It was fortunate I did not become further entangled in Bosnian issues, because something much more important to DEA, and to me, occurred in one of my foreign areas of responsibility soon after my excursion to Sarajevo.

25

Ayyaz

That April night in 1997 was warm, quiet, and calm in Islamabad. By eleven o'clock, residents in the working-class neighborhoods of Pakistan's capital city had settled down for the night.

Then a one-block area of a neighborhood lost its electric service. All lights, and telephones too, were out. Several darkened cars converged on one house. Men in military-looking uniforms rushed into the house and dragged a man from his bed. He was last seen by neighbors being hustled into a car and driven off. Then the lights came back on.

Agent Tom Charlier, head of DEA in Pakistan, soon received a late-night call from an anxious DEA employee's wife. Her husband, Ayyaz Baluch, had disappeared.

Ayyaz Baluch, a stocky, caring man with a gift for languages, joined DEA in 1985. The son of a Pakistani police commander, Ayyaz was a former police officer himself. He stayed busy translating the DEA agents' manual into the Urdu language and making it available to the Pakistani ANF (Anti-Narcotics Force), DEA's counterpart police force in Pakistan. Ayyaz assisted in training courses presented to ANF by DEA and spoke Punjabi, English, Arabic, and Urdu. He soon became a valuable asset to DEA.

Perhaps his greatest worth to DEA, however, was his ability to roam about the countryside recruiting informants, who gave valuable information concerning drug trafficking. Ayyaz was from Baluchistan, a province of parochial, fiercely independent tribes that stretches over the mountains and desert along Pakistan's southwestern borders with Afghanistan and Iran. Ayyaz's efforts earned him a reputation as a resourceful, unfailingly loyal agent. His knowledge and cunning were vital in his home province, home to some of the area's biggest heroin traffickers.

One noteworthy exploit involved Ayyaz traveling undercover to a large heroin laboratory located inside a guarded compound in Afghanistan. He boldly walked around taking photos with a camera hidden in his shoulder bag. That's brass.

Ayyaz's talents extended beyond narcotics cases. He was instrumental in the investigation to find and arrest Ramzi Yousef, wanted as one of the bombers in the attack on the World Trade Center in early 1993 and as the ringleader of the Bojinka Plot, a 1995 plan to explode bombs on several planes flying from Asia to the United States. Ayyaz also had a hand in helping to hunt for Aimal Kasi, the attacker accused of killing two CIA employees in Langley, Virginia, in early 1993.

That skill and reputation brought him to the attention of Pakistan's Inter-Services Intelligence Directorate (ISID). A military intelligence organization, the ISID worked intimately with the CIA during the Soviet occupation of Afghanistan and grew to be a power unto itself. At times, elements of the service had been accused of protecting heroin traffickers. Now, it was considered supportive of the Islamic Taliban government in Afghanistan.

DEA's heroin-control programs in Pakistan had been undertaken in adversity. About 20 percent of the heroin sold in America at that time was coming out of Pakistan, making it an important strategic post. DEA's counterpart in Pakistan, the ANF, listed a force of three thousand agents, but Tom Charlier had once quipped that ANF's force actually numbered one thousand agents supported by two thousand tea wallahs (servers). He was joking, but I got the idea, and understood why DEA's relationship with ANF was strained—ANF's lack of action and its corruption.

Meanwhile, DEA's Pakistani employees such as Ayyaz were taking care of business, showing up the ANF and basically embarrassing them. When DEA presented information to senior Pakistani officials about a corrupt ANF officer's activities with heroin smugglers in Quetta, military officers in the ANF and the ISID became convinced that Ayyaz was the source of the allegations. They complained openly that he was unreliable. Yet it wasn't his reliability that bothered them. The ISID and ANF didn't like the idea of Ayyaz running around knowing as much he did. The ISID wanted to determine if he was collecting intelligence on nuclear or military secrets.

What prompted Ayyaz's abduction had begun only a few months before. In early 1997, Major Qasim Khan flew a Pakistani airplane into Dover Air Force Base, Delaware. He was a Pakistani air force pilot coming to the United States to pick up spare airplane parts. He stopped briefly in the base exchange store at Dover and chose something. He also chose not to pay for it and was caught shoplifting by store security. Since he was a foreign military officer, he was allowed to leave, but not before a report of the incident was sent to the Pakistani air force.

Qasim headed to New York for a few days. There was a sizable Pakistani population in New York and he had friends there, along with a cousin, Tahir Khan. Tahir hosted a party attended by several Pakistani expatriates. At the party, Tahir introduced an acquaintance to his cousin Qasim, and their conversation somehow turned to heroin smuggling. In addition to being a pilot and a shoplifter, Qasim was also a heroin trafficker, as was Tahir. Unknown to them, their new friend was not a trafficker; he was an informant for the DEA in Chicago. Thus began a relationship that was short, but had far-reaching consequences.

When Qasim bragged that he was delivering one kilogram of heroin to a buyer in New Jersey, the DEA informant asked Qasim to sell him heroin. The informant claimed he had a buyer in Chicago who wanted two kilograms of pure heroin. Qasim agreed and promised to bring the heroin on his next flight to the United States.

As it turned out, the New Jersey deal fell through, so Qasim gave the heroin to Tahir to deliver to their new friend. Tahir later met with the informant in Chicago and gave the heroin on consignment to the buyer, a DEA undercover agent.

Qasim was grounded upon returning to Pakistan, his superiors having received the report on his shoplifting incident. He was now an embarrassment to the Pakistani air force, so they punished him by making him stay in Pakistan. No more shopping trips to the United States. It was only a minor problem for Qasim's heroin trafficking operation, though. His friend, Farooq, also an air force pilot, was only too happy to step into the vacancy and take over delivery duties.

Qasim, Tahir, and the Chicago informant kept in contact and negotiated for Tahir to make another delivery. But Qasim demanded payment for the consignment kilogram delivered earlier before sending along the new two-kilogram load. The informant complained that the one-kilogram package had been of poor quality and they were having trouble selling it. Qasim agreed to send on another two kilograms after he was paid something. That was when DEA in Chicago asked DEA in Pakistan help out and make a payment to Qasim for them.

I first heard of the case soon after, when Tom Charlier called me from Islamabad on our secure phone and related the details of the case thus far. "Chicago has a buy into Tahir, but they need something on Qasim to tie him in, since he is the real source of the heroin. Qasim is grounded in Pakistan so they can't get at him, but they want us to get a meeting with him, pay him some money owed for the heroin, and get that all on video. Then he will send two more kilograms to the States. We could use one of our investigative aides here in Islamabad to make the payment and get some dialogue tying him in to the Chicago delivery. But there is one problem."

"That all sounds reasonable to me," I said. "What's the problem?"

"Here in Pakistan, the military is the real power, and the air force stands on a high pedestal. If we go to the ANF with this, they'll go crazy. They are powerless against the military, and there is no way they would allow us to involve a pilot in any dope deal. If we share this with them, they'll just grab Qasim and we'll never hear about him again." Tom paused to let that sink in. "Our other option is to cut out the ANF, say nothing, and just do this on our own. After we get Qasim on video talking about the heroin and taking the money, we'll tell the ANF. It'll be too late to bury it, and they'll be forced to do something then."

"You sound hesitant," I said. "What's your concern?"

"My concern is whether we need to SARC this first. I don't want to, but I'm worried the Pakistanis won't be happy if we do this without their knowledge"

SARC was the special activity review committee. DEA had formed it to allow DEA's legal counsel to review potentially controversial or high-risk actions—it existed to prevent operational screwups.

Tom and I discussed it after he spoke with the US ambassador and I conversed with my boss, Mike Howard, chief of foreign operations. In the end, everyone agreed the SARC was not necessary. Our decision seemed reasonable. Qasim had been the one to approach our informant and had already been smuggling heroin into the United States before meeting our informant. He needed to pay for his crime, and we didn't want to allow his escape. If we reported it to the Pakistanis first, they would merely slap his hand and likely ship him out of sight.

Tom's words of concern were prophetic, though. The Pakistanis did take exception to our unilateral activity.

Tom asked Ayyaz to serve undercover as the money man. Ayyaz called Qasim, saying he was a friend of the Chicago informant and had been told to pay Qasim $5,000. They met in the lobby of the Marriott Hotel in Islamabad. Ayyaz was carrying a briefcase and placed it on the coffee table in front of them. The small video camera hidden in the case recorded everything—Qasim's spoken knowledge of the heroin delivery and acceptance of the money from Ayyaz. It was the evidence Chicago needed.

Two days later, Qasim's friend, Farooq, flew to Dover in a Pakistani air force plane carrying two kilograms of heroin. At Penn Station in New York, Farooq met with the Chicago informant, who introduced the buyer, a DEA agent. DEA agents arrested Farooq after he handed over the heroin. They then found Tahir and arrested him for his previous delivery in Chicago.

Following those events, Tom Charlier went to the ANF to advise them what had transpired. They were not pleased. He handed over a copy of Qasim's videotaped interaction with Ayyaz. ANF accepted the information unsmiling. They got right on it, however, and ISID agents soon after arrested Qasim Khan at his home.

Qasim rolled over under ISID grilling. Four days later, the Pakistani embassy in Washington notified our State Department they were taking steps to extradite Farooq back to Pakistan to answer drug trafficking charges. Ayyaz's payment to Qasim had highlighted a problem and sent notice to the air force. It seemed the Pakistanis realized they had a serious problem and had gone into damage-control mode.

Within a week of Tom's disclosure to ANF, ISID carried Ayyaz away from his home. The Pakistani military had delivered notice of its own.

Initially, the US embassy in Pakistan heard nothing about Ayyaz's fate. The day after his arrest, Harry Michaels, who ran the Pakistan desk at the State Department, called me to go with him to the Pakistani embassy in Washington. We met with Ambassador Hafeez, and he gave us the first confirmation on Ayyaz. "Yesterday Ayyaz Baluch was arrested by military authorities in Islamabad."

He was formal, well-spoken, and polished. Listening to him speak, though, I found him a little too smooth. And my reservations were valid. Throughout our relationship, he gave me precious little reason to trust him.

"What are the charges against Ayyaz?" I asked, waiting to hear some trumped-up accusation, but he stonewalled us.

"Ayyaz has not been charged yet. We will have to wait to see what transpires in the investigation."

We found out the military had the highest authority in Pakistan, if it wanted to exercise it, and Ayyaz could be held indefinitely. To help bolster Ayyaz we gave Ambassador Hafeez a copy of Farooq's confession obtained by our DEA office in New York. Farooq had rolled over right after his arrest and had given complete details of Qasim's trafficking activity. We wanted to show the Pakistani authorities that Ayyaz was not the problem; he was only the messenger.

Ambassador Hafeez could see we were concerned. "They are only holding him while they try to find out what type of corruption, if any, there is in the Air Force. Don't worry; no harm will come to him."

But harm did come to Ayyaz. After being handed over to the military jail, Ayyaz was kept shackled in a cell. Qasim Khan, a key witness against him, was in the same jail, occupying a nearby cell. The military held Ayyaz in solitary confinement and out of touch. From ISID, he received their usual interrogatory treatment: no sleep, cattle prods, drug injections, and numerous beatings. Ayyaz suffered severe damage to his back and knees.

Strangely, or perhaps not, their line of questioning dwelled on the premise that the United States was out to destabilize or overthrow the Pakistani government. He was not questioned about heroin trafficking.

His inquisitors promised to stop the pain if he signed a confession. All he needed to do was agree to appear before the press and admit he had been hired by the US ambassador to spy on Pakistan. Or he could say he had been tasked by the United States to seduce Pakistani air force officers to betray Pakistan's nuclear capability. They grilled him to identify any Pakistani leaders who visited the US embassy and may have been recruited as spies. ISID wanted to know what Ayyaz was doing in Quetta and who he knew there.

We didn't yet know about Ayyaz's suffering. He was still incommunicado.

After a week, his wife and father were allowed a brief visit with Ayyaz. DEA was still kept away, but his father told us what Ayyaz was enduring at the jail. At that same time, several newspaper articles appeared in the Pakistani press. They all depicted Ayyaz as an instrument for the United States to entrap a member of Pakistan's military in order to destabilize the government.

We had obviously underestimated the sensitivities of the Pakistani military when we asked Ayyaz to meet with Qasim. Meantime, Ayyaz continued to sit in jail without charges and without legal counsel.

It was time to take off the gloves and put pressure on Pakistan to release Ayyaz. We had by then apologized both to the ANF in Islamabad and to the Pakistani ambassador in Washington. We had furnished complete disclosure of our criminal case against Tahir, Farooq, and Qasim. Farooq had told us Qasim had been selling heroin for the past five years. How did that fact indicate Ayyaz had enticed Qasim?

An unofficial committee, including members from DEA, Justice, State, and the National Security Council, was formed in Washington to brainstorm ideas to diplomatically persuade Pakistan to release Ayyaz. We knew better than to keep asking Pakistan to do the right thing. No; Pakistan was holding us for ransom, and springing Ayyaz was going to cost us.

An act of contrition for our unilateral action would not soothe Pakistan's ruffled feathers or bring back Ayyaz. Our deed had shown the Pakistanis our lack of respect. Left unsaid but understood by all was that this was another case of the United States arrogantly imposing its will. Concessions were in order. Pakistan implicitly demanded restitution for the embarrassment it had suffered when we entangled members of its air force in a drug-trafficking investigation.

Pride was one thing, but money mattered to impoverished Pakistan. The United States, then as now, gave Pakistan hundreds of millions of dollars annually in the form of foreign aid, military training, and other assistance. Our committee tossed around thoughts on making some cuts in those areas. There was also the issue of decertification to consider. That referred to a law requiring the American president to certify that the major drug-producing and drug-transit countries (including Pakistan) had cooperated—taken adequate steps on their own to meet international goals to reduce illegal drugs. If decertified by the president, Pakistan was ineligible for most forms of American assistance.

While we held frequent committee meetings, I conversed almost daily with Tom in Islamabad. We all fought frustration trying to find a way to help Ayyaz. The resentment many of us bore was tempered by concerns among a few that excessive pressure might worsen Pakistani antagonism. American efforts to contain Pakistan's nuclear weapons program and limit its support for the Taliban were mentioned. But, as someone said during one of our meetings, "Let's keep our focus; we owe this man a lot."

State drafted several letters, trying to resolve the issue diplomatically. Pakistani authorities remained silent other than to report the investigation was continuing. They were not budging, but still Ayyaz had not been charged. I was learning a lot about international diplomacy and about what it takes to get our way without giving up too much. In the end, compromise proved to be the water that primed the pump of agreement.

Two weeks after Ayyaz's arrest, Mike Howard and I marched upstairs to brief the administrator. He wanted to know what had happened and what was going on. I knew I was in trouble, because in hindsight, what we had done didn't look good. I had screwed up; I should have run the case through the SARC before we sent Ayyaz in with that money. We had never anticipated the Pakistanis reacting as they had. But, I knew not to evade or offer justifications; the administrator did not countenance excuses.

The moment called for me to fall on my sword. I told him it was my fault. An apology was owed and I gave it. However, I told him I would work on the problem until it was fixed—until Ayyaz was free.

The administrator did his part to help get Pakistan moving. He made a call to the head of US Customs asking for a favor. Starting on May 1, every Pakistan International Airlines flight landing at Kennedy Airport in New York was tossed; that is, combed stem to stern by customs agents. Every Pakistani air force plane and crew coming to the United States was also searched.

On May 20, Pakistan acted and charged Ayyaz with antistate activities for attempting to subvert a Pakistani government official. Conviction carried a possible life sentence. A military court would hear his charges and decide his fate. As for Qasim, he was tried in closed military court, convicted of subversion, and sentenced to life in prison.

DEA obtained a local attorney to represent Ayyaz, and we worked on putting together a defense. On paper, it looked easy. We had unquestionable evidence that Ayyaz acted properly and that Qasim was a known heroin smuggler. We didn't yet realize Ayyaz was headed into a kangaroo court.

Ayyaz's trial began in August. It was a closed court, and Ayyaz was not allowed any defense witnesses. Qasim was the chief witness against Ayyaz and his story placed all blame on Ayyaz, painting himself as a victim. The condemning videotape of Qasim talking to and taking money from Ayyaz was not allowed as evidence. Under cross-examination, Qasim said the videotaped verification was made under duress.

It was apparent Qasim had made a lifesaving arrangement with the air force, because after the trial his sentence was reduced from life to sixteen years. That was a pretty good deal for a day's work.

The court reluctantly allowed Tom Charlier to appear and testify only after rigorous complaining by Ayyaz's attorney. Sitting in the closed court, Tom spoke through an interpreter and gave a statement on behalf of Ayyaz. The members of the court never batted an eye or raised a question. Tom's testimony was held to be not relevant.

At the closing, the court stated that Pakistan's military code made it illegal to induce an otherwise undisposed officer to commit a crime. It then convicted Ayyaz of the charge.

The court's conviction was direct retaliation for the military's embarrassment at the revelation of a Pakistani officer's corruption. It was also a rebuke against DEA for stepping out of line. As a member of the court declared, "The sting operation organized by DEA was by itself a criminal act under Pakistani law."

The conviction also served to punish Ayyaz, albeit not for the crime he was falsely convicted of. He had refused to talk with ISID about the sensitive information entrusted to him, and he had snubbed any ISID bribery possibilities in his Quetta escapades. He had not behaved as ISID felt he should have. So when it came time to set an example, Ayyaz was chosen as a sacrificial lamb. The air force could not bear to have its own people visibly caught up in drug dealing. Putting Ayyaz away saved face.

The court sentenced Ayyaz to a prison term of ten years at hard labor.

While the trial was dragging on through its frequent administrative delays, the Pakistanis played another card in our poker game. Chaudry Sayed worked for the prime minister and was Pakistan's unofficial liaison with the United States concerning the Ayyaz issue. He came to Washington to offer a deal.

Harry Michaels from State and I went to the Pakistani embassy to meet with Sayed and Ambassador Hafeez. Ayyaz had not been convicted yet, so we were cautiously optimistic. Accompanying Sayed was a member of Pakistan's Bureau of Accountability—a bean counter.

Sayed explained that Pakistan was investigating Asif Zardari and Benazir Bhutto for financial crimes. Sayed alleged that Zardari and Bhutto, husband and wife, had secreted over $200 million in Citibank accounts, money obtained through bribes and kickbacks while Bhutto was in power. Bhutto had been thrown out of office several months earlier, in November 1996, and was succeeded by Nawaz Sharif. Sayed wanted the United States to help find and seize the money.

We took notes and, remaining noncommittal, said we would look at it. On our way out, Ambassador Hafeez, oily as ever, remarked, "Work with us on this, and Ayyaz will get out quietly in a month. He's being held just to rub your noses and teach you a lesson about sharing cases."

We announced our news at a meeting of the unofficial committee. Pakistan was blackmailing us, pure and simple. Since the Bhutto/Zardari money case looked interesting, we decided to cooperate with the Pakistani accounting cell, whose ongoing investigation into the funds was at a dead end. We would trace the funds, line up witnesses, but would not freeze or seize the funds—not until Ayyaz was out.

I placed a member of my staff to work with the cell. The money angle was substantial but not critical to Pakistan; to them it was really all about us helping the prime minister's office get dirt on its political rivals. We realized that by working on the case, we were in effect throwing in with Prime Minister Sharif against his rivals.

I met Sayed a few times during the next several months, both in Washington and in Pakistan. He was Prime Minister Sharif's man and tried to explain to me that there were many political concerns with the Ayyaz situation. The prime minister could not just release Ayyaz but had to go through the legal process. Sharif was in a political dogfight, and his concerns were not limited to Zardari and Bhutto. He was also fighting with the courts, the military, and the ISID. Dealing with the Pakistani government was an exercise in Byzantine complexities.

Despite our assistance with the Citibank investigation, Ayyaz remained in prison. We needed to raise the level of our pressure, to reach a higher office. Shortly after Ayyaz's conviction, several of us on the committee briefed Attorney General Janet Reno and Congressman Gilman, chairman of the House International Relations Committee.

Soon after, Gilman visited Pakistan and handed Prime Minister Sharif a letter from Secretary of State Albright. Another formal letter from Congress to Pakistan gave the same message: release Ayyaz or face monetary sanctions. State and the National Security Council were supportive of recommending decertification for Pakistan if the government didn't release Ayyaz. Trying to cover all possible avenues, Ayyaz's attorney also filed an appeal on his conviction with the Pakistan Supreme Court.

By now Ayyaz had been in custody for almost eight months. Tom Charlier arranged for the embassy doctor to examine Ayyaz. He reported Ayyaz was suffering from high blood pressure, back spasms, a knee sprain, and constant pain. He advised hospitalization.

During my trip to Islamabad in December, I managed to visit Ayyaz at prison. He looked worked over and worn; prison had aged him.

We received little encouragement. Our committee heard from Sayed that the prime minister was making a deal for the release for Ayyaz, but that it was going slowly because of politics.

The real picture was starting to come into focus. Ayyaz had become a pawn in the military/ISID power struggle with Prime Minister Sharif. In trying to create a rift in American/Pakistani relations, the military was looking for an opportunity to take over the government, which it would succeed in doing the following year. ISID had revealed that intent when they didn't ask Ayyaz anything about narcotics but kept pushing to get a statement about American involvement in Pakistan's internal affairs.

Ambassador Hafeez contacted us often, pressing for information on the Citibank money. We had shared much information with them already. They knew how much money there was, where it was, and the procedure to get it. But we told him nothing further would happen until Ayyaz was freed.

The Pakistani government was the first to blink in our standoff. The tipping point was a February 1998 meeting between Attorney General Janet Reno and Ambassador Hafeez. Hafeez was told Pakistan would be decertified on March 1 unless Ayyaz was freed.

It was not an idle threat, since Pakistan had not come close to meeting the antinarcotics standards for certification. Many countries were in similar circumstances, but it was not unusual for the president to waive decertification for economic or political reasons.

Two weeks later, Sayed met with Tom Charlier in Islamabad and told him the prime minister had agreed to release Ayyaz. The release would not occur, however, until after the news of the certification process was delivered on March 1—another Pakistani face-saving move. The timing would not make it look as if they had released him based on a decertification threat.

Whatever; it was starting to look good to us. The news that Pakistan's decertification had been waived came out on March 5.

A small article in the Pakistani press in April 1998 reported without fanfare that Pakistan's air force commander had pardoned Ayyaz Baluch, a DEA employee, after a petition for mercy by his family. Ayyaz and his family were immediately flown to the United States. No mention was made of any government influence from either the United States or Pakistan in achieving clemency for Ayyaz, nor of the heights that issue had reached in both governments. But that action brought to rest the year-long efforts of dozens of people. Ayyaz had spent just three weeks short of a year in prison.

Once Ayyaz and his family had been welcomed to America and settled in, we took him around to meet some of the many people who had worked on getting his release. Almost none of them had ever met Ayyaz, and they wanted to see on whom their efforts for the past year had been spent. They were not disappointed.

The Ayyaz issue was noteworthy for several things, but one aspect of the case was significant for intragovernment efforts inside the Beltway. For once, it seemed, no infighting, posturing, or jockeying for position and influence occurred. The support and advice from the State Department, Department of Justice, Congress, and the National Security Council was something truly appreciated by those in the know at DEA. We never could have accomplished his release without their help. Only a united front and unwavering determination won Ayyaz his freedom.

Just before Ayyaz started his new job with DEA, we held an awards ceremony at the academy in Quantico. The administrator presented a well-earned award for service to Ayyaz. It wasn't much, but it did serve to formally acknowledge Ayyaz's sacrifices on behalf of DEA and America, and to give our thanks to him for remaining steadfast and loyal.

Ayyaz thanked us with a simple gladness.

Holding out for a good job in the field and then getting it, I left DEA headquarters in September 1998 for an assignment in San Diego, where I served as the commander of the San Diego County Task Force. It was a comfortable and stimulating role, and the three years I spent in sunny San Diego were pleasant.

Subsequently, my assignment to Bangkok to take over as program director of the International Law Enforcement Academy (ILEA) came rather suddenly. In preparation, the State Department asked me to come to Washington for a few strategy meetings before heading to Bangkok.

The flight from San Diego was delayed in Dallas, and I arrived late at night at Dulles Airport. After checking in to the Key Bridge Marriott in Rosslyn, I went right to sleep because I had a busy schedule the next day.

The following morning I drove my rental car to DEA headquarters in Arlington. I had a meeting scheduled at the State Department in Foggy Bottom at eleven, but I wanted to stop at DEA headquarters first and visit. It was a beautiful day, and that Tuesday, September 11, 2001, was starting out well.

I picked up a visitor's badge at reception and rode the elevator up to the eleventh floor, meaning to visit with some friends in foreign operations. It was 8:45 a.m., and most employees were already at work.

Entering my old office, I noticed several people gathered around the television monitor next to the desk. Someone said a plane had just crashed into one of the towers at the World Trade Center in New York. We stood watching the coverage of the smoke and flame. Then, in shock, we watched the live video of another aircraft crashing into the other tower. We stood stock-still before the unfolding drama.

An airliner crashing into the Pentagon across the highway from us at about nine thirty created a thunderous explosion, the shock wave shaking our building like an earthquake. We ran to the window and could clearly see the west edge of the Pentagon. It had erupted with smoke and fire.

An alert to evacuate the building awakened us from our spell. The elevators had been shut down, so it was a walk down eleven flights of stairs for us. In an orderly but anxious crowd we made our way. No one had panicked, yet everyone was aware we had come under attack. Billows of confusion and uncertainty swirled among us because no one knew what would come next. It was like the fog of war.

I was enveloped in it too. Although I knew almost everyone on that floor, today I can't remember a single person who started down those stairs with me—except for one.

Clara Billingsley had beaten us to the stairwell. She was an enormous woman wearing a dark blue, velveteen shift that made her look like a La-Z-Boy recliner. You commonly see people in her physical condition riding around on electric carts at Walmart. *And she was taking on the stairs.*

Wearing a determined expression, she gave a pneumatic sigh and slowly started down, one labored step after another. No one could get around her on the steps, so we kept back, bunched up. We let her make her own way down but were poised to assist when the inevitable collapse occurred.

But Clara made it, all the way down from eleven. It is amazing what an adrenaline rush can accomplish.

Outside was pandemonium. Most people held cell phones to their heads, but the phone system was down. I wove through the crowd to my car and decided to go to my hotel—there would be no meetings at State that day.

I managed four blocks on Washington Boulevard before traffic was stopped by police roadblocks. Traffic could only go west, away from the Pentagon. So I continued to Falls Church and parked at the Metro station. The trains were working in Virginia, and I took the Metro back to Rosslyn.

That evening I went out looking for food on the quiet, deserted streets. A small Indian place in Rosslyn seemed open. I was the only customer. The owner, a Sikh, joined me at my table. We spent several reflective moments discussing what had happened, what changes that event would cause in our lives.

EPILOGUE

Change is a process, not an event, and change takes time. After my retirement in 2005, I served as an instructor from time to time for the State Department's antiterrorism assistance program. In 2007, I traveled to Sarajevo, Bosnia, to instruct in an antiterrorism course. My last view of Sarajevo had been eleven years before. Sarajevo had improved in the interim. Although war damage was still visible, it was fading, and life seemed better. The trams ran, the markets were busy, and the restaurants were full.

Our class was held at the police academy, which is located on a hillside above town and was heavily damaged during the civil war. It had been patched up and now served as the workplace for several police officers who had at one time been fighting against each other.

Also patched up were the relations between the three ethnic factions in Bosnia. My students, twenty-four police officers, numbered eight each of Croats, Bosniaks, and Serbs. All were national police officers but posted in their respective areas. I watched them intently, and all the students appeared to get along with each other. During our social gatherings everyone seemed relaxed and at ease with one another.

I knew better than to believe all was forgotten. Who could forget after what had occurred there? But a definite change for the good had come to Bosnia.

Live in hope.

In my story, I have journeyed far and wide, mixing with the best of people and the worst. I have worked in democratic countries, police states, and countries in between. Having seen much of the world, for me there is nothing out there to substitute for coming home to America—scars, scabs, warts, and all.

During a forty-year span, I fought in a losing war and engaged in a losing battle to suppress illegal drug trafficking. However, I don't recall those experiences as defeats. My personal remembrances abound with victories, significance, and holding the line.

The fact remains that the world is a menacing place, and America is not safe today. Illegal drug use has not abated; that possibility is not even imaginable. Many say it's all a lost cause, that we should change unenforceable narcotics laws.

What keeps us going? I don't know. I wish I did. But I believe that so-called lost causes are never lost as long as those who believe in them carry on. Someone always sees those who step forward, and that someone in turn will follow.

Some of us have discovered that duty, keeping up the fight, is not only a burden and an obligation, but deliverance. Duty must endure, if not overcome.

MY THANKS TO

Megan Williams and Sydne Johansen, for your encouragement;

Brad Reed, for your memory;

Erik Lloyd, Terry Potter, and especially Tina
Seamon, for your analytic reviews;

Bank Sinwitayarak, for your art;

and Ayyaz Baluch, for your service.

Printed in the United States
by Baker & Taylor Publisher Services